THE ARAB PREDICAMENT

The Arab Predicament
Arab Political Thought and Practice Since 1967

FOUAD AJAMI

CAMBRIDGE UNIVERSITY PRESS

Cambridge

London *New York* *New Rochelle*

Melbourne *Sydney*

Published by the Press Syndicate of the University of Cambridge
The Pitt Building, Trumpington Street, Cambridge CB2 IRP
32 East 57th Street, New York, NY 10022, USA
296 Beaconsfield Parade, Middle Park, Melbourne 3206, Australia

First published 1981
First paperback edition 1982

Printed in the United States of America

Library of Congress Cataloging in Publication Data
Ajami, Fouad.
The Arab predicament.
Includes bibliographical references and index.
1. Arab countries – Politics and government – 1945–
I. Title.
DS63.1.A35   320.917'4927   80–27457
ISBN 0 521 23914 1 hard covers
ISBN 0 521 27063 4 paperback

Portions of Part 2, "Egypt as State, as Arab Mirror,"
have appeared in *Foreign Policy,* no. 35, Spring 1979.

To my son
Tarik F. Ajami
ಬಾ

Contents

Preface

Because of the way they work and the circumstances of their lives, some incur more debts than others. I owe so much to so many that I was tempted to skip the acknowledgments for fear they might be inadequate. But I decided against it.

Five Princeton friends and colleagues served as teachers and examples. Richard A. Falk was there from the beginning, and I want to express my gratitude and appreciation. Henry Bienen, an Africanist and more, always asked the right questions and always cared. Robert Gilpin saw the possibility of the enterprise a few years before it was visible to others. Robert C. Tucker's work on Russia served as an inspiration, and I was flattered and encouraged that he cared. Manfred Halpern's path as scholar and teacher, his relentless quest to combine understanding of and compassion for the follies of human beings and their dilemmas, left their mark on me. Ali Mazrui, of the University of Michigan, was always generous with his time and ideas and his work on Africa a source of pleasure and many ideas.

The Lehrman Institute in New York City provided financial support for the writing of this book, but that was not the main thing it did. It brought together a number of scholars and friends who battered my pride at times but who taught me a number of things and forced me to rethink some conclusions. I wish to acknowledge my debt to all of them: Stanley Hoffmann, Nicholas Onuf, J. C. Hurewitz, John C. Campbell, David Calleo, and Lewis Lehrman. Tahseen Basheer and Nadav Safran cleared up some of my confusions about matters Egyptian, and I am grateful to both of them. I owe a special personal and intellectual debt to the director of the Lehrman Institute, Nicholas X. Rizopoulos. A master stylist and perfectionist, he was merciless at times but always inspiring.

Ali Dessouki, Abdulaziz Fahad, Saad Ibrahim, Hassan Hanafi, Tawfic Farah, Malcolm Kerr, and John Waterbury shared with me their insights into Arab politics. Even when I disagreed I always learned.

Three people were there, in a personal and intellectual way, and they have a unique place in the development of this book and in my life as well: Richard H. Ullman, Susan Sorrell, and Terrayne Crawford. All three of them listened to many reflections, laments, and memories. All three have my love and gratitude. Richard's help and interest were absolutely pivotal to this project.

Walter Lippincott, Jr., editorial director of Cambridge University Press, was a patient and supportive friend and critic. He had his own unique way of disbelieving my many self-imposed deadlines but retaining faith in the ultimate product. His staff and associates at the Press were unfailingly helpful, always efficient.

Marcia Carlisle helped in many ways. Martha Curtis and Theresa Taylor Simmons provided badly needed assistance with typing and administrative matters.

The connection between past and future is one thread running through the inquiry. There is such a connection in my own life: my mother and my son. My mother is of the previous land in my life, Southern Lebanon. She knew its history and traditions and wounds. From her I learned more about politics and about the way men and women dealt with defeat and power than I did from anyone else. My son is of the other land in my life, born in 1969 and raised in America. The troubles of the world I write about here are unknown to him, but it is my hope that some of its wisdom will reach him. It is to him that this work is dedicated: small gift indeed for so much that he has shared and given.

Much of what I have written here has personal meaning to me, and there is no use hiding behind academic objectivity. Scholars are not some kind of neutral umpires. Their reflections, experiences, and judgment are part of their work. As I wrote the pages that follow, I tried to record as honestly as possible the perseverence and disillusionment of so many people I knew and so many public lives I followed. Some of what is stated here is painful to reflect upon and painful to read, but it is stated neither as some kind of massive indictment nor with any sense of moral and political superiority. I have only tried to the extent possible to depict the thoughts and deeds of men and women caught in what seem to be difficult times for them and for us all.

January 1981   FOUAD AJAMI

Note to the
Nonspecialist Reader

People familiar with a particular subject often write as though their readers ought to be equally familiar with particular names, movements, and dates. What follows is a selective glossary of names and concepts that appear in the text with a brief note as to their significance.

Adonis: An Arab poet and essayist of great depth and sub-stance. "Adonis" is the pen name of the Syrian writer Ali Ahmad Said, born in 1930. He did battle with the formalism and stilted-ness of Arab poetry and writing. His concerns, like those of so many of his generation, became more political after 1967. In 1968 – 1969, he helped found a literary/political magazine, *Mawaqif,* which became one of the leading forums for young intellectuals. Readers interested in his poetry should consult a translated volume entitled *Blood of Adonis,* University of Pittsburgh Press, 1971.

Michel Aflaq, Sami al-Jundi, and the Ba'th Party: Michel Aflaq is a Paris-educated publicist and teacher of Greek Orthodox background, founded the Ba'th Party in the 1940s with his friend Salah al-Din al-Bitar. The Ba'th was part of what can best be de-scribed as a radical, nationalist alternative to the Communist Party. This was part of the post–World War II middle-class na-tionalist evolution in the Arab world. Syria was the base of Aflaq and his associates, but their horizons were pan-Arab and they de-veloped a substantial base in Iraq. They were committed to Arab unity and to a vague and mild socialism. Much as Aflaq and the Ba'th talked about political mobilization, it was their success in re-cruiting military officers that gave them whatever power they knew in the 1950s and 1960s. Aptly enough, it was their alliance with the military that proved to be their undoing. After a turbu-lent period, Aflaq and the other theoreticians of the Ba'th were driven out of power and banished from Syria in the aftermath of a military coup in 1966. Aflaq went into exile in Beirut to lament and write; the Ba'th—military alliance turned into full-scale military rule in Syria. Eventually Aflaq was invited to settle in Iraq, home of the competing branch of the Ba'th Party, and to serve as a general secretary of the shell that remained of that party.

But the ideological tale and the polemics no longer mattered. In Syria under Hafez Asad and in post–1968 Iraq, power belongs to the military. To a very limited degree, a man like Michel Aflaq can buttress Iraq's claim to preeminence over Syria and to being the true and legitimate heir of yesterday's Ba'th, but power in both countries now belongs to the military. Of the Ba'th there remains the pamphlets, the symbols, the icons. A historic footnote to their tale was provided in July, 1980, when Salah al-Din al-Bitar, Aflaq's friend during his Paris schooldays and his partner in politics, was murdered in Paris. By then Bitar had broken with his own past, dismissed the polemics of the Ba'th, declared it as dead and finished, and founded an exile magazine for which he wrote some cogent pieces about the crisis of authority in Syria and the Arab world.

Sami al-Jundi was one of the Ba'th's articulate founders and members a colleague of Aflaq and Bitar. He left a set of remarkable books and memoirs, examined in Part 1 of this study. He left the world of politics to practice dentistry in Tunisia.

Sadeq el-Azm: A Syrian, Azm was educated in philosophy at Yale University. He taught at the American University of Beirut and wrote some substantial studies on Kant. Radicalized by the 1967 experience, he went on to write *Self-Criticism After the Defeat* (1968), *The Criticism of Religious Thought* (1969), and, later, a critical study of the thought and practice of the Palestinian movement. Azm's writings cost him his post at the American University of Beirut and made him a target of the Lebanese religious and political authorities. He came from a distinguished aristocratic Syrian family. His drift to the left and membership in one of the more radical Palestinian movements in the early 1970s were part of the broader radicalization that took place after 1967. Both those who agree and disagree with him credit him with having made noteworthy contributions to the debate after 1967. There is a novel theme to his life — novel in the Arab context of this period: It is the story of affluent young men who could have chosen acquiescence and security but instead chose to oppose, to dissent, and to lose out.

George Habash: A physician, a Palestinian of Greek Orthodox background, Habash was educated at the American University of

NOTE TO READER

Beirut, and now heads the Popular Front for the Liberation of Palestine. His story illuminates the Palestinian drama after 1948: first
the period of individual salvation as the Palestinian refugees tried
to put together personal careers and lives, assimilation into the
Arab World in the 1950s and 1960s, then radicalization and the
struggle for Palestinian autonomy after 1967. His political begin-
nings were in the pan-Arab nationalist movement of the 1950s,
which drew together small groups of university teachers and students. The stirrings were those of postcolonial nationalism. Then
he and like-minded Arab nationalists were drawn into the orbit of
Nasserism in the late 1950s and early 1960s, only to be rudely
awakened by the 1967 defeat. Habash split off from the Arab nationalist movement to lead the more radical, Marxist-leaning Popular Front for the Liberation of Palestine.

The verdict of Habash and his associates on the Syrian and
Egyptian regimes was particularly harsh. Henceforth, they declared in 1967, one had to fight not only against Israel, the West,
and the Arab monarchies but also against the "petty bourgeois" regimes of Syria and Egypt. Habash's group survives as a counter to
the more strictly Palestinian nationalist perspective of Yasser Arafat and the Palestine Liberation Organization. The dominant
state system in the Arab world accepts Arafat's position and for
obvious reasons rejects that of Habash.

Ahmad al Shuqairi: If George Habash tells part of the Palestinians' story, Shuqairi tells a different and older one. Born to a Palestinian upper-class background, Shuqairi was active in the Palestinian politics of the 1930s and 1940s – in the struggle for
Palestine that culminated in the victory of the Zionists and the establishment of Israel in 1948. The politics that Shuqairi knew were
the politics of clans and notables that were hardly a match for the
modern, committed politics of the Zionists.

With a gift for words, the demogogic, venal Shuqairi went on to
serve as a delegate of Syria, then of Saudi Arabia, to the United
Nations. When an Arab summit established the Palestine Liberation Organization (PLO) in 1964, Shuqairi was designated its
leader thanks to his latest patron, Gamal Abdul Nasser of Egypt.
The defeat of 1967 sealed Shuqairi's fate, and power passed to a
younger generation of Palestinians who pushed Shuqairi aside and
took over the PLO. Shuqairi died in Beirut, a broken and forgotten
man. He is remembered for his oratory. Some students of the Arab
–Israeli conflict still argue over whether Shuqairi said or did not
say in 1967 that he wanted to "drive the Jews into the sea." Few

others remember him. The world he knew and the politics he represented have passed from the scene and become memories.

Sulta: The term recurs throughout the text, particularly when
I reproduce the arguments and concerns of Arab intellectuals. It is
an evocative term used to describe political authority and power.
Though used by conservatives as a somewhat neutral term, radicals and critics use it to conjure up the capricious, heavy-handed
nature of political power in the Arab world. To refer to authority
as *sulta* and to today's ruler as the *sultan* is to underline how little
has changed over centuries in the relations between ruler and
ruled.

Sunnis, Shi'a, Alawis: Strictly speaking, *sunna* means "the
custom," "the orthodoxy" (the closest approximation in English).
Sunnis are the majority of Muslims, particularly among the Arabs.
The first doctrinal split in Islam took place between the main body
of the community of Muslims and those who became known as
Shi'at Ali (the partisans of Ali). Ali was the son-in-law of the
Prophet; he was passed over for succession after the death of the
Prophet Muhammad in A.D. 632. The battle over the succession
(Ali was passed over three times in a row) became a broader split
as Shi'a served as the focus for disaffected ethnic elements and dis-
sidents.

The Shi'a subscribe to the doctrine of the *imamate,* the infallible leader. As their doctrine has it, the imamate belongs to what
they call "the people of the House" — the descendants of Ali and
his wife Fatima, the daughter of the Prophet. The doctrine of the
hidden imam maintains that someday the imam will reappear to establish the realm of justice. Shi'ites suffered persecution that drove
them and their beliefs underground. Shi'a is the dominant orthodoxy in Iran and has a substantial following in both Iraq and Lebanon, where the Shi'a outnumber Sunni Muslims.

The Alawis (also known as Nosairis) are a heterodox small sect
who are mostly located in northern and central Syria. The practice of the Alawites is a mixture of pagan, Christian, and Muslim
beliefs. Alawites carry the veneration of Ali, the son-in-law of the
Prophet, to extremes that place them, as far as Sunni Islam is concerned, beyond the proper boundaries of Islam. Alawis see Ali as
the incarnation of Universal Soul, and they are said by other Muslims to make Ali either equal or even superior to the Prophet. The
practice of the Alawis is shrouded in secrecy, and much is imputed
to them by the main body of Muslims, who consider the Alawis to
be seceders from Islam.

These doctrinal differences between Sunnis, Shi'a, and Alawis are internalized; they become part of self and history, correspond with lines of ethnicity and class, and matter less for the hair-splitting arguments about orthodoxy than for what people make of them.

IMPORTANT DATES

June 5–11, 1967: The Six Day War. The defeat of Egypt, Jordan, Syria.

Early 1968: The rise of the Palestinian movement as an independent force in Arab politics. Their early base was in Jordan.

March–June, 1969: The war of attrition along the Suez Canal. A war designed to challenge the status quo along the Canal, to give Egypt some diplomatic leverage.

September, 1969: Qaddafi and his fellow officers seize power in Libya. A hitherto marginal country is brought into Arab politics. Qaddafi throws Libya's weight and money behind Nasser and stakes out a position for himself as spokesman for pan-Arabism and for a radical kind of Muslim fundamentalism.

September, 1970: The civil war in Jordan between the Jordanian regime and the Palestinian movement.

September 28, 1970: The death of President Nasser.

November, 1970: Hafez Asad seizes power in Syria.

May 15, 1971: President Sadat, hitherto a titular figure, pulls off what he calls his "corrective movement"—essentially a coup against the apparatus claiming to represent the remnants of Nasserism.

July, 1972: The expulsion of Soviet troops and advisors from Egypt. A straw in the wind for yet more drastic changes in Egyptian policies.

1972–1973: The putting together of the coalition that waged the October War based on an understanding between Egypt and Saudi Arabia and the participation of Syria.

October, 1973: The outbreak of the October War. The deployment of the Arab oil weapon.

September, 1975: The conclusion of the Sinai accord between

NOTE TO READER

Egypt and Israel under American auspices. The accord causes a rift between Egypt and Syria.

1975–1976: The outbreak of the Lebanese civil war, its institutionalization into a way of life for the country.

November, 1977: Sadat's journey to Jerusalem.

September, 1978: The Camp David accords between Egypt and Israel, with President Carter's participation.

March, 1979: The signing of the Egyptian–Israeli treaty.

January–February, 1979: The collapse of the Pahlavi regime in Iran. The rise of Ayatollah Khomeini.

November, 1979: The attack on the Grand Mosque in Mecca, symbolizing the troubles of the Saudi state and the appeal of religious fundamentalism.

December 1979–January, 1980: The Soviet invasion of Afghanistan; the "Carter Doctrine" as an American response affirming the will to use military force in the Persian Gulf; deepening polarization and discord between the superpowers; an escalating ideological quarrel between the Khomeini revolutionary regime and its neighboring states.

Introduction

ᑭᑕ

. . . and yet for aught I see they are sick that surfeit with too much
as they that starve with nothing
> Shakespeare, *The Merchant of Venice,* act 1, sc. 2.

ᑭᑕ

An imitation of European customs including the perilous art of borrowing has been lately affected: but, in the hands of Eastern rulers,
the civilization of the West is unfruitful; and instead of restoring a
tottering state, appears to threaten it with speedier ruin.
> T. Erskine May, *Democracy in Europe*
> (London: Longmans, Green, 1877), p. 29.

ᑭᑕ

What god shall resurrect us
in his flesh?
After all, the iron cage is shrinking.
The hangman will not wait
though we wail from birth
in the name of these happy ruins.

What narrow yesterdays,
what stale and shriveled years . .
Even storms come begging
when the sky matches the gray
of the sand,
leaving us stalled between seasons
barricaded by what we see . . .
> Adonis [Ali Ahmad Said], *The Blood of Adonis*
> (Pittsburgh: University of
> Pittsburgh Press, 1971), p. 48.

ᑭᑕ

THE ARAB PREDICAMENT

THE WORLD CAN BE READ INTO SMALL EVENTS: In Clifford Geertz's imagery, winks can be made to speak to episte-mology.[1] The small event into which I shall begin reading things is the death of the Lebanese journalist and publisher Salim al-Lawzi.

In early March, 1980, Salim al-Lawzi was found dead and muti-lated in Beirut. He had come back to Lebanon on a personal visit from London where he had been living and working for some time. Because al-Lawzi was a critic of the Syrian presence in Lebanon, it was widely assumed that the Syrians were responsible for the deed. In the Beirut of the late 1970s assassinations and murders had be-come commonplace: Politics had degenerated into nihilism and vio-lence, and there was no use trying to determine who and what should be believed.

Salim al-Lawzi had not been a particularly talented or honest journalist. Nor did he have to be. He was a great success in a world in which success was its own vindication. He mingled with the mighty; he openly spoke of and flaunted the gifts given to him by this or that Arab ruler, this or that embassy. In the time-honored tradition of Lebanese journalism (where newspapers reflected the views of particular embassies), he had served a variety of patrons and offered his services to the highest bidder. At the height of Nasser's power he had served Cairo; then he shifted his services and loyalty to Saudi Arabia.

When the Arab world found its way to London in the aftermath of the October War of 1973, al-Lawzi moved there and launched a new magazine, *Events* (the exact English translation of his Arabic magazine, *al Hawadith*). *Events* picked up where the old *Hawa-dith* had faltered. It catered to the Arab presence in London; it showed that men could use new garb but remain themselves. *Events* discoursed in English, but it was moved by the old spirit. It catered to the winners, to the consumers; it flattered those who mattered and displayed their life style. There was no investigative journalism, no analysis, only the banalities of what passed for truth, the version of the world dictated by al-Lawzi's latest pa-trons. In its pages was that unique mixture of Arab life in the mid and late 1970s — the horrors of the civil wars, the tribalism, the breakdowns together with items about banking and business op-portunities, real-estate deals and speculations. One foot in the hell of the old politics resurgent, one in the benign utopia of finance. It spoke of the wounds and the incoherence and of the new possibili-ties. Back to back were the latest apocalyptic deeds and words of the Lebanese Phalanges and the deeds of the great Saudi financier Adnan Khashoggi. And, of course, *Events* offered a steady flow of anti-Egyptian polemics from the safety and distance of London: criticism of Egypt's "betrayal" of Arabism, its abandonment of the sacred struggle.

A few words said in eulogy by a friend of al-Lawzi suggest one reason why I open with al-Lawzi's death: "Freedom," he said, "is a plant alien to our part of the world. Whenever implanted, it dies . . . We used to blame the colonialists. Then some of us colonized others and the plant of freedom died over and over again. Each time it died a dreamer who inhabited his own world would try to revive it only to perish along with it . . . all those who made the effort rode against powerful windmills with wooden swords."[2]

This had not been a world that took responsibility for its own deeds. The invented nationalist historiography of the Arab kind had always pointed outward: It accused others – Ottomans, Europeans, and others – of causing the ills of the Arab world.[3] T. E. Lawrence had once expressed and helped spread that stereotype. The Arabs were once free; then the Turks came, who "choked the life out of the body politics." "Happiness," he romanticized, "became a dream" as the spirit of the Arabs "shrivelled in the numbing breath of a military government."[4]

But now the world the Arabs lived in was more nearly an Arab world. The Ottoman empire had become a fading memory, Turkey herself a failing society. The external scapegoats had been cut down to size. The wounds that mattered were self-inflicted wounds. The outside world intruded, but the destruction one saw reflected the logic of Arab history, the quality of its leadership. The divisions of the Arab world were real, not contrived points on a map or a colonial trick of divide-and-conquer. No outsiders had to oppress and mutilate. The whip was cracked by one's own.

In the way he lived and the way he died, al-Lawzi told volumes about what I shall continually refer to as the Arab predicament in the modern world. In the Beirut where al-Lawzi had earlier practiced his brand of journalism in the 1950s and 1960s, things seemed reasonably benign and harmless. No one took seriously what his and other magazines said. Much more was said about Beirut's parties, its joie de vivre, its elegant weddings, than about its slums, about the despair of that so-called belt of misery around the city, or about the real antagonisms that separated the Lebanese. Al-Lawzi's brand of journalism reflected the place assigned to the written and spoken word in Arab politics. It also reflected the peculiar nature of that Levantine city where men lived on charm, by their wits, where "principles" were things that men could not afford, where men seemed to push things to the brink and then pull back to keep the game going, to keep things the way they were.

Then grimness crept into this world – part of the broader grimness that came into Arab life in the aftermath of the Six Day War. The sensitive could sense the gathering of the storm. In the preface to the third edition of his *The Arab Cold War,* Malcolm Kerr lamented that Arab politics "had ceased to be fun. In the good old days most Arabs refused to take themselves seriously and this made it easier to take a relaxed view of the few who possessed intimations of some immortal mission."[5] When these words were written, the ordeal of Lebanon that sent al-Lawzi to London and the unraveling of Arab society that jumbled past and future, fundamentalism and technicalism, the cultural anguish and the business deals had yet to come.

There is no "fun" in the material handled here: It is a chronicle of illusions and despair, of politics repeatedly degenerating into bloodletting, of imagined transformations followed by despair that there is some immutable core that disfigures it all, that devours all good intentions, that mocks those who would try to change things. The seemingly harmless games played by the preceding generation, the hair-splitting arguments of Arab ideologues gave way to a deeper and more terrifying breakdown. One generation had sown the wind and the other was now reaping the harvest. The stock-in-trade of men like Nasser, the Syrian Ba'thist theoretician Michel Aflaq, the braggart Ahmad al-Shuqairi of the Palestine Liberation Organization, was symbols and words. There was ample room for maneuver, a margin for errors. In the decade or so that followed the Six Day War, words were replaced with bullets, which now seemed the final arbiter. This generation, writes one observer, split into two groups: those who saw authority growing out of the barrel of a gun and those who packed up and left.[6] The young thugs roaming the streets of Beirut and the snipers on its tall and modern buildings that once stood as a monument to Lebanon's "cosmopolitanism" exposed the tribalism of a deeply sectarian country whose civilized forms were only a cover for biases and prejudices, an escape from realities intuited and known by its inhabitants.

The 1970s of Lebanon, wrote an analyst in a bitter commentary, are the 1980s of the region as a whole. Just as Lebanon led the Arab world into the bourgeois age (it was really Cairo that did so, but the writer is a Lebanese), it now leads them to the new age. It shows them the hell that lies in their future. Its storm will spread to their skies. Which country will be next? Which country will perform the "dance of death"? Will it be Turkey or will it be one of the states of the Arabian peninsula?[7]

Two great events dominate the period that concerns us: the Six Day War of June, 1967, and the October War of 1973. Men fought, worked, and reflected in the shadow of these events. In a curious way, the defeat of 1967 was better handled in the Arab world than the so-called victory of 1973. In the aftermath of the June defeat, the dominant order sought to put together an answer of its own to the defeat, as it had to if it were to survive. That it did in the form of an organized, large-scale war in October, 1973. Between 1967 and 1973, the dominant order could rely on patriot- ism; it had the "safety" of a limited task. Grim as its task was (for it knew that a military victory against Israel was not in the cards) it operated from givens shared by the overwhelming majority of the masses. The defeat was culturally, psychologically, and politically unacceptable, and it had to be dealt with. The managers of order patched up their differences and descended from the world of metaphysics into a more concrete world. They knew that the de- feat was intolerable; they sensed the growing despair and tried to stem it. In the process they acquired some badly needed facts and rules about the way the international system worked: They learned how to speak to the outside world; they displayed some skill in a subdued coming-to-terms with the world. To be sure, the 1967– 1973 interlude had its dreamers, those who thought that the world could be unmade and remade with a pamphlet, but on balance cau- tion prevailed and the social order hung together.

The "victory" in October, 1973, proved more difficult to con- trol, more difficult to live with. For some, that historic watershed promised an instant remaking of the world, a settling of the great score with the West, a great revenge for past injuries. The long view of this can be appreciated from the following passage by histo- rian Bernard Lewis:

> This confrontation [between the Arab oil producers and the West] is the culmination of a long process which has been going on for centuries. It began with the expansion of Europe from both ends in the late 15th century, the Rus- sians from the East, the Portuguese and other maritime na- tions from the West. This expansion, and the ascendancy to which it gave rise, eventually affected the whole world. It took different forms in different places. In some areas it led to direct colonial rule. In the Middle East this only happened in few places and for relatively brief periods. In

most of the countries of the Middle East the impact of Western domination was indirect but, nevertheless, powerful enough to shatter the old society beyond repair and to initiate a process of violent social, economic, and political change which disrupted the traditional order, destroyed traditional loyalty and relationships, and engendered a deep resentment against the Western standard-bearers of the civilization from which these changes originated.[8]

The world brought about by October 1973 blew away the cobwebs of Arab society. Buffeted by mighty winds and propelled by temptations and possibilities unknown before, its cultural container ruptured. It strutted on the world stage for a brief moment; then the breakdown came. There were great victories on distant stages and paralyzing wounds at home. A world seemed to back into the past because the new terrain looked unfamiliar as old verities were challenged, old limits broken and violated. An essay written in 1978 from Cairo expressed my own attempt to understand the anguish and disillusionment that accompanied the great victory of 1973. I reproduce it here because it foreshadows my own analysis in the pages that follow:

> To those so inclined, divine will must be sending a message to the Muslim people of this region and making known its disapproval of what has come to pass in the age of affluence and "petro-power." Since the oil embargo of October 1973, the moment of that perceived great triumph over the West, there has been the tragic collapse of Lebanon, disarray in Arab politics, and of course the recent eruption in Iran. In Muslim and Middle Eastern cosmology, there is a particular emphasis on the fate of those who ride and aim too high and who come to suffer as a result of having dared to break sacred limits and having entertained false pride and ambitions. Since October 1973, the principal malady has been cultural and psychological: a growing imbalance between men and things and the rupturing of the normative order. This may sound a bit poetic and elusive, but it is not intended to be. It has to do with some very concrete things: traffic jams and inflation, growing inequalities, the wearing thin of patience and tradition, and the aftermath of an economic boom that has raised some men to new heights of grandeur and power and demeaned the dignity of others.

Five years ago, the Arabs won what seemed to be a victory over the West: The oil weapon was seen as providing the dawn of a new age of grandeur and power, a revenge for the injuries inflicted on this part of the world. The true age of "petro-power" has visited on the Arabs — as well as on Iran — great suffering and dislocation. Oil money spawned great dreams, but those were inevitably of power and "things." The recurring theme in the tales of "The Thou-sand and One Nights" is that of the beggar becoming king and the king a beggar. The oil victory was to be that kind of theme: a world that had structured a whole moral and so-cial order around poverty could now do unlimited things. It could humiliate those who had once humiliated it and resurrect a great imagined past grafting onto it the power of the modern West. But the new age was not to be. Unable and really unwilling to import the West as "process" — such features as the accountability of rulers, as well as per-sonal and cultural freedom — the oil states would import the West in the form of "things." The strategy has back-fired. When it is in the West, the machinery of the West makes sense: It emerges from a larger social and political order. But imported, the same machinery poses serious problems: The narrow streets of most Middle Eastern cap-itals are as inhospitable to the machines of the West as are the hearts and habits of men.

The dilemma leaves those engaged in it in the midst of pow-erful crosscurrents. The mighty wind from the West promises power, glamour, and the possibility of doing away with what once seemed to be unbreakable bounds. But there is also the voice of authenticity and tradition with its own compelling message. It promises to sweep away injus-tices and troubles and to erect a more caring and true order. It raises the banner of brotherhood at a time of mounting inequalities, hence its power and relevance. Some men have prospered in the new order and many have lost out in the boom. And the losers have not been con-vinced that the winners deserved all that they have accu-mulated. This has colored the relation between the win-ners and the losers both within the Arab countries and Iran and among the Arab states themselves. It is responsi-ble for a deeply felt wound in Egypt and the widespread feeling that richer Arabs want Egypt, as one Egyptian writer put it, to starve alone, die alone, fight alone and go bankrupt alone. The sight of Arabic newspapers in London and Paris that cater to the Arab rich attacking Egyptian policies has a pathology all its own that has not been lost on Egyptians.

The phenomenal wealth of some has made a mockery of the brotherhood of man and man. One does not have to be unduly old or nostalgic to recall better times for this region — times when people had less but shared it more equitably and when the normative order had its own balance. This area's vast depths of compassion and humanity that survive and escape breakdown and violence will have to be tapped if the current malady is to be shaken off. For, as Muslim theology maintains, Allah will help and sympathize only when the believers do their part.[9]

In a useful periodization of recent Arab history, the Moroccan scholar Abdallah Laroui identified four distinct phases:

1. The *Nahda* (the Arab Renaissance) from 1850 to 1914. This was dominated by the quest to "assimilate the great achievements of Western European civilization."
2. The struggle for independence. This phase began with the collapse of the Ottoman Empire at the end of World War I and lasted until the mid-1950s: "It gave rise to popular parties that played an important cultural role by promoting the spread of democratic ideals and, to a lesser extent, of socialist values."
3. The "Unionist movement" that flourished after 1948 and found its leadership in President Nasser of Egypt and the Ba'th party in Syria.
4. The "moral crisis" that followed the 1967 defeat. This "culminated in a period of anguished self-criticism, a searching re-appraisal of postwar Arab culture and political practice."[10]

The post-1967 years of concern to us can be arbitrarily divided into four brief cycles. The first lasted from 1967 to 1970. In this phase, the Arab state system tried to clean away the debris of the defeat and worked out a reconciliation between the "radical" states and the conservative ones. The deal was worked out between President Nasser of Egypt and King Faisal of Saudi Arabia.

What Malcolm Kerr labelled the "Arab Cold-War" was thus liq-uidated. But this cycle's dramatic heroes were the newly radical-ized Palestinians: It was their guns and pamphlets and their chal-lenge to both radical and conservative states that dominated this cycle. This was brought to an end by the Jordanian civil war of September 1970. King Husein's army may have carried the fight to grim limits and thus frightened off those who had commissioned him to take on the Palestinians. Local grievances and offended sen-sibilities in Jordan forced a particularly grim battle to erupt. The Jordanian army had watched the erosion of its authority, the growth of a state within a state as the Palestinians turned Jordan into a sanctuary for attacks against Israel and into a political base. But the fight was not Jordan's alone. Save for the pariah Syrian re-gime (which was brought down by Hafez Asad in November of the same year), all the Arab states had either directly sanctioned the Jordanian effort or simply looked the other way: This was true of Nasser and Qaddafi and of the radical regime in Iraq, as it was true of the conservative states.

At stake was the state system's sensitivity about outsiders who play by a different set of rules. King Husein's army performed the grim service and carried it out with more zeal than some of those who had acquiesced may have wanted: As the casualties ran into the thousands, the Arab states wanted the carnage to stop. But there was no doubt as to their acquiescence in the project. The audacious radicals had to be taught a lesson; the Arab world had to be purged of Marxists; free-lance guerrillas had to be disciplined if the states were to negotiate with Israel or to respond to the diplo-matic initiatives offered by outsiders. States are jealous entities: They protect their monopoly on violence and on order, and the Arab state system was no exception. The Arab states had to main-tain their hold over their populations, redeem their battered pride, prove themselves to the young at home, and prove themselves to superpowers and assure them that they could deliver their constit-uents and make good on their promises — either promises of diplo-matic deals or threats to go to war if Israel persisted in its occupa-tion of the land they had lost.

In the second phase (1970–1973), the dominant political order bounced back. The deradicalization of states begun in the first cycle was completed. Nasser's death and his replacement by Sadat in 1970, the coming to power of Hafez Asad in the same year, and the defeat of the Palestinians, gave the dominant political order a breathing spell. The states used the time to put together the trilat-eral alliance — Egypt, Syria, and Saudi Arabia — that waged the

October War. The deed was done against overwhelming Israeli military power, in the face of the superpower detente that had pretty much frozen the status quo in the Middle East, and against mounting pressure in the Arab world for some kind of solution.

The third cycle (1973–1975) involved the ascendancy of the dominant political order. This was a brief moment of elation. All, including Palestinian self-determination, seemed possible. Great and sudden wealth spawned all sorts of dreams about development, about military power, about the resurrection of the Arab world. All this happened against a promising global background: the revolt of the Third World majority at the UN, disarray in the West, nuclear proliferation (with its promise of greater equality), the illusion that modernity and power could be bought off the rack. This was also America's moment in the Middle East: the United States was to serve as broker in the peace and as a protector of the moderate Arab order. Like all periods of euphoria, none of the troubles vanished; worse still, new and unprecedented troubles were brought about by the new wealth. This phase came to an end with the Sinai accord in September, 1975, concluded by Israel and Egypt under American auspices, which confirmed Egypt's determination to go its own way and was a harbinger of things to come. That same year also witnessed the outbreak of the civil war in Lebanon in which all Arab states were directly or indirectly involved. The great wealth was helpless to arrest the drift toward interstate discord or domestic upheaval in the Arab world. Egypt's diplomatic defection and Lebanon's collapse ended the great historic moment of triumph.

The last cycle (1975–1980) saw further crystallization of the trends of the previous one. Sadat's search for a separate Egyptian path took him to Jerusalem — there were no more subtleties and half-hearted measures, but a fall and dramatic break with the Arab world. The bloodletting in Lebanon became institutionalized, and there was a definite drift toward de facto partition between a Muslim Lebanon and a Christian one. The Syrian "assignment" (shades of the Jordanian assignment of September, 1970) drew Syria into the Lebanese quagmire. Politically and intellectually, this cycle witnessed the greater salience of religious fundamentalism, all the more so in the shadow of the Iranian upheaval of 1978–1979 that ended the reign of the Pahlavis. The frenzy and wrath of Iran mattered less for the material power of Khomeini's regime (which was quite limited) than because of the lure of fundamentalism and virtue represented by Khomeini and because the issues of corruption, of cultural dualism, of vast pillage made possible by the new wealth, of social inequity that brought down the Pahlavis were remarkably similar to the ones plaguing the Arab world.

The Six Day War is not refought in this book. The path that Nasser took need not detain us long. With this great event, as with the later one in October, 1973, we are interested in the political and cultural questions involved; in the way participants sought to think through and respond to dilemmas, in the social and political orders those two great upheavals left behind.

As the well-known chronology of the Six Day War has it, Nasser had mobilized his troops and moved them to Sinai on May 14 as a result of Soviet warnings about a pending Israeli attack on Syria. On May 18, his foreign minister asked the secretary general of the United Nations to withdraw the United Nations troops that had separated Egypt and Israel since the Suez Campaign of 1956. Then, choosing to push things further, Nasser closed the Gulf of Aqaba to Israeli shipping, thereby undoing the consequences of the 1956 defeat. Euphoria gripped the Arab world as the hero seemed to regain his touch.

By June 4, 1967, the hero-leader of Suez and pan-Arabism stood at the apex of a political career full of reversals and triumphs. His Ba'thist rivals in Syria, who had long taunted him about hiding from Israel behind UN troops, were now in his shadow; so were his reactionary enemies, the monarchs of Saudi Arabia and Jordan.

On June 9, the great charismatic figure acknowledged a defeat larger in scope, more dramatic in impact, than that of 1948. The achievements of his reign stood in question and so did the logic and symbols of an era of Arab political thought and practice. The die was cast. The dominant political order could not go back to business as usual. The territorial losses were too sweeping, too historically and strategically significant, the verdict of the defeat too culturally troubling to resume the old game. Because political man is by nature contemplative and probing, some sense had to be made not only of what went wrong, but also of what lay ahead. Great historic crises feed the normal desire to contemplate a nation's essence; they also open up unexpected horizons and opportunities.

Part 1 is an attempt to listen to the society's dialogue with itself, to its anguished self-appraisal. With or without the Six Day War, an audit of the post—World War II generation was overdue. That generation, represented by the Nasserite Free Officers' regime in Egypt and by the Ba'th Party/military officers' alliance in Syria, had seized power in the aftermath of the Palestine war of 1948. The case they had made against the ancien régime was the standard case made by broadly based middle-class nationalists against older, more narrowly based political regimes: that they were embarrassingly weak and compromised, prone to collaboration, disconnected from aspiring social classes, and easily torn to shreds by outsiders.

In rivalry and in alliance, Nasser and the Ba'th had dominated the 1955–1967 period. This was the era of Suez, of the fight for Algeria, of the collapse of the Iraqi Hashemite monarchy in 1958, of the great crusade for nonalignment, and of the fight against the West. In that battle the older, more feudal regimes were on the defensive: The new ones had the capacity to mobilize; they could promise socioeconomic justice, political participation, and the capacity to take on the outside world without defeat or collaboration. Like other such nationalists elsewhere, this generation's symbols had thrown young men and women into a whirlwind of excitement and frenzy. They had stressed how radically different they were from the old world; their experiments with state capitalism (packaged as socialism) had tinkered with the old economic order and proclaimed the dawn of a new world. And of particular relevance to the Arab world, this was the generation that was to liberate Palestine and bring about pan-Arab unity. If the defeat sustained in 1948 was due to treasonous monarchies, to feudal orders that had kept men and women on the margins of history, the new men were bound to do better: They would create modern states and modern armies; they would somehow arrest political decline and stagnation.

Eventually, promises have to be redeemed and delivered: Sooner or later, the real limits of the experiments in Egypt and Syria would have had to be forced. What the 1967 defeat did was to force an audit during a moment of great stress and clarity. And what a spectacle it was! The normal capacity of political orders to deny and to evade, to conceal decline behind a facade of smug and hypocritical assertions that all is well, that the enemies are vanquished, that the order is sound – all those things that all political orders resort to – were denied to the heroes of yesterday. There on brutal display was the world they had wrought: They could not lie to the young and unsuspecting. In a hypermasculine political culture, a small state had displayed their historical inadequacy, had seized massive chunks of land, and had devastated the armies whose weapons and machismo had been displayed with great pride for the last decade or so. There was no place to hide; men had to contemplate where they had been and what it all amounted to. The debates and autopsy reproduced here were in many ways a unique intellectual episode in Arab thought: This had not been a society used to self-appraisal and self-criticism. Whether it was the banalities of the old custodians of tradition or the bravado of the post – World War II generation, political debate had been sterile, formalistic, and disconnected from social realities. In the harsh light of the military defeat, a younger generation came to ask tougher questions and to make greater demands upon political categories and discourse. This was a generation that was no longer sure of anything. The military defeat had rendered a harsh verdict on the world erected by the post – World War II nationalists. In the dialogue and appraisals presented here, we can observe some of the trends that were to crystallize in the decade that followed the 1967 defeat: disillusionment with pan-Arab doctrines on the part of critical populations in the Arab world – the Palestinians and, in their own way, the Egyptians; disillusionment with secularism and the turn toward Islamic fundamentalism; and, of course, disillusionment that gives up on politics and searches for personal escape and safety.

This, then, is the more "intellectual" side of the inquiry in Part 1 – an attempt to see how politically sensitive people depicted the Arab crisis, the questions they asked, the solutions they put forth. On the level of interstate politics, Part 1 deals with the political scramble that followed the 1967 defeat as the radical states (Egypt and Syria) ran for cover and sought an accommodation with the old Arab order (the oil states, Jordan) and as both sought to put down radicalism and unrest that came to rally behind the newly mobilized Palestinians. Here too can be found trends that were to become clearer with the passing of time: the deradicalization of the Egyptian state; the greater influence in inter-Arab politics of the conservative states; the fight between the dominant political order and younger, more disaffected elements; the attempt of the Arab states' system to climb out of that Arab – Israeli ditch that had partly been its own making.

Part 2 grapples with the wounds and choices of Egypt and Egyptians; it is also an attempt to see the Arab world in Egypt – hence the title "Egypt as state, as mirror." As stated there, Egypt is where Arab history comes into focus. The country epitomizes the possibilities and limits of Arab history. For the last two centuries, from Muhammad Ali to Anwar el-Sadat, Egyptians have been experimenting with statehood, with national manufacturing, with sorting out their ambiguous and difficult relationship to the West, with bourgeois ideas, with state capitalism (and its dismantlement), with large-scale wars (and their conclusion). If theirs had not been a particularly successful quest, it has been a historically gripping drama, complete with heroes, villains, tragedies, and, here and there, some solid achievements.

On Egypt's performance — sometimes a desperate trapeze act — other Arabs have been and remain fixated, applauding at times, full of derision at other times. Egypt gave the Arab world Abdul Nasser, its mass hero, during that exciting phase of populist nationalism, and it was Egypt that broke him in 1967. One side, one dimension of Egypt — its resourceful media, the security of its statehood, its stout lungs, its cultural preeminence — raised Nasser to great heights and gave the Arab world the hero it wanted and needed; then the other side — Egypt as a poor society, as a state with a weak army — brought him tumbling down. Egypt gave Nasserism to the Arab world, then treated other Arabs to a fullscale inquiry into it, a smashing of its symbols, under the label of deNasserization. If the first act was thrilling theater, the second left the spectators baffled: How did the worshipped hero of yesterday become the villain of today? The offer made by Qaddafi in 1980 to have Nasser's remains removed to Libya to build a shrine for the faithful in return for $500 million to be paid to Egypt is a judgment on Egypt and on Nasser as a memory and an idea. Nasser belonged to others — to nonEgyptian Arabs. And Egypt was not worthy of him. Besides, in a poor country all things are up for sale if only the price is right.

Egypt led the Arab wars with Israel and was then able and willing to say that the fight was mostly psychological anyway, that the solution that eluded everyone on the battlefields could be hammered out at peace summits.

Egypt led the revolt against the West in the 1950s — we can now begin to appreciate the impact of Suez and of Nasser's challenge to the West on the place of the Third World in today's international system — said no to foreign pacts, broke through military embargos and then succumbed to a puzzling dependency on America as the 1970s drew to a close. Was that a strictly Egyptian weakness, or was there something amiss in the Arab world that made it vulnerable to the ideas, to the wares, and to the approval of the West? Were the Arabs more vulnerable than China or India? Were they only an intermediate crossroads civilization, or did they have something uniquely theirs? Were their ideas authentically theirs, or were they, like the borrowed machines that litter their landscape, mere imports?

Egypt is both the Arab world's most accomplished state and one of its poorest — a tough combination, difficult on Egypt's pride and on those states in the Arab world that have to deal with Egypt. Egypt makes a fascinating study of the role of perceptions in politics as the world changes and power and wealth slip away to others but the memories of centrality and preeminence remain.

Finally, Egypt is a theater for an interesting dialectic between the solutions and world views of millennarians and fundamentalists on the one hand and those who want to find their way into the outside world on the other. In the Arab world's most bourgeois society there exists a nostalgia for purity that survives in every vanquished civilization that sees in the idea of return a solution for its ills.

To all these culturally and intellectually compelling justifications for focussing on Egypt may be added some practical motivations. Egypt is a highly articulate society: It thinks aloud; its intellectuals slug out the great issues of the time; its gifted novelists show us men and women trying to live in the midst of chaos, dealing as best they can with remote authority, with questions of war and peace, and, where they can occasionally afford it, with questions of individual and collective purpose. This is a society that not only tantalizes but also does something that those seeking to write and understand find irresistible: It takes the outsider in, it bares its soul and answers his questions. There is both a strictly Egyptian struggle that we try to understand here — for nations ultimately belong to themselves — and then a wider Arab drama focused on Egypt.

Part 3 addresses the questions debated in the aftermath of October, 1973. It seeks to illuminate the contradictions, the jumbling of elements, brought about by a sudden infusion of wealth. The main concern of Part 3 is the question of Islamic fundamentalism and return. Rather than the dark and archaic causes it is given by some interpreters, the phenomenon is rooted in two critical areas: first, in the relations between ruler and ruled. In the remarkable language of the Sudanese scholar Dunstan Wai, in the fight between those who have "fallen into things" and acquired "economic and political kingdoms," and those who have not.[11] The turning toward religious symbols is in very small measure explained by the doctrine itself, by Islam's classical teachings and its scripture; above all, it is rooted in the failure of secular elites, in the lack of alternative channels of expressing socioeconomic and political grievances.

The second principal explanation of Muslim fundamentalism has to do with the integration or malintegration of the Arab – Muslim order into the modern world system. Let me suggest the drift of my argument by citing two perspectives: The first, with which I am in disagreement, suggests a basic incompatibility between Islam and the Occident, a great binary division. In this view the revolt of Islam becomes a revolt against modernity that reflects the incapacity of Islam and Muslims to connect with others. This is the position, for example, of the great anthropologist Claude Levi-Strauss: It is the view suggested in the aftermath of Iran's upheaval in a great deal of commentary. In Levi-Strauss's words:

> The truth is that contact with non-Moslems distresses Moslems. Their provincial way of life survives, but under constant threat from other life-styles freer and more flexible than their own, and which may affect it through the mere fact of propinquity.

Again, deeply troubled by Islam, Levi-Strauss goes on to say:

> This great religion is based not so much on revealed truth as on an inability to establish links with the outside world. In contrast to the universal kindliness of Buddhism, or the Christian desire for dialogue, Moslem intolerance takes on an unconscious form among those who are guilty of it; although they do not always seek to make others share their truth by brutal coercion, they are nevertheless (and this is more serious) incapable of tolerating the existence of others as others. The only means they have of protecting themselves against doubt and humiliation is the "negativization" of others, considered as witnesses to a different faith and a different way of life. Islamic fraternity is the opposite of an unadmitted rejection of infidels; it cannot acknowledge itself to be such a rejection, since this would be tantamount to recognizing that infidels existed in their own right.[12]

Less distinguished and more partisan minds than Levi-Strauss have made and continue to make similar interpretations.

The second and more sophisticated position can be stated succinctly: Power engenders resistance. In this context, the power of the West, of an ascendent civilizational model, often forces others to look for means of resistance:

> Where there is power, there is resistance, and yet, or rather consequently, this resistance is never in a position of exteriority in relation to power. These points of resistance are present everywhere in the power network. Hence

there is no single locus of great Refusal, no soul of revolt, source of all rebellions, or pure law of the revolutionary. Instead there is a plurality of resistances, each of them a special case: resistances that are possible, necessary, improbable: others that are spontaneous, savage, solitary, concerted, rampant, or violent; still others that are quick to compromise, interested, or sacrificial; by definition, they can only exist in the strategic field of power relations. But this does not mean that they are only a reaction or rebound, forming with respect to the basic domination an underside that is in the end always passive, doomed to perpetual defeat. Resistances do not derive from a few heterogeneous principles; but neither are they a lure or a promise that is of necessity betrayed. They are the odd term in relations of power; they are inscribed in the latter as an irreducible opposite . . . Hence they too are distributed in irregular fashion: the points, knots, or focuses of resistance are spread over time and space at varying densities, at times mobilizing groups or individuals in a definitive way, inflaming certain points of the body, certain moments in life, certain types of behavior. Are there no great radical ruptures, massive binary divisions, then? Occasionally, yes. But more often one is dealing with mobile and transitory points of resistance, producing cleavages in a society that shift about, fracturing unities and effecting regroupings, furrowing across individuals themselves, cutting them up and remolding them, marking off irreducible regions in them, in their bodies and minds.[13]

This perspective helps capture the ambivalence of defeated civilizations: They enter the modern world, they fail, they retreat into their shells. But some things – preferences, languages learned, addictions to goods and ideas – remain with them. They play with traditions, improvise upon them as modes of resistance. Multiple identities have indeed been "furrowing across individuals" and whole societies in the Muslim world. Part of them, part of their loyalty, is fixated on a world that once was; part of them has been dragged into the outside world, leaving them ambivalent, confused – in the words of the Syrian writer Adonis [Ali Ahmad Said], "stalled between seasons." The attraction to lifestyles freer than their own draws people into the network of the world economy, into currents of world thought and culture. Then guilt asserts itself as they begin to think that the imports are not really theirs; or they experience a change of heart when their efforts to plug into the world fail, when their skills prove no match for the more polished skills of others. And it is this ambivalence, this anguish and hesitation, that is missing from much of what has lately been offered us by way of insight into the agony of the Muslim world. We have been paying attention to doctrine, to the display of militancy, and missing the hesitations and doubts of so many who continue to tell us, and above all, to tell themselves, that they wish to break with the codes of the modern world, to leave its techniques and possibilities behind. For the intense civilizational drama of the Muslim world, we have tended to substitute a smattering of easy stereotypes; to deal with it we have come up with fake geostrategic doctrines precisely at a time when so many states in the Muslim world stand indicted in the eyes of their own citizens.

Men and women have not been marching into the past because of the character of their civilization, because of the visceral passions and archaic sentiments that they have stubbornly held onto. It is in the push and pull of political life that political choices have to be situated. The detours that societies take are not to be explained by the driving habits of those in the vehicle, so to speak, but by the forks in the road they come to and by the dangers that a particular journey presents them with. That is why an interpretation of the *apparent* resurgence of Islam (my treatment in Part 3 will explain why I use the term "apparent") must make its way past the stereotypes of the millennarians in the Muslim world and then the stereotypes of those in the West ready with easy explanations that place fundamentalism on one side and rationality on the other.

As a social force, nostalgia exists in all societies. There is always a point at which societies feel that they are losing their hold on the world and begin to recall better times – times when the world was whole and reality made sense. This is true of the most sophisticated societies as it is of the most technologically backward. The past is always there as a reminder, as a weapon, as an invitation for a promising detour. As the British philosopher Michael Oakeshott so sensitively put it:

> The past in history varies with the present, is the present . . . There are not two worlds – the world of past happenings and the world of our present knowlege of those past events – there is only one world, and it is a world of present experience.[14]

Thus the interpretation of tradition and fundamentalism put forth in Part 3 of this inquiry is rooted in the present experience.

It too (like the phenomenon it seeks to explain) backs into Islamic
fundamentalism after an analysis of the other options resorted to in
the last era — all the secular ones, the ones presented by the dominant political system, the ones presented by revolutionaries. But it
does so with skepticism as to how far the experiment can go, for
there is, when all is said and done, a difference between apparent
worlds and real ones, the worlds and systems created by nostalgia
and the ones that exist.

Each political culture connects its political ideas with its practice
in a unique way. Some deduce ideas from political practice; others
come at the practice with ready-made conceptions and schemes
and the ideas have a certain freedom from empirical realities. Some
trust in the practicality of the political process — you try, and
then you learn and emerge with lessons. Others begin with the
scheme itself. These are ideal types and societies fall somewhere on
a continuum.

The meeting ground, the relationship between thought and
practice, is the thread running through this inquiry. The empirical cases, the political encounters and episodes discussed, are all
approached with an eye as to that relationship and a concern that
the mix between theory and practice in Arab political culture is
susceptible to a recurring belief in grand shemes and ready-made
doctrines. As Qaddafi observed to a Western interviewer,

> In your gospels it's written: "In the beginning there was
> the word." The Green Book can destroy the world or save
> it. Carter can wage any war against us: to defend itself, the
> Third World needs my Green Book, my word. One word
> and the whole world could blow up. The value of things
> could change and their weight. And their volume. Every-
> where and forever.[15]

Some of this is vintage Qaddafi style; some, however, is the long-
standing dream that some doctrines, some words might do it all —
exorcise weakness, make the world right again. This propensity
was illuminated by Claude Levi-Strauss in a discussion of the
parallels between French and Islamic political thought:

> I am only too well aware of the reasons for the uneasiness I
> felt on coming into contact with Islam. I rediscovered in
> Islam the world I myself had come from: Islam is the West
> of the East. Or, to be more precise, I had to have experi-
> ence of Islam in order to appreciate the danger which

today threatens French thought. I cannot easily forgive Islam for showing me our own image, and for forcing me to realize to what extent France is beginning to resemble a Moslem country. In Moslems and French people alike, I observe the same bookish attitude, the same Utopian spirit and the stubborn conviction that it is enough to solve prob- lems on paper to be immediately rid of them. Behind the screen of a legal and formalist rationalism, we build similar pictures of the world and society in which all difficulties can be solved by a cunning application of logic, and we do not realize that the universe is no longer made up of the entities about which we are talking. Just as Islam has kept its gaze fixed on a society which was real seven centuries ago, and for the problems of which it then invented effec- tive solutions, so we are incapable of thinking outside the framework of an epoch which came to an end a century and a half ago.[16]

Behind this "stubborn conviction" lies a desire to escape from poli- tics, to trust it all to grand schemes — at times liberal schemes, for others, Marxist schemes, more recently, fundamentalist, restora- tionist schemes.

There is an apt parable by Kafka entitled "He": It shows "him" struggling with his past and future and waiting for an outcome:

He has two antagonists: The first pushes him from behind, from his origin. The second blocks his road ahead. He struggles with both. Actually the first supports him in his struggle with the second, for the first wants to push him forward; and in the same way the second supports him in his struggle with the first; for the second of course forces him back. But it is only theoretically so. For it is not only the two protagonists who are there, but he himself as well, and who really knows his intentions? However that may be, he has a dream that sometime in an unguarded moment — it would require, though, a night as dark as no night has ever been — he will spring out of the fighting line and be promoted, on account of his experience of such warfare, as judge over his struggling antagonists.[17]

But "he" of course cannot be a spectator to his own destiny, or a judge; "he" cannot step out of the fighting line. His choices and commitments do matter.

It is the lot of the Arabs today to make their choices in the eye of the storm. Their world has become too pivotal to be left alone. In their world can be seen not only their own quarrels and dilemmas but the dilemmas and fights of larger, more powerful entities. Whether a region at once so pivotal to the outside world and so vulnerable can be left alone to shape its own destiny is a debatable proposition. Geography and raw materials − or fate, as a believer would say − placed the Arabs close to the fire, somewhere where the two superpowers converge. One power (the United States) is drawn there by economic needs and by all those psychological motivations that drive powerful entities to try to create a world in their image. For the other power (the USSR), there is the desire to break out of what it sees as a hemmed-in position at a time when it may have come to feel that the world owes it more respect than it has hitherto been accorded. The ambitions, fears, and pressures outsiders bring to bear on a tense region are immense and likely to continue. This makes it imperative upon those caught in the storm to display greater competence than they have shown in recent years.

A Jordanian citizen answering the queries of a team of researchers put his worries in the following way: "We [the Arabs] are worse off in 1978 than we were in 1948 even though we have become more wealthy than we were . . . It is my guess that we will be worse off in 1988 than we are today."[18] The raw wisdom at the disposal of the ordinary man or woman often has more depth than that conjured up by scribes or scholars, more honesty than the utterances of those who govern. The worries of that unnamed Jordanian may reflect and echo the worries of other people in the Arab world. They tell us much about the troubles ahead.

Neither large wealth nor displays of traditions will arrest the drift toward disorder in vast stretches of the Arab world. Wealth has only underlined a painful gap between what a society can buy and what it can be, between the vast means available to buy into things and the limited capacity to create a somewhat autonomous public project, a livable public order. Likewise the escape into tradition can only aggravate the crisis. The contrived past can become a narcotic. Then reality will intrude and shatter the illusion. Men cannot indefinitely live on frenzy or be kept in a trance.

1

One's World As It Really Is

The flute and the lute
do not secure victory;
our pompous speechifying
has cost us 50,000 new tents.

Blame not circumstances, no,
blame not heaven if it forsakes you;
for God, who grants victory to whomsoever He wishes,
is no smith forging spears for you.
It pains me to hear the news in the morning,
to hear the dogs bark.
The Israelis conquer not our borders,
but thrive on our shortcomings.
Nizar Qabbani, *Comments on* The Notebook of Defeat,
in Leo Hamalian and John Yohannan, eds.,
New Writing from the Middle East
(New York, New American Library, 1978), p. 74.

How can a thought melt away before anything other than itself? Generally speaking, what does it mean, no longer being able to think a certain thought? Or to introduce a new thought?
Michel Foucault, *The Order of Things*
(New York: Vintage, 1970), p. 50.

THE ARAB PREDICAMENT

PEOPLE READ INTO THE WORLD WHAT THEY ARE IN-
CLINED TO: There is in great events, defeats, and revolutions
something for nearly everyone. No sooner had the Six Day War
ended than a war of a different sort erupted in the Arab world: a
conflict over the defeat. Who was responsible for it? What did the
defeat say about the basis of Arab society, the quality of the Arab
as an individual? How should the Arab world be organized to cope
with the defeat and its consequences?

The traditional plea in such historical moments to keep the
doubts and questions within reasonable limits was shunned. Some,
as expected, made that plea, but an intense wave of self-criticism
swept the Arab world, mocking the ways of an era, and beyond it,
the burden of history; trying, as it were, to go to the roots of the
defeat. And inevitably the search for answers ranged beyond the
strictly political. We heard from some who wanted a total break
with the past and from others who saw redemption in a tradition
that had once supplied order and meaning.

The notion that societies in crisis have no choice but to leap forward is an arbitrary judgment. In our age this notion is fostered by
the liberal imagery of stages of growth and evolution and the
Marxist imagery of revolutionary transformations. But the temptation to retreat into one's own tradition in a moment of historical
stress can be far more powerful than the tendency to leap into un-
charted territory. There are many conceivable interpretations of a
stressful condition. For a defeated society, the victorious enemy
can be many things, its victory attributable to many factors. This
is poignantly illustrated by one Arab intellectual's commentary on
the June defeat:

> The Imam came forward repeating that we lost because we
> deviated from morality . . . The opposition leader in-
> sisted that we lost because the men in power monopolized
> total power . . . The engineer came forward asking for
> new machines and new factories . . . all found in the
> enemy what justified their argument. The theologian found
> justification in the theocratic orientation of our enemy; the
> politician in the fact that our enemy had a parliament; the
> engineer emphasized the abundance of the enemy's techni-
> cal schools. Only few were able to observe that the reli-
> gious faith of the enemy, his democracy, his technology,
> were all useful instruments but that the principal factor
> was the enemy's social organization, his sense of individual
> freedom, his lack of subjugation, despite all appearances, to
> any form of finalism or absolutism.[1]

The enemy, then, was many things; victory entailed adopting the path that appealed to whoever was passing judgment: democracy, science, return to tradition, Marxist revolutionary transformation, or, of course, a slightly revised version of the pre-1967 status quo. An era in Arab politics had ended, and the struggle for the shape of the Arab order had begun. In the ideological war that erupted we heard the expected apologies of men who had blundered and were now looking for a way out and the recriminations of opportunists who said how much better they themselves would have done. But beyond all that lay a more profound and interesting set of developments: the honest soul-searching of intellectuals for the roots of the Arab ailment; the quest of a younger generation for a new political truth and for concrete solutions to harsh realities; changes in political and intellectual substance and styles; and the desperate attempt of the men in power to deal with altered realities.

Yesterday's radicals — the Ba'th Party and President Nasser — were the principal victims of the defeat: Whereas they once had stood for revolt against an older, more traditional, more compromised leadership, they themselves were now on trial. A younger generation was to see, in the full light of the defeat, the shortcomings of that brand of radical nationalism that had held sway from the early 1950s up to 1967. Some would naturally conclude that a deeper revolt than the one attempted by the Ba'th and Nasser was in order, that the massive dislocations of the June defeat presented an opportunity to effect a radical transformation of society, a break with the past, and the construction of a revolutionary social order of the kind that emerged in China, Cuba, or Vietnam. Short of that kind of conscious commitment to revolution, there was an inchoate groping for something new, a relentless attack on most facets of Arab life, a desire to go beyond Arab nationalism's rhetoric, to transcend the ideological and intellectual framework within which preceding generations had worked. It was suddenly easy to see — by those who were so inclined — that the men who had been yesterday's rebels had just not gone far enough.

THE RADICAL SENSIBILITY

For an articulate and sensitive segment of the intelligentsia and students, Nasser's explanation, given in his first statement on the defeat, that "the enemy we expected from the east and north came from the west"[2] and that the defeat was an error that could have

been avoided, was not enough. In the eyes of a large number of radical activists, the defeat was an indictment of an entire way of life,
proof not only that some deep realities had eluded yesterday's radicals but also that those radicals themselves were part of the problem. Thus, all facets of Arab life were subjected to a ruthless assault: Islam, the Arabic language, the capacity of the Arab as an
individual, the record of the radical Arab states.

Among those who wanted to get to the deep structure behind
the defeat there was a consensus that the heroes of yesterday had
made too many compromises with the past, that they had given in
to that frustrating, hopeless body of attitudes and habits, that immutable thing called tradition. Adonis, one of the most articulate
spokesmen of the new radical sensibility, declared in the first editorial of the lively magazine, *Mawaqif,* that he and a group of radical
intellectuals launched in 1968, that henceforth there would be
nothing sacred and beyond discussion, and that − borrowing from
Marx − it was no longer enough to interpret the world but to
change it.[3] Over the next few years, the radical intelligentsia
would leave very few stones unturned. They were convinced that
the millennium was around the corner, that enough fire, skepticism, and clear theory would plunge the Arab world into genuinely revolutionary politics.

Nothing so clearly illustrates the commitment of the radicals to
get to that deep structure behind the defeat as the radicals' attack
on the Arabic language. The 1950s and 1960s had been immensely
verbal times in Arab politics. The gripping language had been one
of the principal weapons of the pan-Arabists in Cairo and Damascus: It intoxicated and created an impression of great power and
accomplishment. The 1967 defeat created a backlash against the
old style of expression and underscored the need for a more living,
more honest language.

"Even the politicians' phraseology was borrowed largely from
the books they read; it was cluttered up with abstract words,
gaudy flowers of speech, sonorous clichés and literary turns of
phrase."[4] That was de Tocqueville's depiction of eighteenth-cen-
tury France. But the crisis of "sonorous clichés" was far more
acute in the Arab world than it was in the French context. Probably the case most comparable to that of the Arab world was China
in the early years of the twentieth century, where the collapse of
the Confucian order was followed immediately by an attack against
the classical literary language. In both the Chinese case and the
Arab case half a century later, style of expression became an issue
between different generations; in both cases reformers attacked

the classical style out of conviction that the dominant mode of political and cultural discourse enabled old interests to structure the
political and cultural universe, to conceal decay, to flatter. It was
an inevitable process: impatience with tradition and rejection of it
leading to a rejection of the medium through which a political culture expressed and maintained itself.

The Chinese attempt at literary reform was launched in 1917 by
the intellectual Hu Shi and a group of associates, who saw the
dominant ways of Chinese literature and discourse as the root
cause and expression of China's decline. Hu Shi dismissed most of
China's written output as "dead stuff written in a dead language."
A colleague of his linked political reform and the reform of the language by attacking the so-called forest, or esoteric literature:
"These types of literature are both causes and effects of flattery,
boasting, insincerity and flagrant disregard of truth and facts.
Now that we want political reform we must regenerate the literature of those who are entrenched in political life."[5]

The connection between political reform and the reform of language was to become one of the prominent concerns of those who
wanted to get to the roots of the Arab defeat. The Ba'thist Sami
al-Jundi, whose experiences and insights I shall closely examine,
was to root the troubles of the Ba'th Party in the rhetoric and poetry of the party's founder, Michel Aflaq. To read Aflaq's main
contribution to the post-1967 debate, a book entitled *Nuqtat al
Bidaya* (The Starting Point), is to perceive fully the bankruptcy
and incoherence of the politics of the Ba'th. Nearly three hundred
pages of text yield no insight, on his part, into what went wrong
and what needed to be done; there is only the visible infatuation
with words and Aflaq's summons to the party to renounce power
and go back to its "pure essence." Some men had "stolen" the
party and its symbols from Aflaq, and the party's redemption lay in
its regaining its soul.[6] Disaffected Nasserites were to see in the polemics of Mohamed Heikal, Nasser's spokesman, the predicament
of Nasser's ambiguous experiment. The parallel Palestinian predicament would likewise be seen in the bombastic oratory of Ahmad
al-Shuqairi, the head of the Palestine Liberation Organization,
who made and unmade the world in a speech.

This language, observed one social analyst, had provided cathar-
sis and relief and had enabled the Arabs to run away from their
weakness: "Our wars have so far been verbal wars"; Arab society
was basically an "expressive verbal society."[7] Another serious
writer's inquiry into the renewal of Arab society took him straight
to the Arabic language as the root cause and expression of Arab

decline. Arabic, he observed, was not so much a means of expression but an end in itself: A great writer was not measured by the
worth of what he said but by his mastery of the language. The language – its nuances, its rhythm – was an instrument of enter-
tainment rather than a medium for transmitting thought and information. Unless liberated from the spell of the language, the
Arab would remain a captive of a sterile system of thought.[8]

The classical language had been the pride of the Arabs. Like
classical Chinese, it had become esoteric at a particular juncture of
its history, when repression by the dominant orthodoxy forced
thinkers to resort to dissimulation and concealment to escape persecution. In the tenth century, concealment became "a general
pattern for all thinkers who did not conform to the narrow range
approved by the official ulama scholars."[9] Much had changed since
then, but the style had remained static.

Contemporary discourse suffered from the burden of the past –
was stultified by the spirit of a Thousand and One Nights, according to several harsh critics – because the historical experiences
that had transformed other languages had not taken place in the
Arab world. Nationalism had, if anything, compounded the problem: Essentially romantic, it added to the pretensions and the delusions and hence to the escapism of the language. The defeats that
nationalism came to suffer meant that analysis would have no hope
and that expression would alternate between melancholy over setbacks and delusions of grandeur.

Bassam Tibbi, a Syrian scholar educated in Germany, took to
task most of what had been disseminated in the Arab world:
Written work, whether produced by university scholars or by
ideologues, he found wanting in precision, depth, and quality.
"Contemporary Arabic writing," he observed, "is speculative,
non-revolutionary, non-scientific."[10] In his view, the men who had
elaborated the political doctrines of Arab nationalism had inflicted
on the Arab world superficial thought and endless slogans because
they were second-rate thinkers mired in polemics and out of touch
with the experiences that give political thought honesty and relevance. The pan-Arabist publicist Sati al-Husri, who had played an
important part in the dissemination of pan-Arabist thinking in mo-
narchical Iraq and then throughout the Arab League, had, according to Tibbi, offered only a hodgepodge of abstractions, an apology
for nationalism rather than a serious inquiry into it. It was Tibbi's
contention, moreover, that al-Husri's reliance on German sources
was not really authentic: Al-Husri made things up and attributed
them to Fichte and others to support his polemics on behalf of

Arab nationalism. Michel Aflaq, of the Ba'th Party, offered only vague metaphysics: The most eminent theorist of a party that came to power in two countries never wrote a serious book. Tibbi said that Arab Marxists had fallen into the same trap: It was easy to tell from their writings that they had never understood Marx. Tibbi's scathing critique was both a plea for a "living language" that breaks with the past and an expression of what the younger generation thought of the men and the ideas of the preceding generation.[11]

Underlying the torrent of radicalist criticism in the post-1967 years was a simple message: We must confront our heritage, our tradition; we must slay the past if we want to liberate the present. An address by President Nasser at Cairo University in April, 1968, in which Nasser paid lip service to freedom of thought, gave Adonis an opportunity to comment on the responsibility of the intelligentsia and their relation to the dominant tradition: "We must realize that the societies that modernized did so only after they rebelled against their history, tradition, and values . . . We must ask our religious heritage what it can do for us in our present and future . . . If it cannot do much for us we must abandon it."[12]

According to Adonis, such a confrontation was inevitable, for God and religion permeated all aspects of social life: God was not solely a religious matter; the religious message was an "economic, sexual, and political problem in addition to being a spiritual supernatural problem." The supernatural ideas of "paradise, resurrection, hell and the angels" were not strictly religious; they had something to do with "the land, hunger, war." The attitudes and beliefs of popular culture had not radically changed; the "progressives" in power had not been willing or daring enough to challenge the tradition. "Our masses," Adonis lamented, "are not up to the level of the revolution. When the revolution surrenders to them it betrays itself, when it abandons them it dies."[13] He did not say which of the two fates the Arab revolution had met, but it would seem in keeping with the general thrust of his conviction and the conviction of his fellow radicals that the Arab revolution had committed both sins: It had surrendered to popular beliefs and reflected them; it had also abandoned the masses and failed to impart to them new beliefs and attitudes. The progressive Arab states had, as Adonis pointed out in a different essay, talked revolution but done very little about it: Half a century after talking about the revolution and years after the establishment of regimes that described themselves as revolutionary, Arab society was still the same; people did not think for themselves but still succumbed to supernatural thoughts; they were not free agents but followers. True revolution, Adonis wrote, would make human beings the center of the universe; they must above all be free before they can believe in "homeland," "nationalism," "socialism" or "humanity."[14]

In the view of the new radicals, whether or not the Arab revolution had taken place was now beside the point. For some the revolution had aborted; for others it was betrayed. In Adonis's words, the revolution turned out to be "a means to a different kind of end": The end was political power and control, authority, *sulta*. Adonis of course assumed that real revolutions aim at a different kind of end. In so thinking, he was hardly alone. The fear that revolutions will end in betrayal or, short of that, in routine, that yesterday's energy and idealism will end either in terror and oppression or in bureaucracy and routine, has haunted and worried others committed to revolutionary politics. Because the danger of betrayal or routine is ever present, the critical difference presumably lies in whether the revolution, before it settles down, manages to do some radically new things to people's thoughts and habits, to the economic system, and to the distribution of power. The tragedy of the Arab revolution was that it had done none of those things.

Frustrated with the failure of the men in power, Adonis called for a separation between the regimes and the revolution. The revolution, he said, would have to dissociate itself from radical-sounding regimes if it were to succeed. The regimes had robbed their people of initiative and spirit and so overwhelmed them with authority that submission and obedience had become second nature. There was no living, dynamic relation between the citizen and the state, between the individual and society. The most that individuals could hope to do in a culture of that kind was simply to look after their own safety.

The concerns of the new radicals were best expressed in a book by Sadeq al-Azm entitled *Al Naqd al Dhati Ba'd al Hazima* (Self-Criticism after the Defeat).[15] Written in 1968, this book must surely go down as one of the most impressive and controversial pieces of Arabic political writing in recent times. Malcolm Kerr rightly describes it as "the most scathing of all indictments of Arab society and culture."[16] Azm, an American-educated Syrian intellectual then teaching at the American University of Beirut, captured and expressed the new radicalism and dissatisfaction hovering in the air. His courage in confronting such sacred facets of Arab life as Islam and his manner of presentation — direct and to the point — attest to the radicals' commitment to a sharp break with the past and to their determination to succeed where their predecessors had failed. On the level of ideas, they were rebelling against the dissimulation and polemics that had afflicted so much of Arab political writing. On the level of practice, they were out-flanking Nasser and Nasserism from the left.

Azm's *Self-Criticism after the Defeat* belongs to a species of political analysis that major military defeats or great upheavals occasion in a society. Azm's point of departure is military defeat and material weakness: A society fails to stand up to its enemies, to catch up with others. But the "crisis of power and energy" soon takes on another dimension, as a critical segment of that society comes to question the worth of the social order, its capacity for order and justice, its right to survive. The book's initial complaint is that the Arabs failed to win the war, but its central concern is with the inadequacy of the Arab social and moral order. Azm begins by examining the weakness of the Arab as a soldier, but he ends up by evaluating the Arab as an individual — his quality of thought, his capacity to make decisions and to shape a viable social order.

Azm's analysis of the June defeat begins with a telling historical analogue: the defeat of tsarist Russia by Japan in 1904. In the victory of the numerically smaller Japan and Israel over the massive but lethargic Russia and the Arab world, Azm sees the triumph of energy over mass, of dedication and work over pomp and ceremony and the rituals of power. The devastating defeat of the Russian navy is an analogue for the destruction of the Egyptian air force.

Tsarist Russia and the Arab world were both essentially backward but smug societies, sure of victory, contemptuous of their respective enemies. The officialdom of both tsarist Russia and the Arab regimes insisted up to the last moment that they could overwhelm their enemies. Their defeat served a harsh judgment on them: They had failed to modernize and to reform; they had fallen behind, could no longer generate power, and were unable to secure the loyalty of the populace. Azm considers that Russia made the best of her defeat: Defeat triggered the revolutionary events of 1905, fostered radical politics, and set the stage for the Bolshevik revolution.

Ideally, the 1967 defeat should have led to a similar process in the Arab world. But Azm, writing one year after the defeat, saw little reason for hope. He noted the tendency among Arab officials, spokesmen, and even some critics to lay the blame for defeat elsewhere instead of accepting responsibility. Some were quick to ex-

plain away the defeat by pointing to American and British participation in the war. Others went further and accused the USSR of
plotting the Arab defeat. Finally, there were those who declared it
was Allah's will.

Azm finds an extreme illustration of Arab fatalism and of the
wish to escape individual responsibility in the statement of the
mufti of the Jordanian kingdom: The Arab defeat was divine will, a
punishment inflicted by Allah "as a result of our abandoning our
religion." The notion of people as actors, as masters of their own
destinies, is, as Azm and his fellow radicals argue, still alien to the
Arab world. Arabs remain the objects of history. Their supernatural explanations of social phenomena betray their passivity. They
are more spectators than actors. The very term used by the Arabs
to describe their defeat in Palestine – nakba (disaster) – con-
notes the absence of human will and responsibility. Azm is convinced that the choice of terminology was not an accident: It reflected the weakness of Arab society, its desire not to face up to its
backwardness.

Azm carefully shows how the dominant Arab conceptions of
politics and war were at odds with contemporary thinking and
practice. First the Arab states pushed things to the brink, then
they expected an easy way out. When war came, they complained
of Israel's aggression, of the ruthlessness of its military assault –
as though war was supposed not to be grim. In their conduct of the
war and their justification of the defeat, the Arabs seemed saddled
with ancient codes of chivalry, with nearly tribal ways of warfare.
Azm singles out two statements, by President Nasser and the Jordanian prime minister, respectively, that exonerated the Arab
armies. Nasser's statement was that Arab soldiers fight bravely and
well in face-to-face combat with the enemy and that defeat was attributable to the fact that they did not have a chance to encounter
the enemy. The Jordanian prime minister said that the Israelis
know the bravery of the Jordanian soldier when the battle pits soldiers against one another, but that, in this instance, the confrontation was between soldiers and fire that "descends upon them from
the skies." Is it possible, asks Azm, for a people to wage war with
such obsolete notions? Is it possible to enter a modern war that requires movement and initiative when the society is permeated by
passivity and reluctance to initiate decisions?

The intimate connection between war and citizenship lies at the
heart of the modern state. The 1967 defeat revealed the failure of
the Arab states to train and create modern citizens, to inculcate
men with the will to fight and die for the state. Remote and hostile,

the Arab state is disconnected from its citizenry. The latter wish only to be left alone, and they shelter themselves from the capricious will of the state. The state — as is in the case in oriental despotism — reigns but does not rule. When push comes to shove, that state falters, because it lacks the support of its populace. It is not to the state that Arabs owe loyalty, but to their families and clans. And if there is an indisputable verdict rendered by the history of the last two centuries, it is the incapacity of tribal orders to stand up to modern states.

The failure of public politics was demonstrated by the hoarding of goods on the eve of the war, the panic and flight before the Israeli army. Privatized, loyal only to their families, careful to protect the honor of their women, the Arabs were all too willing to flee. For Azm, such behavior does not indict the individual citizen but the Arab state system as a whole. The absence of modern institutions and meaningful bonds of solidarity left individuals at the mercy of their fears. Demoralized, disconnected from others, they took the understandable option of escape, of saving their own skins and the lives of those who form their primary social unit.

Having entered and lost the war, the Arabs conducted postwar diplomacy in the same spirit: They now wished to shame Israel before the court of world opinion; it was believed that their case should move the conscience of humanity and force Israel back to its prewar boundaries. World opinion, wrote Azm, is a factor of some importance; however, there is natural sympathy for Israel in both the capitalist and the socialist worlds — both see Israel as an extension of the Occident, as an embodiment of what human energy and will can accomplish.

No amount of crude propaganda will substitute for the more difficult path of entering the modern world, of making a contribution to the scientific and literary output of mankind. Azm's admiration for energy is readily apparent; it is the Faustian aspect of Western civilization, its capacity to move people and matter, that appeals to him. And precisely because the West is built on energy, Azm finds limited utility in the Arab appeals to Western opinion. The view that the West is deceived and that if it were only to understand the Arab case it would see where justice lies and would change its ways is an extension of a simplistic view of politics into the world of international politics. Azm cites the work of Kamal Yusif al-Hajj, a Lebanese professor of philosophy, as an example of this kind of thinking. Hajj had written that the Arab people were mistaken in blaming the West, because the West was merely deceived by Zionism. He argued that it was up to the Arabs to save the West from the hold of the Zionists. Once that was done, "the formidable powers of the West would then be under our influence instead of the influence of the Zionists."[17] Here, in a nutshell, is the great illusion: The innocent West would be liberated from the hold of the Zionists; the Arabs would then become its manipulators. Demonic powers are at work; one spell is broken and another one takes hold. This explains why the Protocols of the Elders of Zion were taken seriously by some Arab writers. In the Protocols, too, the world is a dark conspiracy; diabolical schemes for control and myths are seen to move the world. If the Protocols are believed, then the Arab defeat would make sense: The Arabs would simply be another deceived, dominated people, and what overwhelmed them would be not a small state but a vast conspiracy.

The brunt of Azm's criticism is focused upon the so-called progressive Arab regimes than on the reactionary ones. Not much could be expected from the latter. It is the failure of the former that highlights the backwardness of Arab society, its stubborn resistance to change, and the weakness of the human element that guides it. The progressive regimes had produced a barrage of noise; they had openly declared their allegiance to the strictures of revolution and socialism. What the defeat did was to show that the Arab revolution was neither socialist nor revolutionary: The Arab world had merely mimicked the noise of revolutionary change and adopted the outside trappings of socialism; deep down, under the skin, it had not changed.

Like radical intellectuals elsewhere, Azm is frustrated with the persistence of tradition, with the fact that the past simply refused to go away. It is when he compares the Arab revolutions to the socialist revolutions he admires that the Arab experiment seems particularly defective and flawed. Unlike the great experiments that worked – China, Vietnam – the attempts of Egypt and Syria were half-hearted and ambiguous. The Arab attempts were afflicted with a middle-of-the-road orientation: They never decided what they wanted – socialism or state capitalism, limited land reform or an agricultural revolution. Did the Arab revolution want to keep the life of the Arab individual under laws codified fourteen centuries ago and to stress values derived from the past, or did it want "a new legislative order derived from scientific, socialist thought"?[18] Did it want a new educational system to replace the inadequate hodgepodge of antiquated programs and stale imports from the days of the Third Republic?

Clarity and commitment are the hallmarks of revolutionary experiments. The absence of those ingredients damned the Arab experiment. Stripped of their mystifications, their noise aside, the Arab socialist states turned out to be traditional orders. This explains the energy these regimes devoted to sheer sophistry, to hairsplitting arguments about the compatibility of their version of socialism with Islam and about their indigenous, authentic form of socialism that dispenses with class struggle in favor of a cooperative path to socialism. Phrases like "Arab application of socialism," constantly repeated in Cairo and Damascus, were a travesty of the notions of socialism. Lacking the will and the determination to wage socialist politics, the Arab states made socialist noises while the bases of their societies remained largely traditional.

There comes a time in the life of societies when they must choose among rival social systems. Penetrated, cross-pressured, and timid, the Arab states were simply unable to choose. They prided themselves on their capacity to integrate different world views. But, as Azm argues, no society, however proud of its capacity to synthesize, can escape difficult choices, all of them having different costs. The Arabs cannot pose as brokers among rival systems; sooner or later they must make real choices. Some choices are irreconcilable. The Egyptian claim of having achieved a so-called Arab—Islamic—Scientific form of socialism demonstrates the depletion of a culture. If all things go together, what then distinguishes one social order from another? The Egyptian slogan, "We must not sacrifice this generation for future generations," served to keep intact the privileges of old vested interests: Inequalities remained, and the whole thing boiled down to putting old wine in new bottles.

Influenced no doubt by Marxist analysis, Azm believes that a strictly political revolution is impossible, that meaningful political change rests upon moral and cultural transformations. This is a crucial issue on which Arab revolutionaries seem to have faltered. There is considerable consensus among young intellectuals of Azm's persuasion that Arab revolutionaries — when they really existed — confined their revolution to the strictly political domain. Young Arabs may rebel politically, but their social relations, family ties, judgment on public and private matters, and attitude toward work all derive from traditional sources.

Because the rebels are unable and unwilling to tackle the cultural and psychological obstacles that impede revolutionary politics, the strictly political rebellion ends either in failure or in state oppression. The state may manage to survive with the help of the whip, but that is a far cry from the revolutionary goals of bringing about a new order and creating the new Arab.

If revolution and socialism became disembodied forms or were disfigured when in Arab hands, it is Azm's judgment that science encountered and is bound to encounter the same fate. In the period immediately following the Six Day War, Nasser and his spokesman Mohamed Heikal seized on the theme of science and modernity and made it their new cause. Azm said that the cause was bound to fail, due to the peculiar view of science held by the men in power: For them science was a veneer, a wrapping around an essentially unscientific culture. It is not enough to stockpile weaponry and modern machines; to be scientific requires a particular frame of mind. Here again it is the human element that decides. The Arabs, says Azm, have been importing the products of science, but this falls short of the dynamic relationship between human beings and matter that a scientific orientation requires. "We have made room in our lives for the refrigerator, the television set, oil wells, MIG airplanes, the radar . . . etc., but the mentality that uses these imported products remains the same traditional mentality that belongs to bedouin, agrarian supernatural stages that preceded the industrial revolution."[19]

The rhythm of Arab life has yet to accommodate itself to the scientific age. Arabs import the fruits of science to increase their power, but the same machines increase their alienation. Others produce and they merely consume. They come in contact with the secondary products of science, but they are far removed from the social process that made scientific breakthroughs possible. How else, asks Azm, can we explain the statement made by one religious thinker in Lebanon that the Arabs were destined to prevail over Israel because the angels that came to the help of the Prophet in one of his battles will descend "to help us today and to secure our victory in our battle with the enemy"? Such a statement may be dismissed by the sophisticated reader, but, contends Azm, it closely reflected the prevailing mentality. It was not merely popular culture that stood between the Arabs and science, but also the nature and orientation of the regimes in power, which had lagged behind the times and were still unmoved by "reform and change." Nor did universities measure up to the task: "For all of us know that our national universities are in reality institutions for administering final examinations at the end of the academic year rather than institutions for preserving, renewing, and transforming human knowledge and putting it at the service of the nation and the people."[20]

Azm's critique expresses the standard radical contempt for tradition: Tradition must be overthrown if people are to overcome their anxieties and inadequacies. Audacity, will, and dedication will liberate people from their chains. Like alienated intelligentsia in other backward societies, Azm embraces the radical notion that the destruction of tradition and the creation of the future are inseparable: Unless the first is accomplished, all ends in futility. So much, Azm concludes, was proven by the record of the regime that had tried more than any other regime in the Arab world to bring about a new political order. The Nasser regime was far too circumspect in its approach to tradition: It made too many compromises, it viewed too many things – religion, popular attitudes – as outside the domain of revolutionary politics; it left largely unchanged the deference of the lower orders to the upper ones. In short, it left standing all the main pillars of a traditional order, and thus in defeat was forced to capitulate to the will of the conservative states and to that stratum of Egyptian society that never accepted the radicalization of politics.

With the post-1967 détente between the progressive and conservative Arab regimes more or less a fact of life, it was clear to Azm, Adonis, and their fellow radicals that the revolutionary claims of the progressive states were a thing of the past. So clear, indeed, that some would go so far as to deny a distinction between the two types of regime. The issue, said Adonis, was no longer the kind of regime that the Arab lived under but the rebellion against one's conditions and weakness. In the conservative as in the radical states, people were disenfranchised and history was made from above. If Arabs continued to submit to their lot, there could be no hope that they could engage in the decisive battle, because submission breeds fear and cowardice. Writing in 1969, Adonis expressed his growing disenchantment with the Nasser regime and his doubts as to the existence of Arab will and power to undertake a serious military effort against Israel.[21]

After 1967, there was a widespread sentiment that unity was no longer the issue. It was not a frontal attack against pan-Arabism; but a deeper agnosticism that saw no utility in banding together so long as the fundamental issues of Arab society were unresolved.

An older Saudi writer, Abdullah Qusaymi, who had long been settled in Beirut, commented bitterly that the single large state that the pan-Arabists wanted would only be a vehicle for bringing to power a new version of the Abbasid Caliph Harun al-Rashid.[22] Instead of wasting the people's bread and money on "maidens, singers and poets," as the old caliph had done, the new sultan would waste people's dreams and lives on "adventures, conspiracies, and armies which would not engage the enemy and if it did would not win." The pan-Arabist dream was a search by proxy for a new tsar: The large unitary state exists only to produce the tsar whose authority derives from the authority of Allah and the Prophet. The new tsar would have all the inclinations of the old ones — "Bedouin habits and values" — with all the trappings, inducements, and instruments of modernity. Why then bother with the large unitary state? It is a frightening possibility rather than a source of hope. The state would enslave without generating power; it would aggrandize the power of one leader at the expense of mass suffering. "The story of the big state and the big empire has never been the story or idea or hope of the masses. It has always been the story of men who wanted to be great men or tyrants by diminishing others." Furthermore, why worry about progressive and reactionary states and indulge in make-believe distinctions? Like Adonis, Qusaymi is obsessed with that immutable core. The Arab remains the same regardless of the differences in regimes; his "vision of himself, of his enemy, of the world, of things around him" has not changed. So much had amounted to so little.

This agnosticism, which we shall fully encounter in the memoirs of Sami al-Jundi of the Ba'th party, was to deliver to pan-Arabism as serious a blow as the frontal attack of separatists. Under otherwise normal conditions, the radicals — by age, sensibility, and education — would have provided pan-Arabism with its faithful crop of believers. They would have gone on to spread the word on behalf of pan-Arabism against Islamic fundamentalists, communists, Marxists, or believers in separate Egyptian or Lebanese or Syrian destinies. The weakness of pan-Arabism, which was to become more obvious a decade later, could already — more so with the brilliance that hindsight always endows — be seen in the attitudes of post-1967 radicalism. At the time, however, the myth of pan-Arabism was still strong enough for the break with pan-Arabism to be made in a conscious and forthright manner.

Two other reasons precluded a frontal attack against pan-Arabism at the time. First, the radical intellectuals themselves had a wide elite audience dispersed throughout the Arab world; they spoke of issues that transcended the boundaries of individual countries. Second, the Palestinian question that was to emerge after 1967 provided another barrier against localism. Where the intelligentsia and activists happened to be Palestinian, they gave themselves a leading role and special responsibility, but they still wanted to engage the energies of other Arabs lest their quest seem too isolated. Where those concerned with the Palestinian question happened to be non-Palestinians, they wanted to rein in extreme Palestinian nationalism — not only to give themselves a role (and that motive was, understandably, present), but also to make sure that different Arab states did not go their separate ways, accept a peaceful settlement with Israel, and solidify their positions (military regimes in Egypt, Syria, and Iraq; traditional monarchy in Saudi Arabia; a peculiar blend of pluralist and feudal politics in Lebanon at home). The new radicals had sufficient contempt for nearly all Arab states that they did not want to see these states try to retreat within their own boundaries to tend to their own problems. The Palestinian question was seen as a catalyst for radical politics, an antidote to the defeatism and conservatism that the radicals believed was all around them.

But the sentiment behind the Palestinian quest, while transcending localized and parochial concerns, would nonetheless differ from the pan-Arabist assumptions of the preceding era. For some new radicals, the Palestinian question was a vehicle for bringing about social and political change; for others it was a confrontation between the larger forces of imperialism and antiimperialism, between an insurgent Third World guerrilla movement and an established state sustained by the West. From the intersection of the Palestinian movement and the new radicalism emerged two currents: One was for Palestinian nationalism that rejected wider Arab trusteeship over the Palestinians; the other was for a broad revolutionary movement of the kind popular in the mid and late 1960s, comprising guerrilla warfare, Third-Worldism, antiimperialism, and commitment to socialist change. In other words, one was narrower, the other more encompassing, than pan-Arabism. Whereas the former dismissed the right of established Arab states to make decisions for the Palestinians, the latter dismissed pan-Arabism as an empty shell — too narrow, too chauvinistic, devoid of socioeconomic content; captured, as the radicals were to state repeatedly, by a petty bourgeois element incapable of bringing about social change at home and of understanding the nature of the international system. If one group was saying, "We are Palestinians first and foremost," the other was saying that the "We-are-all-Arabs" slogan of pan-Arabism was a holdover from the past, that it had done nothing to rid the Arab world of the burden of tradition, to bring about social change, to generate power vis-à-vis other states, to build a viable order at home.

If pan-Arabism had failed, and if the prior attempt to incorporate the Arab world into the liberal order of the West had come to naught, then why not turn to the methods that worked elsewhere — in Cuba, Algeria, Vietnam, China? The radicals would now seek in the translated writings of Guevara, Debray, Marx, Lenin, and Giap what the liberals had sought earlier in the nationalism, the legality, and secular politics of the West. The sentiment was the same as was the frustration and impatience that gave rise to it. What differed were the books that people read and the models they admired.

Thirty years earlier, the distinguished Egyptian writer Taha Husayn had expressed the consensus and the yearning of a genera' tion of liberals when he called upon Egypt not only to partake of Western civilization, but to become European.[23] Now a younger generation — for whom liberalism had become anathema, another word for Western colonialism — would seek a different inspira' tion. The politics that struck at the base of old social orders and constructed new ones was clearly more appealing than yesterday's liberalism. Here and there some liberal voices were heard after 1967, but this was not to be a liberal era. Long before 1967, the liberals had lost power and self'confidence. None of what hap' pened after 1967 improved the prospects for liberal politics. In' deed, the political milieu was to become less hospitable to liberal politics and ideas. If people looked outside the Arab—Islamic tra' dition for models, it was to the radical examples of revolutionary change.

THE BA'TH PARTY: A RETROSPECT

People do not always rebel or follow new orthodoxies after old ones play themselves out. Some get discouraged and give up. Having tried one thing and dedicated their lives to it, they become disillu' sioned, turn inward to contemplate their own experiences, try to put together shattered lives and careers. For them the positive choices made by others are premature, not appealing enough, or too optimistic. Some experiences are searing enough that they leave in their wake nothing but bitterness and disillusionment. When these experiences are deeply felt and fully lived and those who live through them are sufficiently honest and articulate, the revelations can become unique human and political documents, a way of seeing history through the eyes of sensitive participants who felt the elation of momentary success and then witnessed the betrayal of once'bright ideals, the incompetence or the greed that distort or undo political quests.

The writings of Sami al'Jundi capture the experience and trag' edy of Ba'th rule in Syria. The four books he published after 1967 tell his personal story, and, perhaps more important, the story of his generation of Syrian pan-Arabists.[24] Jundi grew up in the interwar period and was one of the earliest members of the Ba'th — the party that came to think of itself as the vanguard of the national movement and in whose name the military was to rule in both Syria and Iraq. He rose to prominence in Ba'thist politics in the early 1960s, becoming Syria's ambassador to France and serving as a minister in several Syrian cabinets. He also experienced the capricious side of national politics: the cruelty of the torturer, the loneliness of the prison cell, the evanescence of so much that his generation had believed in and done.

The troubles and irresponsibility of the Ba'th had played no mean part in the malady of the pre-1967 years. The Ba'thists had urged unity but had conspired against it after it materialized. Their stout lungs and rhetoric had helped push Nasser into a corner and precipitate the Six Day War. While in power in Syria and Iraq, they had plotted, conspired, murdered, and made a mess of things. (The antics of the Ba'th have been denounced in a book by a former secretary-general of the party, Munif al-Razzaz. He had been imported from Jordan to Damascus presumably to head the party, but soon discovered that he was a mere puppet of the military, who brought him to Syria because they opposed the party's principal ideologue, Michel Aflaq.) In November, 1967, the co-founder of the Ba'th, Salah al Din al Bitar, resigned from the party, declaring that a "counter-party" had been established within the Ba'th, and that from 1963 onward he had been living in a state of "internal exile," alienated from the workings of the party and the military men who came to dominate it. The party, he said, had come to suffer from "anemia and the hardening of its arteries"; it was a "backward" party that had become "captive of a demagogic mentality and bureaucratic authoritarianism."[25] But Bitar's statement was too brief and uninformative. It remained for Jundi to write the obituary of the Ba'th and to express the disillusionment with politics and nationalism felt by those who, in the aftermath of 1967, saw no hope for the future and no way out.

Jundi's account has the power of a genre of African fiction produced by writers such as Chinua Achebe, Ngugi Wa Thiong'o, and Peter Abrahams. The theme is the bright nationalist vision ending in betrayal. The main characters begin as aspiring young men full of promise; they turn into tormentors and murderers who end up being tormented and murdered by others. Along the way, they act incoherently, become corrupt and violent; one compromise leads to another; they betray their fellows and are in turn betrayed. The outcome is all the more tragic when juxtaposed with the "beautiful beginning" – the moment of nationalist innocence, the fervor of youth.

The young men who came together in 1940 to form the Ba'th were rebels with a compelling vision. They believed they were the dawn of a new age – "We were strangers from our society, rebels against all the old values." All the leaders of the time were condemned by the new idealists, dismissed as expressions of tribalism that must be destroyed to make way for the future Arab state. The young men saw themselves as "idealists who based social relations on love." They found in European doctrines – mostly German – of nationalism the answer to the decadence of the Arab world. No one who lived through those beginning years would have believed that the Ba'th party would end up as a group of "informers, torturers, murderers." The founders of the party did not believe that they would actually achieve political power. Circumstances enabled them to get there. And once in power, they turned out to be "strangers with new mentality and old methods, with neither experience nor ideology. We believed that the centuries of decline ended with our predecessors, the politicians, and that we were the great beginning of a new culture. But we were the latest version of backwardness, a tragic expression of it. We wanted to be a resurrection of honor and heroism but nothing was resurrected with us – in power – but the age of the Mamluks."[26] While others of their generation tended to personal matters, the young men of the Ba'th lived like true believers. They wasted their youth, as Jundi bitterly remembers, on political work: "A lesson that we would recite to young students, a new member for the party, a talk in a distant village with the peasants, and how generous and attentive they were and how pure was their friendship." The experience of the Ba'th turned out to be "rich and tragic": It yearned for a new world but it was seized by the lure of power.

Jundi's work is an honest and sad portrayal of what has befallen many national anticolonial movements in the Third World. From a distance, nationalism was all glitter and promise. The age of colonialism was destined to exaggerate what people thought they would do when they took matters into their hands. As Clifford Geertz notes in a commentary on nationalist revolutions in the non-West, independence was to show that it was different to live in a nationalist world than to imagine it.[27]

A whole literature of disappointment has been coming out of the Third World; cumulatively it tells what has become of yesterday's nationalist dreams. The ruled now share the pigmentation of their rulers, speak the same language, pray to the same deity, but the new rulers crack the whip with unprecedented zeal, and the ruled have come to wonder what has become of the nationalist promise. This is not to say that they yearn for the days of colonialism — a curious argument often implied and sometimes openly stated by apologists for the colonial order and some critics of Third World politics — but only to note the discrepancy between what the anti-colonial struggle visualized and the state of many Third World polities today.

Disappointment with what political power had wrought, imprisonment, torture, and then exile from Syria give Jundi's memoirs a fatalistic tone: Not much can be done to spare societies the agonies of change; no ideology will make the Alawites and Sunnis of Syria forget their primary loyalties. There is a sense of bewilderment and frustration with an inner core that defeats or disfigures ideologies. In one passage, Jundi writes of the "tribes" or the "clans" of the Ba'th. The press may have given the more modern name of "factions" to the groups that battled for power in Syria, but they were simply "primitive tribes."[28] The Ba'th began with youthful idealism, then surrendered to the intrigues and brutality of the military. It wanted a shortcut to political power, and the military gave it the chance to wield political power, but the bargain demolished the party; the men in uniform used the slogans of the Ba'th and gave some prominent positions to its ideologues, but it was the military men who ruled and eventually pushed the civilians aside.

The civilian ideologues had words and pamphlets and could endow a ruling regime with revolutionary legitimacy. But power rested with the military, which grew increasingly weary with what Jundi calls the "poetry" of the Ba'th and struck out on its own. The military men themselves caught the Ba'thist infatuation with ideology and verbiage; they too were to repeat the term "revolution" until it lost all meaning. In the turbulent 1960s, people got used to the movement of tanks from barracks to government buildings whenever the military announced the rise of a new order and the end of a decadent one. First the people would rejoice, then all hope would vanish and the tanks would reembark on the same journey to take over the same places and repeat the same words. These are the ways of the military and the teachings of their civilian mentors — a degradation of ideology and a demeaning of revolution.

Jundi attributes the Ba'thist infatuation with words to the character of Michel Aflaq, the intellectual founder of the Ba'th party.

Aflaq was more an artist than a leader and politician; he had the artist's propensity for escape from reality to a world that exists only in his imagination. "To him [Aflaq] the party was an artistic creation that took the place of a novel or a poem; he wanted the party as his novel or glorious epic and he loved it as an artist would love his own creation."[29] But politics and art are different things. Aflaq's creation turned into a tale of horror – bloody coups, repression, disillusionment and, finally, the loss of the Golan.

Neither the party's civilian ideologues, with their abstractions, nor the military men were capable of competent; dedicated governance – they were too busy conspiring. Domestically their rule led to economic ruin; their foreign policy led to war and a catastrophe for the Arab world. In both domestic and foreign policies, the Ba'thists were obsessed with one idea: "We must be ahead of Abdul Nasser." Land reform and nationalization of industries were ill considered; the economic dimension hardly occurred to the Ba'thists. Local feuds and rivalries dictated the course of land reform. Slogans determined the issue of nationalization and helped bring about the economic ruin of the country.

No one in the top leadership bothered to say – or even managed to understand – that war and peace and an orderly state required a sound economic base. The tribes of the Ba'th were immune to such considerations; all they cared about was the securing of public jobs for their relatives. Salah Jadid, the quintessential conspirator, the Alawite officer who shunned the spotlight and was at one time the real power in Syrian politics, had every person in his family over eighteen years of age on the public payroll. Clans battled for advantage and conspired to eliminate one another. The state remained an extension of that tribal mentality. Jundi reports an exchange he had with Salah Jadid in which the latter asked what could be done to deal with the "sectarian problem." Jundi suggested that the Alawites, a minority sect shrouded in mystery and accused by the Sunni population of deifying Ali, the son-in-law of the Prophet – hence of being unbelievers – make public their secret books and beliefs so as to remove the Sunnis' suspicions once and for all. "He [Jadid] said, 'If we did so we would be destroyed by the Shaykhs.' I answered, 'You are a revolutionary and you fear the Shaykhs? How then will you deal with the big problems?' He did not answer, but from then on my problems with the regime began and I later learned that he was paying Zakat [alms] to the Shaykhs and that he was endearing himself to them."[30]

Incompetence and irrationality in domestic matters were paralleled by erratic conduct in pan-Arab and Arab–Israeli politics. In these spheres, the Nasser complex was a more powerful obsession. As Jundi tells it, the Six Day War ended in tragedy because the civilian demagogues and the military men in Syria miscalculated: They thought Jordan would stay out of the war, Egypt and Israel would exhaust and destroy each other, and they themselves would come to the rescue, inheriting the Jordanian monarchy and emerging as the true leaders of the nationalist movement.

While the Syrian army was in disarray, paralyzed by conspiracies and counter-conspiracies with hundreds of officers either in prison or on diplomatic missions abroad — regardless of whether they spoke the language of the country to which they were sent — the Syrian head of state, Nur al Din al Atasi, gave ringing speeches of fire and bravado. "We shall feed the Sixth Fleet to the fish of the Mediterranean," was one of Atasi's typical statements. In the Ba'th's distorted and romantic view, the Soviet Union was an instrument at the disposal of the Syrian regime — a giant that appears when one rubs one's ring to one's command. When these delusions turned to ashes — King Husein entered the war, Syria shared in the defeat and had neither prestige nor overthrown monarchies to inherit, and the Soviet Union could not change the outcome — the Ba'th had a choice between the survival of its regime and land — the Golan Heights. Thinking that land could be regained but that the order could not, it chose the latter. And in so doing it destroyed itself.

Jundi's generation had thought that their predecessors lost Palestine because of treason and betrayal — King Abdullah's duplicity, King Faruq's treachery, Iraq's rivalry with Egypt. Now there was an unflattering comparison between the record of the monarchies and that of the pan-Arabists: "What is the difference between stupidity and treason if the result is the same?"[31]

That was not what the young men who had pinned their hopes on the Ba'th thought back in 1940 when they declared war on tradition and committed themselves to Arab unity. They believed that they had put the past behind them, that they had once and for all brought to a close the age of decline. But the generation that was to be the savior bequeathed to its successors impotent thought, a mountain of words, and a legacy of defeat: "We accomplished all the wishes of imperialism while we were shouting against it." Jundi notes that freedom is needed if the Arab world is to make the life or death choice that faces it, but the "world of defeat" does not look kindly upon those who dissent and rebel: "I am sure that the world of defeat will not forgive me, for it rejects the rebellion of the solitary individual. My books are banned in most Arab countries; whether reactionary or progressive, the men in power in these countries prove that rebellious thought is their most dreaded enemy."[32]

Others may see nothing particularly profound in the conclusion that the behavior of a particular nation reflects the substance and style of its historical experience and the durability of its cultural patterns. But it has always been the tendency of revolutionary imagery and ideology to claim novelty and to stress the breaking of chains and the forging of new relationships. In such situations, the discovery of the past emerges as a theme only after a particular experiment overreaches itself, suffers defeat, and fails to build the new Jerusalem.

Discontinuity with the past had been the hope and claim of the Ba'thists of Jundi's generation. But the experience of nearly three decades was to impress upon Jundi the haunting power of the past. Like so many others who examined the 1967 defeat, he was eventually to raise questions about the weight of the past and the burden of Arab history. The discovery of the past underscored the extreme pretensions of novelty and radicalism that had been part of the ideological baggage of the self-styled radical nationalists.

Al-Jundi's discovery of the past leads to a set of remarkable, sober, and insightful excursions into Arab history that break with the dominant nationalist historiography of his time. They warrant attention because they constitute an honest attempt to grab hold of a particular tradition, to see Arab history for what it really is without the cant of nationalism or the glorification of apologists.[33] History was not to be read into a sacred text or to be inferred from examining a society's ideals, but to be derived from the actual push and pull of events, from the compromises made, from the wounds suffered, and the way in which people went about consoling themselves and reconciling noble claims with dismal realities. For Jundi, the thrust of Arab–Islamic history was the attempt to evade the decline of a once ascendant and successful order, to run away from an unflattering and cruel reality to a mythical view that explained away failure and held out the promise of redemption.

During centuries of decline, the Arabs kept alive the image of past greatness. Backwardness and decline were attributed to deviation from religious teachings and to the disappearance of belief. "The image of the past becomes a heroic myth which the Arab compares with his desperate situation."[34] This, in Jundi's views, accounts for the sense of melancholy and tragedy discernible not only in Arab music and literature but also in political theory.

"Roving poets" went from village to village telling "innocent listeners removed from the influence of European civilization and of
the machine" about the past, with many embellishments and an
abundance of imagination. Their stories helped create a heroic
model — the Savior who will appear to restore the glories of early
classical Islam. The model was a simple popular image that embodied all the traits that the Arab — the imagined one, that is — had
lost along the way. Thus history intermingled with myth and produced a "primitive, simple ideology removed from the necessities
of the modern age."[35]

The ruthless assaults of the world engendered even greater escapism as well as largely futile attempts to stave off further decline. After the Napoleonic invasion of Egypt, the Arabs came to
feel that the world they lived in was only a distorted reflection of
the real world. The grave violations to their psyche, values, religion, and sense of historical and cultural integrity inspired a handful of men, such as Muhammad Ibn Ahd al-Wahhab, the founder
of the Wahhabi movement in Najd, Jamal al Din al Afghani, Muhammad Abdu, and Rashid Rida to attempt to revitalize Islam, to
make it capable of resisting the assaults of the modern world, to
integrate parts of the heritage with what they judged to be the
least disruptive features of modernity. These men, says Jundi,
mixed religious doctrines with nationalism. This confusion persisted until the Young Turks tried to impose national Turkish
dominance upon the Arabs at the turn of the twentieth century.
The secular zeal of the Young Turks, the inducements of the West,
and the inspiration provided by new nationalist doctrines finally
broke Muslim universalism and enabled the Arabs to rebel against
the Ottoman Empire and to support the cause of the Allies. But
the Arabs soon learned that they were not considered allies but
"one of the targets of the war." "They were deceived and were
sold like slaves." The scars of that period made the Arabs "doubt
the worth of human values."[36] As a result, many thinkers came to
propogate the logic of force in the world, to argue that the rule of
the strong is the only truth, and to push their nationalist doctrines
in chauvinistic directions. German doctrines of nationalism — romantic, militant — seized the imaginations of a number of intellectuals. These doctrines seeped down to a small number of activists
and would-be intellectuals anxious for a new recipe for glamor and
power. Jundi provides a vivid reconstruction of the ideological climate of the period. He and his fellow radicals read with great admiration Nietzsche's *Thus Spake Zarathustra*, Fichte's *Addresses*

to the German Nation, and Chamberlain's *Foundations of the Nineteenth Century* and were the first to want to translate Hitler's *Mein Kampf.*

How did this exalted view of nationalism work in the Arab world? It presumably filled the ideological void caused by the collapse of liberalism and the growing disaffection with traditional institutions. Where there was weakness, it promised power and glamor; it supplied an anticolonial framework; it gave alienated young men a sense of purpose and mission. But, in retrospect, did it not contribute, among other things, to the extremism of the Ba'th? Is there no connection between the glorification of the nation and the trampling upon the individual that Jundi observed all around him? What of the romanticism, the noise, and the metaphysics that had characterized Arab nationalism? Can they be explained, at least in part, by the Germanization of so much of Arab nationalist doctrine? Jundi does not directly take up these questions, but this much can surely be read into his historical narrative: The exalted theories of nationalism popular in the interwar period and during World War II were to come to fruition in the post – World War II years. The discrepancy between the exalted claims and the dismal realities was only to lead to greater frustration and incoherence.

The Germanization of Arab nationalist thought occurred at a time when liberal notions of nationalism were on the wane in the Arab world. If liberal nationalism was too individualistic, associated with domestic privilege and with the colonial powers, then why not an integral, collectivist notion of nationalism? Long before Arab nationalists were seduced by Germanic doctrines, the intelligentsia and the politically zealous in other nations had felt the almost mystic appeal of those doctrines. Did not the Russian intelligentsia in the nineteenth century find in Germanic thought the answer to the problems of a decaying order? In nineteenth-century Russia, Germanic thought "impose[d] its prestige on minds torn between their desire for vengeance and justice and the realization of their own imposed isolation." Even in France, as Camus reminds us, the nineteenth century was, thanks to thinkers like Michelet and Quinet, "the century of Germanic thought."[37]

Surveying the wreckage all around him, Sami al-Jundi tries to find slivers of hope. More out of despair than conviction, he identifies three signs of hope. The first was Palestinian resistance; the anger of the fedayeen reassured him that the Arabs were still a living people, capable of doing more than simply devouring themselves: "Little by little," he said, the Palestinians were separating themselves "from the world of the defeat."[38] Men are numb in the age of decline, and the capacity of the Palestinians for some action was perhaps a sign of some life. But even they, Jundi prophetically warned, exhibited some traditional ailments: machismo, failure to organize, exaggerated claims, and a bit of escapism. The second hopeful sign was what he judged to be a different Nasser: a man deepened by tragedy, determined to correct his own errors and the errors of an entire generation.

The third sign may reveal the extent of Jundi's despair but may also include some deeper wisdom about the groping for change in post-1967 Arab politics – it was the suicide in mid-September, 1967, of the Egyptian commander Abdel Hakim Amir. Jundi saw that act as a harbinger of a new world. Many, he said, saw the suicide of Amir as an "ordinary event but I saw in it the beginning of a new world of anger and the eradication of old beliefs so that new ones would arise in their place."[39] For Jundi the suicide of Amir revolved around the question of personal responsibility. In the old world, men acted, and when they failed they laid the blame on others or on divine will. Amir, however, in choosing suicide, chose to make a different statement; he saw himself as responsible for

> the defeat of his army, for an occupation of part of his country and then for a conspiracy against his boss, leader and friend, so he tried and convicted himself and passed on himself a death sentence . . .[40]

This may seem like a "normal chain of events to a European," but it is something entirely alien to the Middle East. Muslims, he rightly observed, rarely commit suicide. Amir, although an observant Muslim, chose to kill himself; his sense of personal responsibility overpowered his adherence to Islam. Few notable suicides can be found in the history of Islam – the only case known to Jundi was the suicide of Abu al-Qasim, the conqueror of the Indian kingdom of Sind who was reported to have commanded his victorious army at the age of sixteen. That Amir chose to kill himself may suggest that Arabs were now willing to see the world as a product of their labor and sacrifices as well as of their errors.

The illusions entertained in a more youthful and innocent period were shattered; men could no longer hide behind slogans. The pessimism of Sami al-Jundi goes beyond the boundaries of Syria and the Arab world. A life of political struggle and then defeat led him to rethink the achievements and the failures of his generation of nationalists in what he calls "backward countries." That generation, he says, tried to close the cultural gap with Europe, but the

harvest of so much effort was a good deal of repression and perhaps
an aggravation of backwardness. Trying to do so much in a short
period of time, Jundi's generation saw salvation in political power;
it made many attempts — some sincere, some desperate and
clumsy — to organize backward societies and push them toward
modernity. Troubled by the slow progress of things, it

> thought that power would enable it to fulfill its historical
> role, so it tenaciously clung to it and depended on it and
> forgot its starting point and good intentions until power
> became its goal rather than its means.[41]

Sami al-Jundi's memoirs re-create the desperate search of the intelligentsia for a system of thought that would smash tradition, drive
out Western colonialism, build up the nation, glorify it, and unite
it, as Prussia united the German nation. But as Jundi was to learn,
tradition persists, and theory — imported, immoderate, lacking a
sense of proportion as to the costs, means, and ends of political action — can create plenty of noise without altering the substance
and bases of politics. Worse yet, it can destroy the sensibilities of a
hitherto dominant tradition without imparting new standards and
values. Then there is a change in mood: The earlier confidence in
the easy destruction of tradition is dissipated, and tradition is seen
as an unchanging core that will defy all remedies, mock all solutions, and use as garb anything new that is proposed. Both moods
are conveyed in Sami al-Jundi's reflections and review of his past:
first, the desperate escape to books and doctrines; then, three decades later, the discovery of self, the loss of all hope. With enthusi-
astic, messianic politics there is always the risk that men's belief
that everything can be done will vanish, that men will be left with
nothing but defeated spirits.

THE ISLAMIC RESPONSE: RADICAL FUNDAMENTALISM

In both liberal and radical analyses, religion is denounced as the
dead hand of the past. Because both systems of thought seek to liberate humanity and harness its energy for the reconstruction of
the social order, the hold of religious sentiments is seen as a reactionary force. Modernization puts religion in an unfavorable light;
religion becomes an obstacle to social change. The bias of secular
ideologies is that people must discard their religious faith if they
are to make progress. This is not an analytical judgment on the
part of secular ideologists, but, paradoxically, an article of faith

that is adhered to with the same intensity with which religious beliefs are said to be held. In the imagery and folklore of secular ideology, religious individuals are caricatures: men obsessed with
other-worldly concerns, surrendering to divine will, immune to
science, exploited by a religious hierarchy, willing to forego struggle for this world in order to gain the other. The details of the
caricature may vary from one religion to another, but the compos-
ite is the same: Instead of attending cell meetings, participating in
electoral politics, or giving body and soul to the nation in arms, a
religious man would pray, fast, spend his money on a pilgrimage,
trust in the will of Allah.

For many secular Arab ideologists, the defeat was another dramatic illustration of the crisis of Islam: lethargic, backward Muslims defeated by a modern enemy.[42] The debate about the relation
between Islam and the modern world is of course an old one; it
preoccupied the intelligentsia in the nineteenth century. During
the age of Islamic decline and European ascendancy, the twin
issues of internal reform and external defense engaged Arab intellectuals and men of public affairs and divided their ranks. By its
very nature, this debate did not lend itself to a resolution. Different people went different ways, and some, as usual, juggled many
systems of belief. Thus it was only natural for the debate about
Islam to reemerge in the aftermath of the 1967 defeat.

The defeat provided radical secularists with an opportunity to
express their frustration with the persistence of Islamic sentiments. In the era that preceded the defeat, secular nationalism,
seemingly radical politics, annd the tempo of social change had
somehow created a set of expectations that Islam would wither
away and lose its hold on the believers. That view was never stur-
dily based but rested on the alienation of the intelligentsia from religious belief, on the easy assumption that religion and nationalism
were incompatible and, finally, on the fashionable global assertion
of the time that people were killing their deities and that religion as
a social force was living on borrowed time. The secularists had
read their own alienation from religion into the society at large. To
be sure, a certain segment of the population had rebelled against
religion but the overwhelming majority of people had not. Nor did
the presumed incompatibility between nationalism and Islam hold
for the Arab world. The more popular nationalism became, the
more it identified with Islam. The separation that the secular Arab
intellectual made between Arabism and Islam was not made by the
less educated citizen; for the latter, the two were overlapping, almost identical forces.[43] The power of Islam was attested to by the

fact that the regimes that professed their adherence to socialism had dressed their socialism in an Islamic garb and justified their version of socialism by saying that it emanated from Islamic sources. If Islam could survive nationalism and be grafted onto socialism, the secular intellectuals were no longer sure of the withering away of Islam.

In the aftermath of defeat, the turning of the masses to religion for solace and consolation and the continual appeal, couched in religious terms, for faith and patience on the part of no less a figure than President Nasser, served as a reminder that God may be dead elsewhere — particularly in existential European literature and in Marxist tracts read by Arab youth — but was alive and well in the Arab world. The attempt of the radicals to link Islam with the defeat did not go uncontested. Indeed, Islamic fundamentalism made an eloquent and moving case of its own and turned defeat into advantage. Fundamentalists argued that the Arabs had lost the war not because they were busy worshipping — as the radical caricature would have it — but because they had lost their faith and bearings: Disconnected from a deeply held system of beliefs, the Arabs proved an easy prey to Israeli power.

The argument made by thoughtful fundamentalists was similar to the one made by the radical critics: The latter, too, had argued that a society needs a system of beliefs, an ideology, to guide it. The fundamentalists' contention was that Islam offered that system of belief, that it could do what no imported doctrine could hope to do — mobilize the believers, instill discipline, and inspire people to make sacrifices and, if necessary, to die.

Muhammad Jalal Kishk's *Al Naksa Wa al Ghazw al Fikri* (The Setback and Cultural Invasion) is the work of a prolific writer with Muslim Brotherhood affinities. The notion of cultural invasion seems to be the cornerstone of Kishk's outlook; the term appears in the titles of four of his books — one on general cultural penetration, two volumes on Marxism and nationalism as variants of cultural penetration, and one on the connection between cultural penetration and the Six Day War.[44] Kishk's writings belie the notion that Muslim fundamentalists are reactionaries fixated on the image of a theocratic past that has to be restored. In Kishk's world view, cultures clash for preeminence: Some rise and conquer, and others surrender and are subjugated. An old-fashioned thinker, Kishk has no appreciation for what he sees as a fraudulent kind of cosmopolitanism propagated by the West and subscribed to by fifth-column Muslim Arabs. For Kishk there is no such thing as a

world civilization; cosmopolitanism is the pretension of the ascendant culture "that asks others to abandon their identity and
sovereignty, to dismantle their culture," and gives them a choice
between adherence to its postulates or extinction.[45] According to
Kishk, what we are witnessing now is the third crusade against the
Arab people. The first crusade, using the sword and the cross, realized some victories but was eventually overwhelmed. The second
crusade – the age of imperialism – began with Napoleon's invasion of Egypt in 1798 and succeeded in destroying the self-confidence of the Muslim world. The third crusade picks up where the
second left off: It accommodates itself to political independence;
instead of using armies, it seeks to penetrate the mind of the Muslim and to rearrange it. Once the Muslim accepted the "supremacy of the West – not just material supremacy but cultural and
spiritual supremacy as well – the Muslim's resistance would collapse; he would become like an open, defenseless city, vulnerable to
every plunderer and invader."[46]

   That civilizations clash in a Darwinian manner for preeminence
and survival is fully realized by Westerners. Why, asks Kishk, do
Muslim Arabs fail or refuse to accept that overwhelming historical
fact? In part, they have been lulled into complacency by the West,
which spreads the myth of cosmopolitanism. Then there is the role
played by an imported ideological doctrine, such as Marxism,
which postulates a fake universalism of its own. Afraid of looking
old fashioned before their liberal and Marxist mentors, Muslim
Arabs succumb to the process of cultural invasion and come to accept the myths propagated by the West about the decline of religious fervor and the unity of cultures. Meanwhile, the West brings
to its encounter with the Arabs a *ruh salibiyya* (crusading spirit);
it is as hostile to the Muslim world as ever.

   Sincere people cling tenaciously to their beliefs. Mimics go
whichever way the wind blows. They translate others' works, accept the latest fads, live through others' experiences, try to shed
their biases, apologize for their particularism, adopt the ways of
others. In Kishk's analysis, Muslim Arabs are neutralized, paralyzed by false doctrines of universalism – both liberal and Marxist – pitted against one another by sham ideological divisions con-
cocted by the West. Meanwhile, underneath the sound and fury of
ideology, behind the hair-splitting arguments, the eternal clash of
civilizations goes on, the dominant civilization parading as glob-
alism and subjugating other civilizations. Kishk holds up for his
readers the Sino – Soviet split as an example of the transparency of

ideology. No amount of ideology can bridge the gap between an Oriental country and an Occidental one, the old rivalry between China and Russia.

Kishk argues that cultural and ideological penetration are to the twentieth century what gunboats were to the nineteenth. Marxism, which has succeeded in seducing Arab intellectuals, is but another weapon in the West's ideological assault. For Kishk, it is the westernism of Marx that matters, not his opposition to capitalism. In the duel of civilizations, Marx is clearly on the other side:

> Marx did not call for a new civilization: he is a faithful son of Western civilization who formed his theory out of German philosophy, French socialism, and English political economy . . . Marx believed in the values and the history of Western civilization; he was proud of that history which he considered as a triumph for humanity on its way to its final victory. He considered the crimes of Western civilization a historical necessity and did not trace those crimes to the philosophy of that civilization but, rather, to economic necessities.[47]

Marxism was not the only European affliction forced upon the Arab–Muslim world: Another, earlier one was secular nationalism. Kishk is even more contemptuous of secular nationalism than he is of Marxism, more certain of its disruptive consequences. Arabs were so convinced of the power of secular nationalism, so taken by its mystique, he says, that they were willing to set aside their religious beliefs in pursuit of the nationalist dream. But the history of secular Arab nationalism was a chronicle of defeat and setbacks. It does not strike Kishk as a paradox that the force that generated power for Europe brought weakness to the Arab world. Europe needed secular nationalism, which provided an effective way of organizing a community. But things were different in the Muslim world. Under the banner of Islam, disparate populations and ethnic groups had long been organized into a community. A unique kind of socialist ethos had been part of this community's creed and practice. At the height of its glory, it had laid siege to Vienna and outstripped Europe in the realms of science, philosophy, and culture, as well as war. Then the Muslims caught the germ of nationalism. The Ottoman Turks were the first victims of nationalism; the Arabs were next. The house of Islam was now divided, and Europeans could easily subdue the Muslim world. Minorities were now warring against one another. The concept of nationality, held in check by Islamic universalism, had shattered the basis of the community.

All this, it could be said, is the remote background of the June defeat. Had the Arab states waged the war along the only true lines – religious lines – victory would have been theirs, Kishk argues. Certainly the Israelis had seen their conflict with the Arabs along these lines. Kishk's image of Israel allows of no ambiguity: It is a religious state through and through. In Kishk's account there is grudging admiration for the clarity with which the Israelis saw the war, for the fact that young Israeli soldiers prayed behind their rabbis at the Wailing Wall after their capture of Jerusalem. Why did Muslims fail to exhibit the same religious zeal? Kishk believes that they were too embarrassed to do so: False doctrines about the class struggle and progressive nationalism had blurred their vision. He blames the regimes in Syria and Egypt for leading their people astray, for making cowards and inept soldiers out of a community that had a history of glorious victories.

A war society should organize itself in a roughly egalitarian manner: Bread and hardships should be divided in such a way that men are convinced of the justice of the social order. Such was not the case in the Arab military regimes, in which class arrogance and social stratification precluded a fighting society. The military class, placed at the apex of a social order of inequality, appropriated the public wealth for its own privilege and edification. The Arab armies were too busy living off the public treasury to stand up to the enemy. Furthermore, the military was riddled with factionalism; officers spent far more time watching and plotting against one another than they did thinking about the enemy. The Arab officer, according to Kishk, costs his society far more than does his American counterpart, but he hardly gets a chance to put to practice what he has learned. Sooner or later he finds his way to prison, or he becomes a corporate director, or an official responsible for fouling up industrial production in some factory, or someone who sabotages politics in some embassy.

Unimpressed with the ideological claims of the military and their advocacy of socialism and revolution, Kishk finds in medieval dynastic history an apt explanation of the military in power. These men, he says, are "socialist Mamluks." The new men, like the Mamluks before them, consider the land and those on it the property of the sultan.[48] For the military establishment, socialism means the military's dominance of the wealth of the country. None of this is new or modernizing. Kishk was exposed to Western writings that, in the early 1960s, saw the military as an instrument of modernization, as a vanguard of social change. In alluding to the Mamluks, he places the ascendency of the Arab military in proper historical perspective. It is not a new, modernizing phenomenon but a retrogression, a resurrection of the politics of dynasties and intrigue. In the age of Islamic decline, "military gangs" assassinated, usurped power, and established dynasties that were subsequently overthrown by other soldiers of fortune. A keen student of Islamic history, Kishk can see through the claims of the military who proclaimed themselves – and were accepted by many analysts – as a repository of the national will. He can find the thread that connects the new military with its predecessors.

The new Mamluks have misunderstood and distorted the meaning of revolution. For them revolution is mere seizure of power; they see no difference between a coup d'etat – *inqilab* – and a revolution – *thawra*. Had they appreciated the difference, they would have realized that revolution does not occur with a mere attack on a radio station. In the practice of the military, the sole determinant of revolutionary politics was control of the radio station. Whoever controlled it was a revolutionary socialist, and whoever lost it was denounced as a reactionary agent of imperialism. None of this of course had anything to do with war and preparation for war. The military cliques were disinterested in it and unprepared for it. And when they lost in 1967 their main concern was to rush back from the front to hatch new conspiracies and prepare for the coming purge.

Kishk does not consider the military officers the only culprits. He also blames the radical intellectuals who hammered at the foundations of belief, imported false doctrines, and unleashed the moral confusion that paved the way for the defeat. The radical intellectuals put their faith in concepts such as world peace, brotherhood among nations, and humane socialism, but such beliefs put nations that take them seriously at the mercy of aggressive ones. In this world, the eagle and the sparrow cannot coexist; there can be no brotherhood between the killer and the victim. Human history is built on strife. Islam recognized this truth. The Muslim battle cry *"Jihad"* was the only thing that frightened the Europeans; it drew the boundaries between belief and unbelief, setting Muslims apart from other men. But Islam has long been on the defensive, and in its own house men preach its obsolescence and inadequacy and call for its destruction.

Each society must analyze its own predicament; each people must proceed from its own reality. For Kishk, the overwhelming reality is the existence of Muslim people who want to be true to themselves and to withstand the assaults of outsiders. Thus, Islamic movements that proceed from the objective social conditions of the Muslim world are the only ones that can claim to be authentic. Movements that attempt to read into the Islamic world the predicament and the solutions of other societies can lead only to estrangement and mimicry. Kishk's opposition to the radical intellectuals is based more on utilitarian concerns than on concerns about heresy. Our soil, he says, is Islamic; a nonnative plant is destined to die. Nor will attempts at cross-fertilization work: The plant will not survive.[49] Revolutions, Kishk insists, must be authentic. For all its polemical output, he points out, Arab radicalism has yet to produce a single volume, like Mao's, that analyzes local realities independent of the thoughts of foreign masters. No translators have ever transformed societies.

Kishk singles out as an example of the output of the radical intelligentsia Nadim Bitar's book on the 1967 defeat, *Min al Naksa ila al-Thawra* (From Setback to Revolution). Bitar, a Western-educated sociologist, proposed a typically radical argument about the defeat. He saw Islamic loyalties as the primary factor behind it. He also called upon the Arabs to revolt against their religion and adopt a truly revolutionary ideology: Arabs had to "stand naked before history" if they were to break through their dismal situation; they had to recognize that Islam and the traditional thought from which it emerges and that it sustains had led to a stagnant, superstitious society that looked for guidance in a classical text and in the lives and thoughts of men who inhabited a different world.

Other modern revolutions, Bitar argued, understood that the first revolutionary act was to liberate society from the hold of religion. The French Revolution was unambiguous in its denunciation of religion; it understood and taught future generations that the notion of divine transcendence was a pillar of a reactionary political order. Brissot, Chalier, and Saint-Just had set an example for others: To sanction a new order one must slay the God that had long sanctioned old arrangements. Bitar urged Muslims to do the same for Islam too, in his view, had served as a pillar of reaction.

Kishk spotted a paradox in Bitar's presentation. The latter had chided the ordinary Muslim for surrendering to a system of authority outside his will. But, asks Kishk, what is the difference between a traditional Muslim who says that we lost the war because we disobeyed the will of Allah, and Bitar, who asserts that we lost it because we disobeyed Marx's teachings and the teachings of the other messengers whose testimonies he has showered on us? Different people, different prophets: The Muslim looks to the Hadith of the Prophet; Bitar finds truth in Marx's writings. Bitar is as much a captive of a closed ideological system as he presumes the Muslim to be.

That authenticity alone can secure victory is confirmed for Kishk in Algeria's struggle against France. Where others see in Algeria's triumph a victory for a radical ideology, Kishk sees the triumph of Islam. Islam alone, he maintains, preserved the integrity of Algeria and gave it the will to survive. The French had succeeded in seducing the intelligentsia, in remaking that layer of Algeria in France's image. Shelter, escape, and resistance were provided and made possible by Islam. Islam was one fortress that the French could not conquer and the rock on which their plans for integrating Algeria with the Metropole faltered.

The Algerian case and Kishk's views of it substantiate Clifford Geertz's depiction of the role of Islam as a language of refusal. Because the colonial encounter had been, in Geertz's words, a "clash of selves," religion became a safe haven, a way of defending one's integrity, for the "only thing the colonial elite was not and, a few ambiguous cases aside, could not become was Muslim."[50] That was why Muslims increasingly became oppositional Muslims at the height of the anticolonial struggle: When other routes of escape and resistance were cut off, religion provided the will to revolt and the language of dissent.

The many faces of the Algerian revolution were examined in this and countless other exchanges that took place in the Arab world after the June defeat. For the radicals, the Algeria that had triumphed was the Algeria of Frantz Fanon — guerrilla struggle, militant Third Worldism. They believed that the Arabs of the mashriq (the Arab East) had only to emulate the heroic resistance of the Algerians and adopt their ideological commitment. For Kishk and other fundamentalist writers, Algeria's triumph was a vindication of indigenous tradition, the triumph of militant, anticolonial Islam.[51]

Fundamentalists as well as radical critics held up the example of Algeria, not only because it was a case of Arab success on the battlefield, but also because it signaled their opposition to the politics of compromise and to the pursuit of a diplomatic settlement with Israel. Both groups reasoned that the Arab world had no bargaining power, that negotiation was tantamount to surrender. World politics is not decided by appeals to the court of world opinion, warned Kishk; the system of stages is a cruel one, and Western thinking is particularly Darwinistic. This was not a theoretical discussion as much as an attack against the view that what was lost on the battlefield could be recovered at a peace conference, that world public opinion would arbitrate the matter in a spirit of fairness and justice.

Kishk's analysis, which takes as its premise the clash of civilizations, has very little patience with appeals to the conscience of humanity. The edifice of Western civilization, he observed, was built largely through violence and through the near extinction of many native populations. The Arab stands vis-à-vis the Israeli in roughly the same manner as the native American stood vis-à-vis the white settler. It is folly to expect sympathy for Arabs suffering from Western civilization – "the civilization of Tarzan and the cowboy."[52] For two thousand years, Jews grieved over their treatment by the West. That brought them very little sympathy; indeed, it invited greater persecution. The enemy is again an example of how people should struggle to alter their situation, a reminder that the world feels no sorrow for the losers, that it accepts the realities created by the victors.

The Arabs, once winners, are now losers, and their capacity to survive is at stake. In an interesting appropriation of Israeli imagery, Kishk sees Muslim Arabs threatened with extinction. More than a century ago, European imperialism denied the Arab world the opportunity to enter the modern, industrial system. Since that time, the gap between civilizations with power and those without has increased at an alarming rate. The pace of growth threatens to widen the gap; it may make the gap impossible to bridge, something akin to the gap that separates man from the ape. Israel is part of an ascendant, powerful Occident; the Zionist invaders will try to subdue this part of the world in the name of white civilization. This is the central challenge to the Arab world, a threat to its foundation. If the Arabs are to continue to misinterpret their predicament, their survival will be called into question.

Kishk's diagnosis of the Arab ailment and his prescriptions cannot be dismissed simply as reactionary, fundamentalist, or theocratic. Kishk's quest is not just the resurrection of a lost and ideal past. For some time, indigenous Third World traditions have been on the defensive against Western analysts and young intellectuals in Third World societies who openly ridicule indigenous traditions and assert that these traditions are incompatible with the needs and issues of our time. Indeed, the consensus on the obsolescence of traditional orders has been so overwhelming that those who hold it have felt no obligation to supply proof or to look into the tradition in question. In simplistic fashion, tradition and modernity are

seen as two radically different worlds. The supremacy of modernity is an article of faith. It has never been fully explained how and
why traditions should be shed or whether they can be shed. The
intellectual who asks people to stand naked before history perpetu-
ates a false myth: He or she fosters the illusion that such a thing
can be done and that others elsewhere have done it to get where
they are today. But Kishk and those like him are perceptive: They
not only reject the intrinsic moral worth of such an act; they know
that it is impossible.

The radical Arab intellectuals whose ideas I have sampled had
an indifferentiated view of tradition, and their view was that tradition should be smashed. Daniel Lerner's once-influential book
The Passing of Traditional Society[53] took for granted the supremacy of modernity over tradition. Lerner was sure that modern
man was a superior species and that tradition was doomed to extinction. On the whole, what has been missing from both radical
and liberal perspectives on traditional orders is the appreciation
that fundamentalism of any kind comes with variations, that traditions have multiple usages.

The virtue of Kishk's analysis was to demonstrate that tradition-
alist thought can be penetrating and unapologetic and can be
turned onto social and political problems without excessive piety.
For a society that came to doubt itself after a massive defeat,
Kishk's brand of fundamentalism offered a vision of the future out
of a certain reading of Islam.[54] And the product that emerged was
far from reactionary or static. In an oft-cited passage, Wilfred
Cantwell Smith, a leading student of Islam, speaks to the multiple
usages of traditions and the potentially radical impact of the kind
of fundamentalism represented by Kishk and the Muslim Brotherhood:

> To regard the Ikhwan [the Muslim Brothers] as purely
> reactionary would, in our judgment, be false. For there is
> at work in it also a praiseworthy constructive endeavour to
> build a modern society on a basis of justice and humanity, as
> an extrapolation from the best values that have been
> enshrined in the tradition from the past. It represents in
> part a determination to sweep aside the degeneration into
> which Arab society has fallen, the essentially unprincipled
> social opportunism interlaced with individual corruption;
> to get back to a basis for society of accepted moral stan-
> dards and integrated vision, and to go forward to a pro-
> gramme of active implementation of popular goals by an ef-

fectively organized corps of disciplined and devoted idealists. It represents in part a determination to sweep aside the inactive reverence for an irrelevant, static, purely transcendental ideal; and to transform Islam from the sentimental enthusiasm of purely inert admirers or the antiquated preserve of professional traditionalists tied in thought and practice to a bygone age, into an operative force actively at work on modern problems.[55]

This is why radical fundamentalism has posed so formidable a problem to ruling regimes and why it manages, despite repeated crackdowns, to survive in a country like Egypt. The shock of the military defeat created a deep need for solace and consolation, and Islam provided the needed comfort. That phenomenon was strongest in Egypt, but the same thing happened throughout the Arab world. Sensing the new mood, the previously more or less secular pan-Arabists began to display greater piety. The officially guided media in both Egypt and Syria recalled the great achievements and adversities of Islam and the deeds of the Prophet and his early followers.

In Egypt, this may have begun as early as June 6, as soon as the defeat had sunk in. A cable from President Nasser to King Husein giving Nasser's consent to the evacuation of the Jordanian troops from the West Bank had a heavier dose of religiosity than was customary in Nasser's statements: "We believe in Allah and it is not possible that Allah will abandon us and perhaps the coming days will bring us a victory from Him. May Allah help us and let his will be a guide for us."[56] A mere two months after the defeat, the Eqyptian press reported that booklets explaining the meaning of jihad and recounting the campaigns of the Prophet had been distributed to the armed forces. A fundamentalist writer noted the change of heart on the part of the Egyptian regime, which, on the eve of the war, had reported that one hundred and sixty thousand pictures of an old musician, a matinee idol, and two popular actresses had been sent to the soldiers at the front "as though the faces of these singers were going to secure victory."[57]

The same change of heart could be observed in Damascus. Despite the homage Michel Aflaq paid to Islam — as a Christian what else could he do? — the Ba'th had been, on the whole, either hostile or indifferent to Islam; it was committed, as its theorists repeatedly stated, to the destruction of "tradition," and tradition in the Arab world was deeply and ultimately Islamic.

Only a few weeks before the outbreak of the Six Day War, the official magazine of the Syrian armed forces, *Jaysh al Sha'b,* had published an article by a military officer that stated that belief in the old values, both Islamic and Christian, was in vain, that these values had made the Arab "a fatalist, a defeatist" who submits to his destiny, and that the only way to build Arab civilization and society was to create a new socialist man who would believe that God, religion, feudalism, capitalism, and the old values that dominated Arab society are nothing but "mummies in the museum of history." This new socialist man would reject heaven and hell; he would accept that man had to toil for his nation and humanity and that his toil would be an end in itself and not something he had to do in return "for a small corner in paradise."[58]

Popular outrage within and outside Syria over the publication of this article forced the government to dissociate itself from the statement and to punish the writer and the editor of the magazine. But the article's appearance confirmed the schism between the predominantly secularized official class and a deeply religious popular culture. Defeated on the battlefield, the official class would now retreat and show greater deference to popular sensibilities. Rather than leave the religious sentiment to be turned into protest by fervent fundamentalists, the regime would try to do what ruling regimes had done throughout Islamic history: coopt the religious sensibility, identify it with the interest and the stability of the nation, and channel it into less destabilizing endeavors. And as had been the established norm, the official religious hierarchy that had long made its peace with the men of the sword would be ready to pitch in: bless the men in power and urge believers to trust the men who had it within their power to order and presumably change things.

But this is not the Islam of the Muslim Brotherhood. Coopted Islam and populist Islam are radically different. The first has always been willing to compromise: When soldiers usurp power, it accepts the supremacy of the sword. It asks men to obey their rulers or at least to refrain from rebellion against them. It also counsels patience in the face of material inequalities, for they are Allah's will, part of His design for the universe.

Populist Islam of the kind represented by Kishk and the Muslim Brotherhood is an activist, militant brand of belief, however. It keeps alive — and takes quite seriously — the notion that legitimate rule must be Islamic rule, and — to the discomfort of the dominant order — it preaches opposition to corruption and inequalities.

Much of what is attributed to Islam by radical Arab critics is easier to hang onto official coopted Islam than onto the populist strand. At any rate, it has always been official, traditional Islam that troubled the radicals. It is easy to understand why this is so if one keeps in mind not only the radical propensity for wholesale, innate condemnation of religion, but also the balance of power between the populist strand and the official, coopted one. What worried the radicals and the ruling elites in Damascus and Cairo was that the official conservative strand of Islam was claimed and manipulated by the monarchies. As interpreted by the monarchies, traditional Islam became a pillar for their kind of order, a prop for the monarchies that had been warning against wild men, imported ideologies, and subversive movements. The struggle over the role of Islam was an extension of the profane struggle for power.

CONSERVATIVE FUNDAMENTALISM

The power of traditional Islam was one of the weapons that the traditional states brandished against Nasser's regime. This was the Islam that King Faisal of Saudi Arabia invoked against the pan-Arabists at the height of the Arab cold war. (Faisal called for an Islamic Pact in late 1965 to combat the radical pan-Arabists. Its leitmotif was clearly not Islamic piety, for the pact included the Shah of Iran and Habib Bourguiba of Tunisia — men not particularly known for their observance of Islam.)

Nasser and the Ba'th could brush aside King Faisal's brand of Islamic solidarity before 1967, but they found it harder to do so in the aftermath of their defeat. Traditional Islam was heard from as soon as the dust of the battle settled. King Hassan of Morocco lectured the rulers of Cairo and Damascus about the error of their ways, attributing the radicals' ineptness to their deviation from religion.[59] That peculiar institution, the Moroccan monarchy, saw in the defeat of the upstarts and the ideologues divine confirmation of the rectitude of its own position: The Arabs had turned away from God, and God had turned away from them. On a less exalted plane, the Moroccan monarch volunteered that the Arabs had been defeated because they were divided by ideologies and because they relied upon the Soviet Union.

Among some diehard traditionalists the failure of the radical Arab states was taken to mean the bankruptcy of the entire framework of secular politics. In 1969 one fundamentalist writer called for the extreme solution of resurrecting the Islamic caliphate and bestowing it on King Faisal. As the call had it, a traditional *bay'a*

− the acknowledgement of a new caliph and a pledge of loyalty to him − had taken place in Saudi Arabia, and Muslim scholars and *ulama* now had to spread the word to the believers that obedience was due King Faisal as the new caliph.[60] When a radical critic stated that this showed that Islam was a handy instrument at the disposal of the traditional Arab states, the same fundamentalist writer responded that it was a legitimate way of taking on communist influence and ideas, and that opposition to this move was based on the communists' full awareness that "the call for an Islamic Caliphate in the Kingdom of Saudi Arabia meant putting Muslims beyond the reach of Western or hostile currents and the mobilization of the Islamic community on a worldwide basis to liberate it from socialist and capitalist systems that have engulfed the world."[61]

That call died out − the caliphate was not restored − but it was an important statement on the mood and the climate. Sa'd Jumah, who was serving as Jordan's prime minister at the time of the Six Day War, issued his own independent call for the resurrection of Islamic rule with the aim of saving the Arab world from "barbarism and unbelief." There was, he said, a "contemporary living experiment" that could serve as a model for the Arabs − namely, the Pakistani experiment, which was, in his view, a full and living Islamic system. Arabs had to return to their cultural sources "to eradicate class and sectarian differences, to realize the justice, freedom, and equality decreed by our *Shari'a* eleven centuries before they were known to Europe."[62] Secular nationalism, Jumah insisted, was forced upon the Arabs and not really suited to them; it was imported by minorities that had erroneously believed that Islam looked down upon them. The revolutionary socialist and nationalist slogans were motivated by a desire for self-improvement on the part of ambitious, misguided minorities and by the schemes of the West. Bad intentions aside, the very model of the state system developed in the West, with its separation between church and state, was inherently unsuitable for the Muslim world: The separation might have made sense in its original habitat, but it did not in the Arab−Muslim world because of a fundamental difference between Christianity and Islam − the first was a system of morality, but the second was a complete social, political, and economic order. Christianity, Jumah said, was born at a time when the Roman Empire was politically at its zenith and required only moral reform − hence the ethical thrust of Christianity. Islam, however, emerging as it did out of a backward, bedouin setting, had created from scratch an entire social order in which the separation between secular and religious realms made no sense at all.

From such lofty considerations, the former Jordanian prime minister descended to the grubby details of inter-Arab politics that concerned him by advancing conspiracy theories about revolutionaries and minorities. He was told — by whom he does not say — that the ambassador of a great power (he leaves no doubt that it was the Soviet Union) met with a Syrian official on the first day of the war to convey a message from Israel. The message sought to reassure Syria that Israel had sympathy for "Alawite Ba'thism" and that, if Syria stayed out of the war, power and leadership in the Arab world would pass to Syrian hands after the defeat of Egypt and Jordan. The innuendo was all too clear: Revolutionary minorities would not fight; only true Muslim believers rallying under the banner of Islam and inspired by the cry *"Jihad"* would do so. The revolutionary state had been a total failure: It had torn asunder the fabric of the social order and was cowardly and treasonous in war.

These and related conservative Islamic themes coalesce in *Amidat al Nakba* (The Pillars of the Disaster), a widely read book by Salah al Din al Munajjid, a pamphleteer working in Beirut. Munajjid, as we shall see, is a bitter critic not only of radical nationalism and of the Soviet Union but also of those who restrict "freedom of commerce and industry."[63] His vision of what is properly Islamic differs from the more radical and egalitarian outlook of Muhammad Jahal Kishk. Munajjid's Islam inveighs against those who nationalize the people's wealth and make them dependent on a parasitic, godless version of socialism and on the capricious desires of the state. In Munajjid's discourse, property — sanctioned by Islam — would do what Milton Friedman claims it is able to do: give the individual citizen leverage vis-à-vis the state, limit the power of government, and thus expand the domain of freedom.

Thanks to the revolutionary socialists, al Munajjid says, the Arabs have reverted to the age of *Jahiliyya* — pre-Islamic ignorance. Armed with Islam, they had accomplished miracles, conquered kingdoms, enlightened souls, and turned "the solitary individual fighter into a thousand."[64] Islam had once made heroes out of weaklings; it had defeated two powerful empires, the Persian and the Byzantine, despite their superiority in numbers and weaponry. By instilling belief in the hearts of men, it enabled them to fight and die for a just cause. Its power lay in the believers' certitude that Islam was the best message for the world and that the

Muslims were "the best community ever raised up for mankind."[65] Today's Arabs have lost all this: Instead of teaching others, they have become followers of the unbeliever Tito and of "imported ideologies" that are destructive and evil. The West and its local fifth column destroyed the foundations of the community. Nationalism and Marxism are responsible for Arab decline: The first turned fellow Ottoman Muslims into alien occupiers, and the second, so unattractive to the Arabs, was imposed by military rule in Damascus and brought chaos and repression.

No normal, well-adjusted, integrated Muslim would have succumbed to such false and divisive doctrines, asserts al-Munajjid. The people who took the lead in propagating alien doctrines were individuals with "resentments and psychological complexes."[66] Some of them wanted to seize political power; others wanted to destroy Islam. A prototype of the former is Salah al-Din al-Bitar — he loved power, and wanted to rise to the top "even though he was not a Damascene."[67] An example of those whose aim is the destruction of Islam is Michel Aflaq. In both Cairo and Damascus an entire generation systematically embarked upon the Bolshevization of Islam. Even before that misguided generation — Nasser and the Ba'th — others were paving the way for the disaster with their subversive call for nationalist politics. Fifty years of Arab life were wasted on two unsuccessful experiments — nationalism and socialism. Revolutionary socialism was a devastating disease, "more harmful than cholera or the plague."[68]

Munajjid indicts the revolutionary regimes for restricting commerce and industry and reducing to starvation those who were once prosperous, for destroying the spiritual bases of the community (for the first time since the invasions of the Tatars, the sanctity of mosques was violated in Ba'thist Damascus as soldiers entered the mosques with their shoes on and stained the walls with the blood of the believers), and pitting individuals and classes against one another. Particularly objectionable to al-Munajjid is the way the revolutionary socialists had manipulated the masses. They had appealed to emotions instead of reason, and, because the masses are a "willing obedient flock" with no critical faculties of their own, the once stable order that supplied people with meaning and made sense of life and social relations was nearly destroyed: Subordinates began challenging superiors, the young dared challenge the old, and the uneducated demogogic element would no longer honor the notables of the community or the men of intellect. And, presumably, radical officers who defied monarchs and the established order of authority could be included among those who no longer knew their place and no longer played by the rules. To cap all this, the revolutionary socialists then surrendered to the Soviet Union, which stabbed them in the back and abandoned them in their moment of need.

Munajjid's view that the Soviet Union betrayed its radical allies — encouraged them to go to war and then left them to fend for themselves — was a modern, contemporary one. But there was another view of the Soviet Union that was popular among some zealous, traditional Islamic writers and that subsequently seeped down to the public who read their commentaries: The Soviet Union as the incarnation of evil. In this more extreme, diabolical view, the world is Manichean, conspiratorial, a battleground for the forces of good and evil. And in that world, the Soviet Union's Communism and Israel's Zionism are twin evils.

The same publicist who defended the caliphate of King Faisal saw the Six Day War as a Soviet *mukhattat* (plan). He argued that there was an intimate connection between Zionism and Communism: Marx, the founder of Communism, was a Jew, and his solution to the Jewish question was a world-wide socialist revolution. Zionism and Communism were slightly different means for solving the Jewish question and for serving Jewish interests. The guiding force behind their unholy alliance was the desire to destroy the Muslim world. America supposedly acquiesced in this design, but it was more naive than sinister. All the quarrels about strategy and ideology were merely a cover for the old standing duel between Islam and the West.

The subtleties of international politics and the limited objectives of the state system have always seemed unconvincing to some people. In the Arab world, as elsewhere, conspiracy theories of history in which evil forces scheme and distort have always come in handy: They simplify a complex world and justify ancient and visceral quarrels. Far more important than ideas themselves is the climate that makes some ideas more persuasive then others or more persuasive at one point in time than at others.

The ideas of al-Munajjid and of the former Jordanian prime minister had been around prior to the Six Day War, but they were defensive ideas then, the ideas of a discredited past. Pitted against them was the power of charisma, the apparent success of a secular and nationalist ideology that prided itself on its accomplishments and its modernity, and the smug assurance of a younger generation that was in power and that believed that the future was on its side. With the unexpected outcome of the war, the secular pan-Arabists lost their self-confidence and the traditionalists recovered theirs. The latter no longer seemed as anachronistic as the former had said they were. In the minds of the traditional leaders, the modern world had in a sense betrayed those who had made so much noise about their capacity to master that world. To the diehard traditionalists, the defeat of their adversaries was a message, an omen: Radical leaders had turned things upside down and now divine will had made known its disapproval.

Modern human beings are far more superstitious than they think they are. Success seems like a vindication, a confirmation that what individuals and nations are doing makes sense, conforms to some higher law — which, depending on one's inclination, may be the dialectics of the class struggle, the stages of economic growth, or divine will. Conversely, setbacks are warnings: Something is not going well or not going according to schedule. People begin to feel that they are swimming against the current, that they are trying to do too much, or that they are on the wrong track. Without the daring they once possessed, leaders and movements suddenly discover the limits that exist in the world, all the obstacles that stand in the way of what they are trying to do. The superpower that yesterday was told to go drink the ocean becomes an awesome reality whose will you cannot defy. The power that you were going to feed to the fish of the Mediterranean becomes an unassailable entity. The monarchs who appeared so vulnerable and doomed to extinction become formidable rivals to whose will you must bend if you are to survive. And the arguments that were previously mocked as reactionary or xenophopic or archaic become believable.

It is not sufficiently appreciated that the images and doctrines that people and movements manufacture are more for internal consumption than for persuading others. Failure or weakness relative to others is usually preceded by loss of self-esteem, by inner doubts: People cease to believe their own utterances before others doubt them. We know the phenomenon quite well — aristocracies lose their belief in their inherent superiority; colonialists begin to doubt their right to empire; ideologues are no longer confident that their doctrines have the capacity to explain and order the world.

Something like this was to happen to the rulers of Cairo and Damascus in the aftermath of the June war. Their traditional rivals gained a new lease on life while they themselves stood exposed. The Ba'th became a shell of its former self after the desertion of the party's founders, the revelations of men like al Razzaz and Jundi, and the doubts raised everywhere about Syria's participation in the war. The region was no longer hospitable to the poetics of Michel Aflaq. A regime claiming the Ba'thist label did survive in Damascus. One year after the Six Day War, a clique of officers calling themselves Ba'thists seized power in Baghdad, and, as if to underscore that they were serious about their claim, imported the ideologue Michel Aflaq, who had been banished from Syria.

Over the course of the next few years, the two Ba'thist regimes battled one another more than anyone else, and there was an intense struggle over who represented the Ba'th. Their polemics were, as usual, passionate, but there was no longer an audience to take their exchange seriously. Soldiers seizing power and proclaiming revolution no longer fooled that many people. Michel Aflaq wrote a few more articles and gave a few more speeches, but people wearied of his style and of his kind of politics. The game became far too serious and grim for slogans such as "Arabism is love" to catch anyone's attention. Three years after the Six Day War, another Ba'thist officer, Hafez Asad, toppled the Syrian regime, but his stock in trade was not the ideology of the Ba'th. Asad was a shrewd man with a remarkable instinct for survival, but he had not read the books that the earlier Ba'thists had read. His instinct was for the center of Arab politics as he sought to govern what has traditionally been an ungovernable society.

Each political order has its own kind of political style and expression. The style and expression of the pan-Arabists gave way to a subdued language that was more in line with the sensibilities of the conservative states, more deferential to the heritage, less threatening to the prerogatives of wealth and power. The political discourse of the established leaders now emphasized inter-Arab solidarity rather than ideological splits and assigned a more central place to Islam than had been the case in the previous era. The style reflected the change in the material distribution of power: The traditional states were no longer defensive and off balance; their new power would make respectable their style of discourse, their symbols, and their language.

The discourse of the traditional Islamic view was laced throughout with a greater emphasis on Israel's religiosity. This point is essential to an understanding of the resurgence of Islamic sensibility in the aftermath of the Six Day War. The Arabs had been poorly informed about Israel: In the dead language of the preceding era, Israel was only a bridgehead of imperialism, a gathering of Zionist gangs. Israel was mostly seen as a technological, scientific power, and a whole generation in the Arab world had been taught to believe that religion and modernity were mutually exclusive.

The Israeli capture of Jerusalem and its significance for the Israelis gave Muslim believers ammunition in their debate with Arab secularists: Modernity and religion can be brought together; man can fight for religion just as well, if not better, than he can fight for the modern state — and definitely much better than he can fight on behalf of a thin cosmopolitan ideology such as socialism, whose slogans can be repeated without great feeling or authenticity. The principal lesson that the religiously inclined Arabs drew from Israel's victory was that people can both go to the laboratory *and* worship. Israel combined what an entire generation of liberals and secularists had assumed to be incompatible things. It was both more religious and more scientific than the Arab states. Israel, writes Ahmad Baha'a al-Din, one of a handful of Egyptian establishment journalists, poses a "strange challenge" to the Arabs: it challenges in them "the ancient and the modern, the past and the future." In Israel's arsenal are modern weapons and technology as well as ancient visions and claims. What are the Arabs to make of such a challenge? How are they to reconcile the modern side of Israel and the ancient one, which "indulges in archaeology not to write a history but to plan a future"?[69] It was probably no accident that the Nasser regime began after its defeat to pay homage to the modern scientific state and urge greater adherence to Islam at the same time. Israel had demolished the easy superficial distinction, taught by a generation of Arab liberals and embraced as well by younger radicals, that religion is a reactionary force, that the scientific state is built on the debris of an extinguished religion.

But hard as they tried to identify themselves with the resurgence of the Islamic sentiment, the regimes in Cairo and Damascus could not really hope to claim it as their own. This was a battle that the traditional states were destined to win. The matter would not be decided on grounds of true Islamic piety, for some symbols lend themselves to certain individuals and groups more easily than they do to others. The people who benefit from the symbols need not necessarily honor them, at least not fully; they need only honor them more than their rivals are seen to do. Most ideologies and belief systems are not savored for what they are; they are more appreciated for what they do, for their utility in taking on others who manipulate other symbols. Giant corporations thrive on the myth of private enterprise — they feed off attacking bureaucracies and red tape, conveniently forgetting that they themselves are giant bureaucracies and that a corporate technostructure has replaced the brave creative hero of the private enterprise story; they dwell on the myth because they want to have a lofty vision of themselves — the individual entrepreneur taking risks and facing nar row-minded bureaucrats. Moreover, they need the myth as a weapon to use against other bureaucratic systems, such as labor unions and governmental agencies.

As it is with the corporate technostructure and the myth of private enterprise, so it is with the traditional elements of society and the banner of Islam. It is not so much that those who brandish Islam have to be good Muslims, rather, it depends on the day and the issue. What the myth does is raise one's self-esteem and then turn it against others – religious minorities, self-styled radicals, Marxists who in a religiously steeped culture foolishly dismiss religion as the opiate of the people, secular regimes that allow the sanctity of mosques to be violated.

For men who wage political struggles, as well as for those who are brave and curious enough to try to interpret the struggles, the ideas that are thrown around are less important than the material struggles that underpin them and give them value and importance. The tangible issue that arose immediately after 1967 was the new balance of power between the traditional conservative states and their rivals, who had just suffered a major defeat. With or without the issue of Islam, a fight to determine the postwar configuration of the Arab system of states was next on the agenda. The radicals' loss was bound to be the conservative states' gain: The latter had the money, and the former had been in error, had lost the war and the land, and had to worry about their survival at home. But few struggles for power are ever waged without pretensions to ideological or normative stakes. The protagonists drag ideas into the game both because they take the ideas seriously and because they wish to invest their quest with moral worth and to provide a cover for what otherwise would seem to be narrow and selfish goals. The oil states could not have stated openly that the fight was about stability, that they were on some level relieved that the people who had disrupted stability for so long had paid for their sins, that as a result of the defeat they could now enjoy a period of relative peace. They might have said that they felt more secure because the radio stations and the media that had blasted them daily and accused them of treason and reaction had finally lost whatever credibility they once had, that Israel's victory – though painful on one level – had worked to their advantage.

But of course they would not say so. Like all others engaged in such struggles, they would wrap their interest with what E. H. Carr called "convenient morality."[70] In their case the convenient morality was Islam – a particular kind of Islam, to be sure. The monarchs of Saudi Arabia, Libya, and Morocco and the emir of

Kuwait were – as far as they saw it and as far as they wanted others to understand it – engaged in an attempt to reconstitute a community that had lost its bearings, to liberate a people from imported doctrines, to correct the errors of a misguided generation, to exorcise the region of the irresponsibility of pan-Arabist doctrines. That in doing so they would protect their own dynasties and interests went without saying, for political struggles are not waged by individuals who renounce the world in favor of transcendent ideals. The transcendent ideals that the monarchs would put forth were the *turath* – the heritage. And in their reading of it, it was a conservative, cautious *turath,* which upheld the authority of elders and notables and kept individuals and classes in their places.

At this point, the conservative states had a choice: They could either push their victory too far in order to avenge the injuries and the abuse of the past and try for a full restoration of the ancien régime, or, sensing the new storm – far more militant enemies than Nasser, Marxist Palestinians, embittered youth had been – they could accept a reconciliation with a former rival in the interest of overall stability. The revolution that the Arab radicals waited for after 1967 did not take place, largely because – as we understand with the benefit of hindsight – the conservative states took the second option and because the man at the helm in Cairo would swallow his pride and adapt himself as best he could – and that was not easy, given his own personal makeup – to a new set of realities.

Several factors were to bring about an alliance between the traditional states and the Egyptian regime: the radicalism of the new revolutionaries (George Habash of the Popular Front for the Liberation of Palestine, and young men who were far more relentless in their opposition to tradition than the regime in Cairo had ever dreamed of being), the emotional appeal of the slogan "a war of national liberation," and the dangers to a totally discredited Arab system of states of a military outcome that had dishonored all the regimes and ridiculed all those in power. The regime in Damascus would continue to snipe at the system, but the arrangement that mattered would be worked out between Nasser on the one hand and King Faisal on the other. A frightening generation gap developed in the aftermath of the defeat: The language, the symbols, and the world view of the men in power were losing their grip on the young, who were now marching to a different drum. In the circumstances, Nasser no longer seemed as much of a troublemaker as he once had – or, more accurately perhaps, as he once had been. With the threat posed by the new radicals, it was easier for Nasser to work with King Husein than with someone like George Habash, who was declaring to receptive young men that Nasser's experiment was "petty bourgeois" and no revolution at all and that the answer lay in a popular war of liberation and not with armies that had proved their incapacity to fight.

It was at this point that the logic of the state system – limited resources and capabilities, and the knowledge, to which outsiders are immune, that great and popular crusades must be checked against messy and sobering constraints – asserted itself. Faisal, Nasser, and Husein headed established states, and they wanted some control over what they saw as a situation of great danger. Their adversaries were free from governmental responsibility: They could agitate; they could ask for the impossible; they could endlessly cite Debray, Fanon, and Giap; they could hijack airplanes and make a mockery of the regimes' standing in the eyes of the citizenry. The men in power operated from vastly different premises, but they would, to the extent possible, patch up their differences to ensure that turmoil, frustration, and radicalism did not go beyond reasonable limits.

DeTocqueville's classic discussion of the French intelligentsia rooted their totalism in the marked separation between precept and practice in French political life: "One group shaped the course of public affairs, the other that of public opinion."[71] This separation between precept and practice was to become a particularly severe problem in immediate post-1967 Arab politics. The intelligentsia, who shaped public opinion, were for the most part radical outsiders: They gave precept a revolutionary tone, and they wanted total and bold solutions – nothing less than a new society and a new human being. The people who shaped public affairs were far more cautious and restrained: They had economies to keep afloat, defeated armies that had to be reequipped, two superpowers that had to be appealed to for weapons and diplomatic support, and a more powerful enemy holding occupied soil and showing every sign that it was digging in for a long stay. The radical outsiders were a more impatient, younger breed who thought a war of national liberation would do it all – transform the domestic order and defeat their more powerful enemy.

It should be recalled that post-1967 radicalism began with a profound rejection of the unfulfilled, empty slogans of the previous generation. But the radical intelligentsia and activists soon succumbed to a typically intellectual affliction: conviction that revolution was imminent. Whether they rallied to the cause of the new revolution – the Palestinian movement – or simply believed that the dominant order was about to collapse from its own weight, their talk of revolution came to dominate the political and intellectual marketplace. Was history repeating itself? Were the radical intellectuals and activists playing the same game that the Nasserites had played in Egypt and the Ba'th in Syria? The radical intellectuals would have objected to such a portrayal. They knew that they were different and that they would escape the errors committed in the preceding era. At any rate, it was their belief that they were living in a situation that was soon to give rise to revolutionary politics: Out of the debris of the defeat would emerge new people and new politics.

That wars and defeats can speed up the dissolution of a social order is received wisdom that is underscored by great revolutionary upheavals. But a revolutionary outcome is neither inevitable — as Arab politics were to show in the years that followed the Six Day War — nor even the norm. A revolutionary situation has to be appropriately defined and seized upon if the potential inherent in it is to be realized. Extreme situationism is unpersuasive, for there is always a range of outcomes inherent in a particularly fluid situation.[72] This is where circumstances, luck, clear thought and, above all, gifted leadership can make a difference. If the gifted leadership is on the revolutionary side, it can activate the processes that conduce to the collapse of a reigning regime. If the gifted leadership is in the saddle, it can outmaneuver its opponents, seize the initiative, and offer a more compelling justification and a way out of a particularly acute crisis. Whatever revolutionary potential existed can thus be defused as the dominant order is given a chance to correct its previous errors.

Fear of uncertainty and chaos can help the established order: In a dismal situation, a familiar voice and face can be soothing and reassuring. Particularly gifted leaders can rise above the ashes of regimes that they had ruled and promise a new beginning. In a dark and frightening hour the old order can bounce back with new slogans and promises: Give the leader another chance and he will find, as he did in the past, a solution of some kind, an honorable way out; he will renew himself and the nation. To lose the leader at this particularly traumatic moment is to plunge into the dark and to be set adrift. This is the way events evolved after the June defeat: Faith in the imminence of revolution collided with President Nasser's determination to survive and to keep the Arab system of states from taking too radical and dangerous a turn; the talk about the bankruptcy of traditional orders and the revolutionary nature of the masses met its test in Jordan when the Palestinians faced

King Husein's army. It is one thing for a political order to face military defeat and loss of credibility; the capacity to push it over the brink and replace it with a new order is an altogether different endeavor:

> And was all that . . . intoxication, delirium? Perhaps —
> but I do not envy those who were not carried away by the
> exquisite dream. The sleep could not last long in any case:
> the inexorable Macbeth of real life had already raised his
> hand to murder sleep . . .[73]

The writer was the great Russian publicist Alexander Herzen, the dream that of the European revolutionaries in 1848. On a far lesser scale, to be sure, there was "intoxication" and "delirium" in the Arab world during that radical interlude that followed the June defeat. But here too the "Macbeth of real life" would appear to slay the dream, and we would see all the standard ingredients that devour dreams: "revolutionaries" who turn out to be far less radical than they presume themselves to be; a dominant order that turns out to be more powerful than it looks; an international system that hems in radical movements and reiterates the fact that nationalism is a far more real question than revolutionary delirium.

2

Egypt As State, As Arab Mirror

There was but one dominant discussion at Al Karnak [a Cairo cafe]: Day after day, week after week, month after month, year after year, we had no other topics to discuss. Exhausted by boredom one of us would say: Let us choose another topic. We would show enthusiasm for that suggestion, raise some topic, deal with it with carelessness and then go back to our old topic, devouring it and it devouring us, without interruption and with no end:
  - "The war, there is no option but war."
  - "No, it is the Fedayeen [guerrillas] struggle."
  - "A peaceful settlement is also possible."
  - "The only possible solution is that which is dictated by the great powers."
  - "Negotiations mean surrender."
  - "Negotiations are a necessity. All the nations negotiate – even America and China and Russia and Pakistan and India."
  - "Peace means that Israel would dominate the entire area."
  - "Why should we fear peace? Were we swallowed up by the English and French?"
  - "If the future proved that Israel is a 'good state' we would coexist with her and if it proved the reverse we would eradicate her as we eradicated the crusaders' state before."
  - "The future belongs to us. Look at our numbers and our wealth , . ."
  - "Our real battle is a civilizational battle. Peace is more dangerous to us than war."
  - "Let us then demobilize the army and rebuild ourselves."
  - "Let us declare our neutrality and ask other states to recognize it."
  - "What of the Fedayeen? You ignore the real catalyst in the situation."
  - "We have been defeated and we must pay the price and leave the rest to the future."
  - "The real enemy of the Arabs are the Arabs themselves."
  - "Everything depends on the unity of the Arabs in the effort."
  - "Half the Arabs . . . were victorious on the fifth of June [1967] "
  - "Let's begin then with the internal situation. There is no escape."
  - "Great. Religion, religion is everything."

> Najib Mahfuz, *Al-Karnak* (Cairo, 1974), pp. 95 – 96.

Egypt is neither the beginning nor the end . . . If the Arab nation is great with Egypt, Egypt cannot be great but with the Arab nation.

> The Tripoli Summit Communique, in *The Middle East Reporter*,
> December 10, 1977, p. 17.

THE ARAB PREDICAMENT

BURSTS OF ENTHUSIASM have a way of sweeping away things that have been around for a long time, defying incredible odds, challenging time-honored traditions and continuities. Then the enthusiasm fades or is thwarted by the superior resources of others, by incompetence or an overwhelming defeat: The old doubts and fears return, and the old battles have to be refought; paths once abandoned or thought unworthy in the revolutionary movement are rediscovered, as societies hemmed in by difficult circumstances reach out for solutions and possibilities.

Nasser's Egypt lived a revolutionary moment, or so it believed. Its defeat in 1967 broke that revolutionary wave; it added a new wound to a deeply scarred civilization; it threw new constraints in the face of a society whose history has been a frustrating struggle to push back — or to ignore and avoid — what seemed to be eternal constraints. And because the new constraints had to be dealt with, the attempt to deal with the 1967 defeat forced upon Egyptians yet another encounter with their classical themes and vulnerabilities. It threw out questions that the revolutionary order had confidently declared to be obvious and settled.

Egypt's centrality in the Arab world made it inevitable that Egyptian thoughts and second thoughts and Egyptian choices would become wider Arab concerns and dilemmas. The Palestinian question may have been the public issue of post-1967 Arab politics; but there has been an equally serious concern with the Egyptian question. The latter may not have generated the sound and fury of the former, but it has been a deadly serious matter that has touched upon fundamental civilizational sensibilities and fears. And just as the Egyptian struggle with the pan-Arab identity was in a way an internal debate about one's own society and civilization, so too was the wider Arab speculation about Egypt a proxy debate about the harvest of Arab history, about the capabilities of the Arabs and their place in the world.

The people who in the aftermath of the Six Day War denounced Egypt's incapacity to rebel, to become another Cuba or Vietnam, to win a war, and to build an austere society were really debating what they saw to be the frustrating incapacity of the Arab–Muslim order to shake off a stultifying legacy. A decade later, the concern with Egypt's despair and surrender was yet another debate about the failure of the Arab world either to win its fight with Israel or to come to terms with it. No other question — not even the Palestinian question — raised for the Arab world as a whole the magnitude of cultural and political issues generated by Egypt's agonizing struggle with herself, her search for a way out of military stalemate and economic breakdown, her attempt to deal with far-off powers that have the means, and the illusions that tempt them, to shape Middle Eastern realities.

Other Arab states may have derived some satisfaction from Egypt's troubles. Egypt's crisis — dwindling resources, military defeat, loss of energy, economic and political stalemate — may have given other Arab states added room for maneuver, and a greater chance to neutralize Egypt's demographic weight, cultural lure, and traditional political preeminence. But there is more to the world — even the world of politics — than the harsh calculus of power. In civilizational and psychohistorical terms, Egypt's crisis was a trauma to other Arabs. If Egypt was faltering and its society was falling apart, what then was to become of the Arab world? If Egypt was the hub of the Arab system, its decline and hardships at a time of Arab affluence and its surrender to the West are damning indictments of the state of the Arab world. Then there was the conflict with Israel: If Egypt were to disengage from that conflict, what hope was there for seeing that conflict to some kind of honorable solution?

Latecomer as it was to pan-Arab politics, Egypt was slated to head that movement once the nation entered it. When pan-Arabism had an anti-Ottoman thrust, the Egyptians, who were then worried about the British occupation of their country, had low regard for a movement that was not only anti-Ottoman but also burdened with a British connection. Early advocates of pan-Arabism moved between Damascus and Baghdad, but it was in Cairo that the league of Arab states was headquartered when it finally came into being in 1945. It may be true that Egypt simply waved an "Arab flag which fell into its hands,"[1] but there is no denying that it was Cairo's leadership that gave Arab nationalism the concrete reality it came to possess. This may strike other Arabs as peculiar, but Egyptians have generally taken for granted their preeminence in the Arab system. In the first half of the twentieth century, bourgeois Egypt could rightly feel that sense of preeminence: It had a relatively developed economy and sophisticated cities, its exposure to the liberal ideas of Europe had put it decades ahead of the rest of the Arab world and its literary and cultural output far surpassed the achievements of other Arabs. And when it shifted leftward during the Nasser years, it became the Mecca of Arab radicals and progressives. Whatever his domestic faults, Abdul Nasser was an Egyptian, and his hold over the masses of Syria and the young of Saudi Arabia and Beirut was another confirmation of Egypt's preeminence. In the view of the Egyptian middle classes and the politically conscious, Egypt's centrality to the Arab world was natural and inevitable. Whether Egyptians were dealing with liberal ideas, building a modern army, making movies, writing books, exporting revolution, or conducting diplomacy with Israel, they were convinced that they of course excelled and led and that other Arabs would follow.

But preeminence has its risks and price. There are responsibil-ities to be shouldered; the allies and dependents one acquires can limit one's freedom and drag one into all kinds of troubles. Precious resources can be wasted in vain attempts at securing the gratitude of others. One ends up fighting others' fights only to be denounced when one grows weary of a long-drawn-out battle. Preeminence can also distort the view of the leading member of a community. Weariness has a way of rewriting history, as the emotions and in-terests that led people to fight are forgotten and the preeminent see the fights in hindsight as selfless sacrifice on their part in pur-suit of others' dreams and in defense of others' interests.

The scarcity of material resources can make things particularly difficult for nations — as well as individuals — whose ambitions, memories, standards, and claims to preeminence overreach their power and resources. Others who have more resources at hand are seen as crass newcomers who either cheated or were lucky or grubby enough to succeed. The imbalance between one's cultural achievements and one's pretension is a nightmare for individuals as well as nations. Behind Egypt's struggle with its sister Arab states is the all-too-familiar human rejection of downward social mobil-ity. Egypt's power and wealth vis-à-vis other states in the Arab world have declined; the world outside interfered in October 1973 and played havoc with the Arab order and its ranking; it conferred immense riches on those who had historically been in Egypt's shadow. In so doing, it challenged the geography of the mind within and outside Egypt: It left gloom and a sense of betrayal in Egypt, but among the lucky states, there were the dreams of a new order and unlimited possibilities.

This jolt to the mental geography and sense of self must be seen against the background of a deeply held Egyptian belief in Egypt's centrality to the region around it. Nasser had given the Egyptian claims a radical thrust, but the material with which he worked predated him — Egypt's belief in its supremacy and its urge to pursue its destiny in places such as the Sudan, Syria, the Arabian peninusla. The same urge that had taken Muhammad Ali, the builder of the modern Egyptian state (ruled 1805–1848), and his son Ibrahim to Syria and the peninsula would operate on the radical Abdul Nasser. There may have been deeper historical roots than were suspected in Saudi Arabia's response to Nasser's thrust into Yemen. After all, Muhammad Ali had undertaken a similar expedition in the early nineteenth century against the Wahhabi forefathers of the present dynasty.

Currents borne by the wind and the constant of geography underpin what may seem like modern ideological contests. Egypt, long an established state, saw it as its burden and privilege to lead others around it. In a seminal and rich study on Egyptian personality, culture, and ecology, the Egyptian scholar Jamal Hamdan expressed that kind of innate belief in Egypt's centrality: Leadership in the Arab system was not open to debate and speculation but has been once and for all determined by geography and location – once Egypt entered the house of Islam, it was destined to lead.[2] Even when other Islamic empires arose elsewhere, they were transient. They collapsed because they were built on the periphery of the Arab–Muslim order. In Hamdan's mental geography and reconstruction, the Umayyad and Abbasid empires were marginal: The first ended in the escape of Umayyads, and the second was vulnerable and susceptible to destruction, as seen in its fate at the hands of the Mongols in the thirteenth century. Centrality belonged to Egypt, and that is why ambitious dynasties and rulers sought to make their home in Egypt and why repelling the crusaders had to be launched from Egypt by the Mamluks and Saladin. Geography placed Egypt between the Asian part of the Arab world and Arab Africa. Egypt introduced the two parts to one another and was a magnet for the talented, the ambitious, the dissatisfied, the oasis of the Arab world.

Hamdan's view is partly warranted by the objective facts of history; it is partly myth and imagery. But myths have their own power and reality, and in the years that followed the Six Day War both the reality and the image of Egypt's ascendancy were to be tested – sometimes consciously and openly, sometimes in the deep recesses of the mind, where things are more sensed and intuited than seen. Few Arabs stated this with the clarity that the Egyptian writer Muhammad Jalal Kishk did when he wrote that the June defeat marked the end of the Egyptian myth in Arab life.[3] The objective inter-Arab struggles and the cumulative Arab debate of more than a decade – all the way from the polemics of the intellectuals after 1967 to the Arab diplomatic conferences of 1978 and 1979 that sought to bring Egypt back into the fold – revolve around Egypt's pride of place and the imbalance between her material resources and her psychological esteem of herself – between her old glory and current poverty — and around the attempts of other Arabs to sustain, limit, or oppose Egyptian choices.

All the currents in the region battled to win Egypt over, to save it from itself or from others. The Arab radicals wanted Egypt to go beyond itself and become genuinely revolutionary; the Palestinians first wanted it to step aside and accept that there was a new revolution on the Arab horizon and then to commit itself and its resources to the creation of a Palestinian state. The third bid came from Qaddafi, offering the Egypt redemption through radical fundamentalist Islam — return to the sources — and a cure for its poverty through a union with Libya. Then there was the bid by conservative Arab wealth offered by Saudi Arabia and the smaller oil states: Arab wealth was willing to help, and in return it wanted from Egypt an expulsion of the "atheistic" Soviet Union, a dismantling of the public sector, greater deference to Islam, an end to the pan-Arabist zeal, and the patience and willingness to abide by collective Arab will in diplomatic matters. Finally, there was the duel of the two superpowers in the region, which culminated in the eclipse of one and the engagement of another.[4] Here too Egypt was a coveted prize and a main arena. The Soviet Union had to concede its incapacity to comprehend, let alone control, this costly and peculiar ally, while the United States moved from being a friend of the enemy to President Sadat's and Egypt's full partner. The United States had tangible interests to protect, but there were intangibles — the desire to be wanted, the excitement of a new frontier — that played a part in Sadat's successful courtship of America. Ancient civilizations (witness America's attitude toward China) stir the imagination: They have a kind of malleability that enables others to read into them what they want; they can be hotbeds of revolution or fragile entities ready to be courted and redeemed. They invite those who have a sense of destiny. From Napoleon to Kissinger, powerful societies and leaders have seen Egypt as a natural zone of their influence: "It is proper for this country (Egypt) to attract the attention of illustrious Princes who rule the destiny of nations," wrote Jean-Baptiste Joseph Fourier, the secretary of Napoleon's Institut d'Egypte.[5]

Lesser figures than Napoleon had equally vivid imaginations, and Egypt was sufficiently ambiguous to allow them all their moment. For commissars, it was a candidate for socialism to be imposed on from above; for an Arab–Muslim soldier like Qaddafi, it was home of the Arab–Muslim world's leading university, and it was there more than anywhere else that Islam fashioned a civilization, made its peace with the world, built a great city, and debated the issues of the day. For a bourgeois, cosmopolitan liberal, Egypt was the place where the West as process left its deepest marks as well as its most durable scars in the Arab world. For those states with wealth – either a faraway superpower, a militant soldier next door, or a nearby conservative dynastic state – Egypt's poverty stimulated the imagination. It suggested the possibility of conquest and conversion, of buying into a major undertaking. In having Egypt see it one's way, there is a tangible interest to be served – stability or revolution or a base in a turbulent region, depending on the viewer – and the intangible gratification of having an ancient civilization on one's side.

Through it all, Egypt's path has been navigated by two men, and there is a temptation to see the choices the two men made as idio-syncratic, personal ones. Both men have been the subject of a great deal of speculation. Nasser was a hero, a tragic figure who occu-pies a special place in recent Arab history; Sadat is an enigma who surprised the Arab world first with a remarkable deed in October, 1973, and then with a psychohistorical shock in November, 1977, with his journey to Jerusalem. But a king, wrote Tolstoy, "is the slave of history. History, that is, the unconscious common swarm of life of mankind uses every moment of the life of kings as an in-strument for its own ends."[6]

That is why the temptation to go after the personalities of the two "kings" in order to explain Egypt's path must be checked, for there were constants that both men had to deal with: (1) an unac-ceptable military defeat that both men had to try to break out of, (2) a revolutionary legacy that had generated a great deal of noise and that now had to come to terms with the world. In the case of Nasser, the revolution was his own work; in the case of his succes-sor, it was an inheritance that he had to pay homage to and then try to transcend. There was also the question of growing economic dependency: One leader faced it in 1967 and the other capitulated to it; and there was the difficult matter of Egypt's relation to the Arab system of states, both during the stalemate years of 1967 to 1973 and, later, at a time when the oil revolution had created new realities and rival centers of power. The last question was the old issue of the Arab–Muslim order and the West. Where Nasserite Egypt once led the rebellion against the West, Sadat was to move all the way to a special relationship with the United States. Some of the drama can be understood by focusing on the two "kings." But it is important not to let their performances and the passions about them overwhelm us, for even in one of the most centralized of cultures – a place where men once worshipped rulers as deities — the logic of a society's history and its predicament can use the life of kings for its own ends.

THE LEGACY REASSESSED

Great charismatic figures have, as it were, two careers: one while they live, and another after they pass from the scene and their legacies are fought over by their followers. The fight over what they leave behind is often more intense than the fights they generated when they were alive. The great leader is more flexible than those who seek to emulate him; he has no text to follow, no chapter and verse to cite; he can make up the text as he goes along. Different claimants to the great leader's legacy pose another problem: Are the real heirs the ones who fill the institutional void he left behind? Or are there more legitimate claimants who, although removed from the position once held by the great leader, may nonetheless be able to claim his mantle? Finally, there are the endless problems posed by concrete policies: Would the great man have handled it that way? Have his successors deviated from his path?

Eventually these debates are transcended. The leader ceases to be remembered with the same passion and intensity; once-timid successors go on to assume power in their own right; one faction decisively wins, and it either turns the legacy into an incantation that loses its evocative power or it slays it. But before that occurs, there is that critical period when the legacy is a potent weapon and a real issue, when people talk about the memory of the leader but have something else in mind: their own interests, the distribution of power, this or that compelling issue on the agenda.

Nasser's legacy persistently haunted and troubled Sadat; it became a weapon brandished by his rivals in the Arab system and by his critics at home. But legacies can become inflexible when they are brandished as weapons and when they are remembered by those who want something to hold up against what they see as a compromised world. Qaddafi's Nasser is a hero, a rebel, a modern-day Saladin who in time would have redeemed the Arab world; Sadat's post-1967 Nasser is recalled in Sadat's autobiography as a "living corpse."[7] That is why legacies have to be rescued from true believers and harsh critics and why we need a basic reconstruction of what the "great man" left behind and how he responded to the wounds inflicted by the June defeat.

Part of Nasser no doubt died on June 5, 1967, but the "living corpse" somehow survived for another three years at the helm, assumed his role as a "resister," was given a new mandate of sorts with the popular demonstrations of June 9 and 10, and went on to preside over the redefinition and transformation of Nasserism. The charismatic relationship between him and the masses formed during the bright youthful days of Bandung and Suez was shattered with the defeat; another variant, born out of despair and a sense of loss, sustained him until his death. He would stay in power not as a confident, vibrant hero, but as a tragic figure, a symbol of better days, an indication of the will to resist.

Sadik Abdul Hamid, a character in Najib Mahfuz's *Al Maraya*, conveys the way in which the leader manages to survive: Sadik Abdul Hamid was an educated man who believed in the "July 23 Revolution" and was willing to overlook its errors. When the "thing" happened on June 5, he was overcome with grief and despair; he wondered why no one was going mad or committing suicide. But then he recovered his composure and came to believe that the continuity of the revolution was the central issue: "The more he heard of the enemies' wish to liquidate the revolution the more firmly he became committed to it until he sincerely believed that the continuity of the revolution was more important than the recovery of the occupied Arab land, for what good is it to recover the land and lose ourselves?"[8]

Nasser's genius and the popular need for belief in someone, in anything enabled Nasser to rise above the defeat. The leader was dissociated from the defeat and invited to go beyond his political apparatus and to purge the elements that had supposedly captured and undermined his revolution. For the true believer, the Egyptian defeat was easy enough to explain. There were really two states in Egypt prior to 1967: One was the state of revolutionary Nasserism with all its accomplishments; the other was the state of power centers, which was doubtless an obstacle in the way of greater accomplishments by Nasserism. The state loses, but the leader rises from the ashes of his regime, supposedly to go on and deepen the revolution.

Beneath that level of metaphysics and belief, Nasser's game was to become purely defensive: how to deal with his own legacy and previous ambitions; how to shore up the popular will in the face of despair; how to absorb the frustrations and anger of youth; how to tackle Israeli occupation, inter-Arab matters, and the frustrations of international diplomacy. All this he had to do while his own health continued to falter. His own health was a metaphor for what had gone wrong — his revolution was, like him, exhausted and finished, the daring of youth had ended in tragedy and an incentive somehow to redeem himself before death caught up with him.

Egypt was Nasser's principal arena, but he had also to worry about the wider Arab theater. The immediate need was to secure the economic help of the oil states; more remote was the need to check the radicalism that erupted in the volatile Fertile Crescent. The first task required a deal with a former rival, King Faisal, and the deal was negotiated by the Sudanese Prime Minister Muhammad Ahmad Mahjub and concluded during the Khartoum summit conference that met in August, 1967. As Mahjub recalls it in his memoirs, he told King Faisal that as a "noble Arab," Faisal should refrain from killing a wounded rival but should instead nurse him to health and offer him a choice between a duel and an understanding.[9] The Egyptian "revolution" was on the defensive; the Arab cold war that had generated so much sound and fury had become banal and irrelevant.[10]

The radical delegates to the Khartoum summit conference – Algeria, Iraq, the PLO delegation headed by Ahmad Shuqairi – had come to the meeting expecting a fight with the conservative oil states, but they now had to contend with Nasser. Their radical proposals were lamely withdrawn: "The Arabs' petroleum," wrote Ahmad Shuqairi with his usual rhetorical flourish, "triumphed over the Arabs."[11]

Nasser's course at Khartoum was novel: He read the situation correctly. While in Khartoum he was to concede privately to Mahjub and Shuqairi that Egypt was on the verge of breakdown, that there were plots and schemes in the military and dissatisfaction among the population, that he was not sure he could keep things under control. "Exporting revolution" and "supporting the progressive forces" were the luxuries of a more youthful era. The Egyptian state was face to face with its limits, and it had to fight for its survival. The notion that revolutions are born out of despair is a naive stereotype (de Tocqueville had devastated it long ago in *The Old Regime and the French Revolution,* but it is still a popular dictum). Pushed against the wall, devoid of hope and resources, men and societies do not rebel: Instead, they give up, they surrender, they make compromises. And that is what Nasser had to do, as much as his history and personality would allow him to. Egypt, he was to tell President Boumedienne of Algeria and the Sudanese Muhammad Mahjub, was the "big fish" of the Arab world and was now "on the hook"; it could die slowly or try to break free. A dialogue with the United States – the United States, he said, had proven a skilled fisherman – was hopeless.[12]

The best he could do was set the stage for his successor, someone who might be able to initiate such a dialogue. Meanwhile, he had to keep the troubles and the doubts within Egypt from tearing the country apart.

The confusions and frustrations of the country found expression in a deep generational split between the custodians of the regime on one side and the students on the other. The youthful revolution had been tarnished; the seemingly invincible leadership suddenly looked vulnerable, and there were all kinds of demands. There were communists on one extreme and Muslim Brotherhood adher-ents on the other; there was a world of difference between those who wanted to liberalize the economy and those who wanted to make sure that the populist gains were not lost, between those who wanted an all-out war of national liberation and those consumed with the understandable human desire to be left alone to pursue normal lives.

Whatever else they did or did not do, the popular demonstra-tions of June 9 and 10 had given the citizenry a sense of their own power. Spontaneous or not, they had become part of the regime's self-defense and, hence, directly and indirectly sanctioned pop-ular initiative. The protests that erupted in February and No-vember of 1968 and that were to become a recurring feature of 1967 – 1973 Egyptian politics served notice on the regime that it had to change its ways, that it was no longer omnipotent, as it used to be. In both of the 1968 demonstrations, trouble erupted over a particular issue, sparked latent discontent, and turned into a full scale confrontation between the regime and the students.[13] The immediate pretext that touched off the February demonstrations was the light sentences, given to the accused officers by a military tribunal that had been looking into the June defeat. The issue was symbolic: the military class that had led the nation for fifteen years and dragged it to defeat would persist in protecting its members. No crime – not even wasting the lives of thousands of Egyptians, losing Sinai, and blocking the Suez Canal – would be adequately punished. In November, 1968, demonstrations started in the city of Mansura, after a clash between the students and the police took the lives of several students, spread to other cities, and escalated into a major confrontation in Alexandria. In both Mansura and Alexandria, the army had to be called upon to put down the riots. The two eruptions shook the self-confidence of an already trauma-tized regime: In a traditionally deferential and stable society, nei-ther deference nor stability could from then on be taken for granted.

The regime tried to put forth the best possible interpretation of what gave rise to youth unrest. Nasser explained it away as the "urgency of youth" and youth's understandable desire for reform. The organs of the regime played up youth unrest that was then sweeping other societies – France, the United States, and so forth. The implication was that there was a worldwide groping among the young and that Egypt was just another society confronted with angry, confused youth trying to make sense out of their own lives. The first outburst was explained away as a spontaneous response to the verdict of the military tribunal – a verdict that the regime quickly proceeded to overturn. But neither this limited explanation or the phenomenon of worldwide student unrest really came to terms with the predicament of Egyptian youth. One explanation was too limited, the other too cosmic.

The verdict of the military provided the spark, but the fuel had already been there. One account by a participant observer, then an engineering student at Cairo University, shows that the verdict of the tribunal was one of eight issues raised by the students and that it was of low priority. The common denominator of the other seven demands was the question of authority and freedom: the regime's style, the rights of youth and other groups in society, the arbitrary power of the state. Two of the demands called upon the state to rein in the power of the police; one called for an independent legislative assembly with real political power; one asked for freedom of expression and for a free press. This last demand, as the engineering student reminds us, was to reappear in all the student declarations of the succeeding years.[14] The semiofficial *Al-Ahram* was one of the student's continual targets, and, under Nasser, there was a particularly deep hostility to his spokesman Mohamed Heikal. The editors and the spokesman were to change under Sadat, but the hostility persisted. At issue was the moral responsibility of the written and spoken word. The spread of mass education and literacy, greater exposure to the outside world, and the June defeat itself as a great teacher, had made it more difficult for the rulers to get away with what they had gotten away with before. A generation that had been systematically lied to, and told that a new world was in the making, was in effect saying, "We have had enough of your distortions, and because we will have to pay for your errors and decisions, you'd better tell us the truth, no matter how difficult and painful."

A message was being delivered to people like Mohamed Heikal: The audience was no longer as gullible as it used to be; it could see through the apologetics and distortions, it wanted a new language and a new style of discourse — one that dispensed with hypocrisy and pretensions. The old school had lost its hold on the symbols, its pretensions had become transparent, its memories almost irrelevant. For fifteen years, it had insisted that it represented the wave of the future, that it broke with the defeat and betrayal of the old world. But now it was clear that this was mostly illusion, that the new forms were empty shells, that the slogans were hollow. So deep was the split between the old school — how bitter it must have been for the youngsters of 1952, for the new nationalists to age before their time! — and the new sensibility that it often seemed that the two sides were using two distinct languages and mental frameworks, inhabiting two radically different worlds at war with one another. As the testimony of the engineering student puts it: "I used to feel that I lived in a different society from the one inhabited by the people outside the college. Here we are free and they are the slaves; we are the judges and they the accused; we are the truthful ones and they the liars."[15]

The political tradition itself was on trial in the encounter between the rulers and the young dissenters. The men in power thought that the state belonged to them and that outsiders could not be trusted with the truth and were not entitled to it. The students wanted the state to trust others and mobilize them, to shed its fears and suspicions. This sentiment was reflected in a remarkable statement made by a student leader in a session of the Arab Socialist Union, the country's legal political party, chaired by President Nasser. Youth, said the student leader, still believed in Nasser, they were still with him. The President was suggestively reminded that the young stood by him in the "darkest hours" of the defeat when he was defenseless, that they were the ones who turned the "shifting sands" beneath his feet into "solid ground" on the days of June 9 and 10, that nothing stood in their way then had they really wanted to undermine him and his order.[16] In other words, the state need not always be on the defensive: Liberate individuals from the tyranny of state power and engage them in a common effort if you want the political order to stand on its feet and to stand up to the outside world. A worker from Suez struck a similar note: Involve the young if you want them to fight and die, inform them of the decisions that affect their lives. The young used to hear about the battle but not directly experience it: They would hear about clashes across the Suez Canal as though they were remote events in Vietnam.[17]

The individual had all along been a subject of history; people had been and remain spectators to their own destiny. The sultan was being asked to share political power, and the daring needed to ask him was supplied by the great defeat of a few months ago. Israel's success lent courage to those who could now insist that people who witness their own destiny, who stand idly outside history applauding when sham political parties ask them to do so and trusting that a seemingly masterful and heroic figure can do it all on his own, will be prey to others.

Economic concerns and anxiety over careers and private lives gave to the encounter between the regime and the students a grim and desperate dimension. Mass university education made possible by the regime's populism had produced a glut of university graduates who had to be employed and whose expectations surpassed the capacity of the economic system. The regime had had a difficult choice to make: It could restrict access to university education, it could expand the educational system but make the graduates fend for themselves in the marketplace, or it could guarantee both university education and employment. For obvious political reasons, it had chosen the third option, and the result was an inefficient, bloated public sector that guaranteed economic survival but engendered deep frustrations and a sense of uselessness. At a time when patience was wearing thin, when the seeming verities began to unravel, the inequity of the system could be more clearly seen and became more difficult to defend. The privileged economic position of the officer corps had been an obvious but more or less tolerated fact of life.

In defeat, the socioeconomic ascendency of the military became unbearable, and the dormant resentments of the civilian graduates toward their military counterparts came to the surface. Because the military officers held such an ascendant position in the public sector, there was now an undercurrent of support for the private sector among the students. The motive was not so much a revolt against socialism but a simple desire, born out of frustration, to encourage a competing system of production wherein the deck was not as heavily stacked in favor of the military. If socialism had degenerated into a rule of the Mamluks, then why not try something else?

The wind was blowing from all directions: On one extreme was the call for domestic austerity, a war economy, and a people's war of liberation. On the other were the enemies of the regime, who saw in the defeat an opportunity to roll back the changes of recent years. In between was the bourgeoisie, whose support the regime had to bid for. This Nasser understood, and he made an offer to share political power — that was the meaning of his so-called

March 30 Declaration. He was willing to change the symbols and style of the regime that had alienated them. Instead of the language of revolution, he would now speak of efficiency and science; where he had previously appealed to emotions and instincts he would use more sober, technical language. Instead of making noise about justice and equity, he would pay homage to efficiency, productivity, work.

Together with the change in symbols went some economic concessions: If the regime could not engage in a full-scale war, it could lower the barriers to imports, bring in more cars and other consumer durables, give the middle-class peasantry more incentives. Whereas the Yemen war had been financed out of consumption – private consumption had declined from 72 percent to 68 percent of GNP during the Egyptian intervention in Yemen – a critical political decision was made after 1967 to keep private consumption stable. Rearmament was to be financed at the expense of the investment sector, which dropped from a high of 18 percent of GNP prior to the Six Day War to a low of 13 percent in its aftermath.[18] This was a decision with awesome consequences in the years ahead: Consumption levels had to be maintained while the infrastructure continued to deteriorate. The moment of reckoning was postponed, and others – Russians, Arab oil states, Americans — were to help keep things from coming apart. The dependency that Nasser had found so repugnant was to become a fact of life. The choices available to the men in command would be reduced to a choice among different backers.

The economic concessions to the middle class were one side of the regime's response to its crisis; the war of attrition across the Suez Canal was another. Whereas the first sought to create a sense of normalcy and to preempt the potential opposition of the middle class, the second appealed to the patriotism of all Egyptians. Moreover, the fight across the Canal served to underline Egypt's role as the critical Arab actor. When the Palestinians struck out on their own in early 1968 and proclaimed the beginning of a guerrilla war of national liberation, they posed a deep psychological challenge to Egypt's sense of preeminence and confronted the Egyptian leader with a set of thorny problems. For more than a decade, it had been an article of faith that the hope for doing something for the Palestinians rested on Nasser and his army: That was Egypt's burden and role. Now, in a dramatic reversal of fortunes, Egypt stood paralyzed and ineffective and the Palestinians were raising bright banners and offering a desperately anxious and demoralized Arab world a sign of manliness and courage. The Arabs, in their folklore a martial race fed on tales of courage and sacrifice, had come face to face with a reality that contradicted that image. At that bleak moment, Palestinian defiance and guerrilla incursions provided reassurance that all was not lost. For a while the Palestinians were able to beat Nasser at his own game: Their communiques exaggerated their achievements, and they offered grand solutions and some hope. Whereas Nasser and Egypt seemed resigned to an unhappy status quo, they rejected; while he pleaded before the world, they resorted to force. They were new and he was old; they were the revolution, and he was a missed opportunity.

A master of street politics who knew the political power of images and impressions, Nasser realized that this was a fight he could easily lose and that sooner or later he would have to give substance to his view that the fight with Israel was an interstate matter that required the skills and weight of regular armies. Afraid of the potential for disorder inherent in the politics of his rivals, determined to maintain the initiative in inter-Arab politics and to keep the fragile balance within Egypt itself intact, he threw the war of attrition into the equation. The enemy's fire and punishment were preferable to domestic and Arab disorder. This was to provide an antidote to his rivals' romanticism, proof that the stable, orderly politics he represented were the Arab world's only realistic hope. Surely the guerrillas could help, and Nasser knew their popular appeal and was not about to risk an open attack against them, but the principal role was not theirs. The fight across the Canal was both a fight against Israel — for by then Nasser had begun to state that Israel was bent upon freezing the cease-fire lines and imposing a new status quo in the area — as well as a response to his new rivals in the Arab world. His calculations were largely accurate: The stiff response of Israel to the war of attrition inflicted great damage, but it bought time; it supplied proof of the will to resist. And when Israeli statements began to suggest that the aim of Israel's deep-penetration bombing was to topple the Egyptian regime and make the costs of the war intolerable, that was the kind of politics that Nasser could thrive on. Bitter enemies are not particularly good at toppling regimes; the more ruthless an attack against a besieged leader, the more heroic he becomes. So the bombing raids that were intended to topple Nasser wound up making him "the symbol of courageous resistance at a time of national crisis."[19]

Caught between the pressures of those who wanted him to negotiate and normalize a world that had been in constant turmoil and those who were fired up by the need for revenge and restoration of pride, between one superpower committed to his enemy and one that now could take him for granted and synchronize him into its global design, between young revolutionaries who could suddenly see that he had failed to be heretical and rebellious enough and a traditional Arab order that had gained a new lease on life after 1967, there was very little Nasser could do but try to juggle all these pressures. There was no longer a big project under way. Worse yet, he had lost land in a country where ownership of land takes on obsessional overtones. Under him, a country that had been plundered, invaded, occupied, where occupiers came and managed to stay long stretches of time, was to witness yet another occupation.

Nasser's intuition, eloquently expressed to Boumedienne and Mahjub, was correct. Others had to get Egypt off the hook. So he died leaving a mixed legacy, enabling someone like Heikal to say that Nasser's story was not yet finished, enabling a Qaddafi to go on with his own brand of Nasserism, to claim as he does on the cover of his pamphlets and books that Nasser designated him as the trustee — *al-amin* — over the fate of Arab nationalism.

But Qaddafi's version of Nasserism and the Nasserism of the die-hard believers in west Beirut share very little with the late stage of Egyptian-style Nasserism. Qaddafi's is more buoyant, because it is the philosophy of loud, rebellious youth, sheltered from the wounds, the constraints, and the traumas of original Nasserism. Qaddafi's is a desert philosophy engendered by wealth and possibilities. Because his baggage is light — a small population, a high income — Qaddafi can fly as high as his imagination could take him. Nasser's base was a more impoverished, more crowded land, and it set limits to his expectations and possibilities, particularly in the latter part of his career. Whereas Qaddafi's philosophy is bedouin, Nasser's philosophy bore the mark of a crowded, wise — some (including Qaddafi) would say cynical — city that had long been used to applauding winners, forgetting losers, and coming to terms with things it did not like. West Beirut's and Syria's brands of Nasserism are altogether different things. The first was an oppositional doctrine, a protest by Muslim Sunnis against the dominance of Christian Lebanon, a yearning for a Sunni Arab order. It was only natural that the young of West Beirut and the pan-Arabists in Syria would respond to Nasser, for he came to embody both pan-Arabism and (despite his secularism at home) Sunni internationalism.

Qaddafi and his fellow officers neatly illustrate Nasser's predicament: However serious he might have been in his commitment to normalize the Arab system, to reopen channels of communication with powers he had alienated, to sober a generation he himself had fired up with excitement, and to turn his attention to Egypt and her troubles, the hero still had a role to play; the script had long ago been prepared and he could only introduce minor variations. It remained for his successor to play the part. Mr. Sadat had never excited a pan-Arab audience; he had never been a hero, and if he lacked the hero's stature, he also lacked the hero's reputation and was free of the chains that tie heroes to their great deeds.

If anything, Sadat – and this is only human – who had long lived in Nasser's shadow, would find it gratifying to slay the myth that was to a great extent the work of his predecessor – a man he had once known as an equal and who had managed to rise above Sadat and other colleagues to almost mythical and heroic proportions due in some part to the love and devotion of people in distant Arab capitals. This is where the psychology of the leader intrudes: Sadat could hope to compete with his predecessor in Egypt proper, but in the Arab world his predecessor was larger than life. There was perhaps in Sadat's Egyptianness a desire to move from Nasser's shadow into a smaller arena in which his predecessor seems more real and less glamorized, more subjects to errors and to a normal, more tangible assessment. In Egypt, as contrasted with the Arab world in general, Nasser was more likely to be seen realistically, to be criticized.

THE EGYPTIAN SEARCH

While others outside Egypt would hold their memories of Nasser, the real-life people who inhabited Egypt – very much like Mahfuz's characters – would go on debating war and peace, civilization and religion, the Arabs who won and those who lost in 1967, the real intentions of the Soviet Union, and so on. The same debates would repeatedly take place in the higher councils. The new man at the helm, less sure of himself, less entitled to his position, would say, as he did during a meeting with his generals, that there was no other choice but to fight, that it was a matter of survival: To be or not to be. But sooner or later the chatter had to end if the Egyptian state was to remain in command at home, to redeem its standing in the Arab system, to check the appeal of Mu'amar Qaddafi, to challenge the detente of the superpowers and the complacency of Israel. Above all, it had to do something to resolve its own doubts about its own capabilities and integrity, to open a new path.

One leader presided, but he seemed paralyzed; he needed his own great act if his Egypt was to come into being. His corrective movement of May 15, 1971, which ended in his victory over the apparatus left by Nasser, was not enough; from the Libyan desert there was a claim that it was the young Libyan — armed with the Quran and with oil wealth — who was more qualified to continue the march. At home there was frustration and skepticism, spilling over every now and then into student riots and clashes between Muslims and Copts; in the Arab system there was a malaise deep enough to prompt a sensitive observer of Arab politics such as Arnold Hottinger to write that Arab radicalism might yet create a social order that resembles "present-day China more than any other society now known to us."[20] Globally, there was a detente between the two superpowers that broke the back of nonalignment that a whole generation of Arab and other Third World nationalists had lived on since the days of Bandung and charismatic leadership such as that of Nehru, Sukarno, Nasser, and Nkrumah.

Politics were now more psychologized than ever: their vocabulary and concerns had nothing to do with concrete policies and issues, but with questions of survival, of *qalaq* (anxiety), of pending storms and confusions. The word that the Egyptian regime and other Arab regimes had used so frequently — the "battle" — had to be made real if these regimes were to survive, and it was in Egypt that the psychological burden of the defeat was heaviest and where the frequency with which the battle was invoked had itself become another political issue. In early January, 1973, a group of the country's most celebrated writers and intellectuals issued a public statement that asked the regime not to further cheapen a word that had "lost its power, effectiveness, as well as credibility." The group said that the references to the battle had confused the young, whose "path was blocked," who worked for their diplomas only to be sent to the front "where they forget what they learned and don't find an enemy to fight." The state had to be honest "if the fog was to be cleared and people were to know what lay ahead."[21]

Recurring like a litany in the statements of officials and critics alike, in works of fiction as well as in more conventional social discourse, was the reference to the path that had to be cleared, the corner that had to be turned. The country's doubts had to be resolved and its fears exorcised, and the leadership was to find in the limited war of October, 1973, a way out of the fog and confusions. It was a gamble; new problems awaited but at least the oppressive stalemate was broken. The war provided Sadat with his great act.

The crossing of the Suez Canal became the mandate to create his kind of Egypt ("restore" may be a better word) and to move from his predecessor's shadow. It was a concrete act — a relief and a needed contrast to the volume of words and scenarios — and an answer to the skeptics in Libya, the Fertile Crescent, and the oil states. The crossing was also a metaphor: Men like Mustapha Amin and Ahmad Abu al-Fath, two ancien régime journalists, the first of whom was imprisoned by Nasser and the other exiled to Switzerland, used the crossing to symbolize the break between Nasser's Egypt and Sadat's. In Mustapha Amin's exuberant style, a style that had once served the monarchy, then Abdul Nasser, and finally Sadat, the crossing was a "crossing from defeat to victory, division to unity, shame to dignity, oppression to justice, terror to security."[22] Nasser's Egypt stood for defeat, socialism, Arabism; the new, triumphant Egypt for a "free economy," a more responsible order, an Egyptian Egypt. "June's Egypt" had lost its way; "October's Egypt" regained its soul. The talk of revolution vanished; *Misr* (Egypt) was to become the new symbol. The Egyptian order began its march forward — into the past.

Such was the logic of one important intellectual verdict made by Tawfiq al Hakim, a man rightly described as Egypt's "dean of letters,"[23] in a book that helped launch the phenomenon of de-Nasserization. In Hakim's hindsight — the book was written in 1972 and published after the October War — the entire Nasserist experiment becomes a moment of madness; a leader mesmerizes an entire nation, "expropriates its mind," creates fake victories, and wastes the bread of a poor society in pursuit of a pan-Arabist mirage. Hakim's second thoughts on Nasser and Nasserism have an interesting twist: Four decades earlier, Hakim had written a work of fiction, *Awdat al Ruh* (The Return of the Spirit), which supposedly stirred Nasser's imagination.[24] The work had the standard themes of its time: the West and the East, the yearning for independence, the glory of the bourgeois-nationalist revolution of 1919, the splendor and miracles of ancient Egypt. The passage that must have caught Nasser's attention was an exchange between an austere English administrator who sees things as they are and a mystic Frenchman who sees the deep meaning behind things. This poor, wretched people, said the Frenchman of the Egyptians, still have the spirit of their ancient temples; all Egypt needs is a man to worship, someone who can "embody all its sentiments and wishes." Then the limitations would crumble and the Egyptians would build modern miracles. Nasser's emergence had made him Hakim's hero, but Hakim now saw it all as illusions.

With Nasser's spell broken by defeat, Hakim's nostalgia was now for another period of Egyptian history: the bourgeois, nationalist revolution of 1919. That revolution was the work of Egyptian society "looking for itself, resurrecting its spirit and civilization," whereas Nasser's revolution was made by the state; it was revolution from above, the will of one man whose socialism turned out to be a mere replacement of an old class with a new one, whose deeds were mere sound and fury, and achievements were nowhere to be seen. The "Egyptian revolution" had come full circle: The Nasserist order had imposed a near blackout on the liberal, nationalist phase of Egyptian history. Sadat's post – October 1973 order was to rediscover that phase – in it the archaeologists saw a better, saner, more proper Egypt, a place where the right men made the decisions, where people knew and kept their places, where the state was kept at bay. Its claims were limited, but so too was its reach into the private lives of individuals. "I thought that Egypt's history began on the 23rd of July," observed one of Najib Mahfuz's characters in *Al Karnak;* "it was only after the *al-Naksa* [the June 1967 setback] that I began to look for what preceded it . . . I will not hide from you that I admired the resilience of the opposition and its freedom, the role that the Egyptian judiciary played during that period. The old regime was not totally worthless; it had many intellectual elements that deserved to continue and flourish. The negation of these elements was a factor in our setback."[25]

This kind of political archaeology was primarily domestic. But it had implications for the mix of Egyptian nationalism and Arabism, for the relation between Egypt, where Nasserism governed, and those in the Arab world for whom Nasserism was an exciting change. The urge of Egyptians to look back at the Nasserist period, the natural rage of those who had been victimized by the Nasser regime, or the skepticism of those who had experienced the Nasserist system as it really was clashed with the nostalgia and fidelity of the Arab Nasserists who still saw Nasserism as a grand epic. In Egypt, observed the astute Mohamed Heikal, Nasserism was *hukm* (rule, a regime), but elsewhere in the Arab world it was *hulm* (a dream).[26] The Egyptian urge to undertake an internal audit of the seamy side of the Nasserist system – the tales of torture, the many tales of corruption that provided a radically different picture from the regime's socialist incantations, the pettiness of the men at the helm, the sordid and banal ways in which men larger than life really behave – was in the eyes of the Arab Nasserites sheer blasphemy.

It was suspected that the internal audit was a disguise, merely a dress rehearsal for an attack on Egypt, on Arabism. If a society blessed with such a great heroic figure would still find it within itself to attack his memory and achievements, then there must be something wrong with the society itself, something craven and unprincipled. In contrast to the lofty world of metaphysics and ideology, the private and tangible concerns of Egyptians were petty and irrelevant. If the Egyptians objected to the record of Nasserism, then they could be seen for what they were: petty bourgeois consumers, bureaucrats who play it safe, squeamish men who fail to see a great historical drama at work and who willingly sacrifice their petty concerns at its altar.

This was the first impasse between the Egyptian state and those who came within the orbit of Nasserist experiment, with those in Libya, Syria, the Palestinian community and elsewhere who wanted Egypt to stay the course, to be, so to speak, larger than it. In large measure, this was the logic of the Nasserist era playing itself out: Revolutions create constituencies, and there are always those who come from afar to believe and to applaud. It takes time to shake off such constituencies, to awaken them rudely to the fact that their expectations are one thing, but difficult realities are another. In some measure this was the predicament of Egypt in the Arab system of states that had been brought about by the defeat in 1967.

A unique blend of pride and weakness seems to have pushed Egypt along in the Arab system since her defeat in 1967; her so-called victory in October, 1973, gave her a margin for maneuver. But the country came up against a new inter-Arab order after October, 1973. This was an order that Egypt helped create. The perception that Egypt did not reap its harvest offers a better guide for understanding the conduct of the Egyptian state than class analysis or the will of the ruler. Behind the Egyptian choices, one can discern more urge and instinct than deliberate policies: a desire to break out, to put the recent past behind, and to turn over a new leaf.

On one level, the Egyptian–Arab disagreements over the diplomatic aftermath of the war – the first disengagement accord, the Sinai accord, the Jerusalem initiative, Camp David – built on top of one another: One step led to the next; the Egyptian leader felt his way through the dark, took a step, raised a storm, then rode it out on his way to the next step. Yet there is a prior explanation that is worth considering: The disagreement can be seen in the different assumptions about the October War itself. The Egyptians fought the war in order to give themselves more maneuverability on the Egyptian–Israeli front, in the Arab system, and between the two superpowers. In their eyes, the October War was a one-shot affair, a way of breaking out of the nightmare of the 1967 defeat. The men who made Egypt's difficult decision in 1973 did not intend that war to be the beginning of a new, sustained war with Israel or of another captivity in inter-Arab politics. Just as Nasser's war of attrition had been a way of regaining initiative in Arab politics, so too was the October War.

Programmatic statements by leaders are not the best way to understand what they do, but Sadat gave a clue as to what lay ahead in his statement, *The October Paper,* published in early 1974. "The world after October 1973," he confidently observed, "was not the same as it had been before." Some homage was paid to pan-Arabism and the brave Syrian "brothers," but the first and primary element in the victory was *al-Wataniyya al-Misriyya* (Egyptian patriotism). The victory, said Mr. Sadat, was the accomplishment of an ancient, homogeneous people that had lived on the same plot of land for seven thousand years. The country had been repeatedly invaded, but it managed to escape the tribal and sectarian divisions that plague other societies. The "seven thousand years" symbol and Egyptian patriotism had been discarded during the Nasserite revolution. Their reappearance in the October Paper was no accident: The Egyptian state was pushing its case for a new deal in the Arab order and reminding others of its advantages — a centralized authority, homogeneous population, an indepedent nationalism.[27]

We know from the memoirs and revelations of some of Sadat's close associates that there was an urge to prove Egypt's capabilities to other Arabs, a realization that other Arab states were not going to help Egypt so long as the country did not perform its role as the Arab world's principal fighting force. That is why the first shot had to be fired and the crossing accomplished before President Sadat dispatched Sayyed Marei, one of his closest associates and a pillar of the Sadat regime, to Saudi Arabia and the other oil states. There Marei and his delegation were to put before the oil states Egypt's accomplishments and needs. As Marei recalls it, he was under instruction from President Sadat not to ask for any specific sums of money: Other Arabs had to be made to face their obligations.[28] And some poignancies emerge from these meetings: how to calculate the value of Egyptian sacrifices, how to reconcile Egypt's grim and terrifying war with the other Arabs' demand — made by

King Faisal — for a "lengthy" and substantial war, how to balance the four hundred million dollars given by Saudi Arabia and Egypt's sacrifices?

These questions were raised as the war itself was being fought on the Egyptian–Israeli front. They acquired greater salience after the guns fell silent and diplomacy began. War, says an Egyptian diplomat versed in inter-Arab affairs, is a "spectator sport."[29] Having helped subsidize the war, the other Arabs wanted it to last longer; they believed that the war was one battle in a sustained military encounter. But the Egyptian elite viewed it as a way of regaining honor, opening up new possibilities and horizons, setting straight the pecking order in the Arab world. What the Egyptian decision makers dreaded most was another stalemate, and that was precisely what the war had produced. A more intractable stalemate still — and probably another war — loomed on the horizon if Egypt were to try for a collective bargain. This was Sadat's reading of the situation; he reasoned that Egypt had enough weight to get its own terms and that was what he opted for.

Sadat could have done other things: He could, for example, have provided the facts about the October War, conceded that the Israelis had crossed to the other side of the canal, and that he needed Kissinger's mediation to save the third army. But he chose not to: Sadat and others in the Egyptian leadership had experienced the trauma and shock of the 1967 defeat. It would have been difficult for them to concede that the battle for which Egypt waited and prepared had ended unfavorably. The national pride of the society, the maneuverability of the state, and Sadat's leadership were at stake. The October War was his war, a source of his own legitimacy, his own great act, a chance to be something more than Abdul Nasser's accidental successor — the meek, inheriting political power. And as the October War took on almost mythical dimensions, Sadat was called upon to make good on the promise of October — his new order of peace and prosperity. This dictated his policies. He had become a captive of his own promises.

THE WAYS OF THE PHARAOH, THE WAYS OF OTHERS

The new order entailed territorial concessions from Israel, help and sympathy from the United States, acquiescence on the part of the oil states, and the cooperation of Jordan and Syria. Sadat reasoned that Syria had no place to go and would be forced to play by his rules; that Saudi Arabia's innate conservatism and its links to the United States would force the Saudis to go along with him. All of this obviously required the cooperation of too many other play-ers. But if some of Sadat's subsequent troubles were beyond his reach — he could not deliver the Saudis and Kuwait, he could not force Jordan and Syria to see matters his way — many other prob-lems were caused by his style.

Sadat's preference for what he proudly called his "electric-shock diplomacy" faced others in the Arab system with serious di-lemmas. Operating from a belief in Egypt's centrality to the Arab world, Sadat tended to underestimate the resources of others; sit-ting at the helm of a stable polity, he underestimated the troubles of other rulers who presided over countries more difficult to gov-ern. His relations with Syria show how conflicting perceptions over national situations helped erode that alliance. Sadat com-manded pliant aides and could take gambles and political risks, be-cause such was the nature of the Egyptian political system. Asad lived in a different world: A member of a minority group gov-erning a volatile country, he had to be more cautious. From Cairo, Sadat could take a relaxed view of Lebanon's troubles, of Palestin-ian radicalism. Indeed, Lebanon bought Sadat time: It tarnished Syria's appeal; it kept the Syrians and the Palestinians locked in a bloody and costly conflict. But for Asad the stakes in Lebanon were different. Lebanon was his next-door neighbor, and he was caught between the sympathy of Syria's Sunni majority for the Muslim — Palestinian — leftist alliance and his own fear that a vic-tory by that alliance would trigger an Israeli intervention.

Lacking Sadat's base and distance, Asad had to stay in the game and play it with caution. He had to prove, at least to his own popu-lation, that he was shackling the Palestinians in order to enhance the Palestinian cause by ridding it of its extremism, and by avoiding the prospects of yet another radical and troublesome regime on the border that might drag Syria into an untimely war with Israel. That is why Asad could not go as far as Sadat and why he disasso-ciated himself from Sadat's journey to Jerusalem. Whoever rules Cairo, observed the astute Lebanese politician Kamal Junblatt in his last political testimony — "his will" — is a pharaoh; whoever rules Damascus is a *wali* (a provincial governor).[30] The pharaoh could go to Jerusalem if he so wished; the *wali* could not. The fight between the pharoah and the *wali* was not primarily over substance: Both had agreed on the limited nature of the October War; both had accepted the harsh logic of Israeli military power; both knew what would play and what would not in the world of states. Neither of the two had radical views on the nature of the socioeconomic order. Their alliance faltered over tactics, over their sense of the permissible in their respective political systems. The battle between the two was narrower in scope than it was made out to be after the two had parted company. There were very few takers for the Syrian argument (made in retrospect) that their split with Sadat was ideological in nature, that rival priorities and philosophies had clashed.

Egyptian patriotism Sadat-style was quick to put Syria beyond the pale of civilized humanity. The "brave Syrian brothers" of October 1973 had become dispensable; they were never understood or appreciated by the average Egyptian. Damascus was far away, its politics and ways not easily understood through Egyptian categories. Syria's politics were volatile and unpredictable, her ways entailed risks and violence; Egypt's way was hailed by the civilized world that sets the codes of behavior, that knows the difference between the politics of despair and violence and the politics of responsibility. In the conservative Egyptian sensibility, Syria's politics (not to mention the politics of Libya and Iraq) were a whirlwind of blood and violence. "They are nothing," said the Egyptian daily Al Akhbar of Iraq, Syria, and Libya; they are closer to being insane asylums than modern states. Syria is a "Soviet colony" that massacres the Palestinians while talking of Palestinian rights; Iraq's leader, Saddam Hussein, loves the "spilling of blood."[31] For Egypt's stability — the oasis of the area — there is Syria's violence and Iraq's bloodbaths. Some of this is second-hand colonial imagery, some the inevitable difference between a society with a strong, centralized tradition and a culture in which people still take matters into their hands.

The image manipulated above is also Sadat's imagery: we see it at work in a critical speech by him to the Egyptian National Assembly in defense of the Camp David accords. "What is happening," he asks, "in the camp led by the Soviet Union? Syria devastates Lebanon; she comes in and liquidates the Palestinians at Tal al Zaatar and attacks the Muslims . . . then she turns against the Christians." The entire "Soviet camp" becomes a land of "torture, imprisonment, murderers, executions." Egypt is a threat to all those states, for it remains a "democratic oasis" that protects the dignity of man.[32]

Dispensing with Syria and Iraq was a relatively easy matter. The impasse with Saudi Arabia was more problematic, if only because the financial stakes for Egypt were considerable. Sadat had assigned Saudi Arabia the role of financier for his new order; he had assumed that Saudi Arabia would bless the shift of his country away from being the Arab world's military force to becoming its cultural and economic oasis. Saudi Arabia's design was different. The Saudis were not interested in turning Egypt into a viable economic entity, even if that was within the realm of the possible. States do not charitably build up other states and create problems and competition for themselves. Egypt's demographic weight is awesome; Saudi Arabia is a sparsely populated society that must worry about the ambitions and claims of its neighbors. In Saudi Arabia's scheme of things, the Egyptian decision maker could move on his own, for the Saudis are firm believers in the right of Arab states to sovereignty over matters that lie within their domain, but the Egyptians must stay within the normative and political limits of the group and the overall Arab censensus. The Egyptian urge to break out and do things on their own was precisely what Saudi Arabia did not want.

Saudi Arabia's tribal ways and Sadat's preference for dramatic, solo performances go a long way toward explaining Egyptian – Saudi troubles. Tribes are collective entities that frown on loners; the order of the tribe must be kept intact and involves patterns of consultation, *shura,* ways of doing things through appropriate channels. Mr. Sadat's irreverence toward the accepted ways, his daring to think and do the unthinkable in going to Jerusalem, could only offend the conservative sensibility of a tribal society that sets strict limits on social behavior. Like a tribe, the Saudis' tendency was to wait and hope for the members who had gone astray to return to the fold. Their participation in the Baghdad summit in late 1978 showed that their hope had vanished. The brother was lost for good; his ways had become too eccentric for a world in which *bid'a* (innovation) remains a prohibition.

Then there were the conflicting perceptions between a rising power (Saudi Arabia) and a declining one (Egypt). Each assumed that it would call the shots: the Saudis because they believed that the new world was theirs, that they had become the linchpin of the Arab system; the Egyptians out of habit. The Saudis' weapon was financial; Egypt's was the "one hundred thousand martyrs, the four wars," and Egypt's centrality. Each power chose to see the weak side of the other. To the Saudis, Egypt was a bottomless pit, a lethargic, scarred country, unable to win a war or to stick to a fight. On the Egyptian side there was the pride of the great city, the traditional urban contempt for the people of the desert. For all the talk of rural values and the mystique of the desert, Muslim Arabs are firm believers in the supremacy of the city: The desert appeals to Westerners, but the Arabs' romance is with the city. The hostility of Cambodia's Khmer Rouge to Phnom Penh as a soulless transplant of the West does not find a powerful echo in the Arab–Muslim order. Some of that feeling can be detected in Qaddafi's sermons on Cairo's nightclubs, her unveiled, liberated women, but Islam has traditionally been a religion of the city and Cairo was built by Islam. It was a monument to Islam's conversion of Egypt to the true religion of Allah.

This has given Cairenes the notion that they can reconcile the outside world and the world of Islam. During the heyday of liberal Egypt's experiment, Saudi Arabia and the Arabian peninsula could be looked at with condescension. Taha Husayn's important manifesto of liberal Egypt, *Mustaqbal al Thaqafa fi Misr* [The Future of Education in Egypt], written in 1938, came close to expressing a kind of "Egyptian man's burden" toward the less fortunate areas like "the Hijaz and the provinces of the Saudi Arabian state."[33] Egypt's financial resources may be limited, he observed, but Egypt should help educate those states if Egyptians were to live up to their "leadership and dignity." Nasser's Egypt had the same low opinion of the Saudi state. Under Nasser the contempt took a radical tone: a progressive, socialist state patronizing a decadent, feudal one. But the result was the same.

The world had changed since Taha Husayn's time, and it was no longer what it was at the height of the Nasserist experiment. But societies do not easily surrender their illusions; they do not adjust to their decline as easily as others would like them to. Social scientists removed from the scene may be able to play with indexes and measurements of power and to determine the ebb and flow in national resources and capabilities, but nations persist in their memories. And the Egyptians remain persuaded that Cairo is the capital of the Arab–Muslim order.

Another Egyptian advantage derived from a fact that non-Egyptian Arabs have rarely appreciated: By classical geopolitical definition, Egypt is the only nation-state in the Arab world. Egypt's rivals in the Arab systems were two kinds of states: either minority-based sectarian societies (Syria and Iraq) or dynastic entities (Saudi Arabia and Kuwait). The daring with which Sadat (and before him, Nasser) conducted matters of state reflected the security that came from an established political tradition. Sadat's repeated violations of Arab sensibilities left his Arab critics baffled, lamely insisting that the next violation would prove to be his undoing. Throughout the great turmoil triggered by the Iranian upheaval and at a time when other regimes were running for cover, Anwar el-Sadat was swimming against the current: openly hosting Begin, offering America military bases, offering asylum to the Shah of Iran, inviting others to stand up and be counted. Some of that was vintage Sadat style, some the security that comes from ruling a relatively stable national entity in which nationalism derives from millennial continuity and from the logic of modern nationalism, which played itself out in recent Egyptian history. Both the personal style and the security of statehood can be seen in one of Sadat's many contemptuous statements: "As for the leaders of the other Arab states, it is enough to look at their problems and the problems of their regimes. Hafez Assad now faces the revolt of his people and Saddam Hussein (of Iraq) faces popular upheaval in addition to his troubles with Iran. Even Saudi Arabia now faces internal difficulties despite its prosperity. There are now leaflets in Saudi Arabia that say that there is no ruler in Egypt with a salary of $8 million, no ruler who gambles with the wealth of his people. As for the states of the Gulf, they are threatened by Khomeini . . ."[34]

Old Egyptian cultural and political claims and political advantages helped justify Sadat's separate diplomatic path in defiance of the Arab rich, and so did new grievances. The simplicity of the image with which President Sadat and those in the intellectual establishment who saw things his way worked had its potency: On one side of the divide (Egypt) there was the blood of the October, 1973, dead and the tears of the survivors; on the other (Saudi Arabia and the Gulf states) there were both wealth and self-righteousness.

Two popular concerns that went beyond the confines of diplomacy and politics gave Egypt's diplomatic defection and battle with the oil states personal meaning and drama. In a country in which land is scarce and valuable, there was concern over land and real-estate acquisitions by rich Arabs, a feeling that Arab wealth was making Egyptians strangers in their own land. In a country in which notions of *ird* (honor of one's women folk) still move, imprison, and demean humans, there was concern that Cairo — to quote one influential editor — had become the Bangkok of the Arab world, that Arab wealth was violating Egypt's honor and integrity. Both the land acquisitions and the question of sexual liberties might have been exaggerated, but they were deadly serious and sensitive matters. The leadership did not have to dwell on these themes, but they were there in the country's popular films and magazines, part of Egypt's endless chatter. Arab wealth challenged Egypt's sense of self: Possessed by *arriviste* bedouins, it underlined the cruelty of a world that had gone awry. The imagined prosperity of yesterday had vanished; the change was not the fault of the Egyptian state; the reasons had to do with the costly wars waged by Egypt on behalf of the Arab states.

Sadat was to ride these sentiments all the way to Jerusalem and to exploit them in the aftermath of his deed. His initiative administered a psychohistorical shock to other Arabs. In its wake they would ask questions about him as an individual, but there were questions about Egypt as well. Was his trip an act of surrender, an expression of his and his country's despair? Or was it, as he himself claimed, an initiation of the Arabs into the modern world of states? Was his act the whim of an isolated sultan or was it an expression of Egypt's will? Was not his embrace of the West proof of his own alienation from the Arab world and by implication of his country's as well? There were doubts about Egypt's integrity, doubts that Egyptians are sensitive to and had heard often enough Qaddafi's description of Egypt as an empty house with two doors, one from which the country "flirts" – notice the sexual metaphor – with the enemy and one with political reaction. The metaphor evokes the moral weakness of a country that changes its ways and where people easily surrender.

Other Arabs have never quite understood Egyptian crowds. The same crowds that once had hailed Abdul Nasser's Arabism were out in full force to greet Sadat's break with it; the same crowds that once had chanted against American imperialism gave Richard Nixon an unprecedented reception in the summer of 1974; the people who once had acclaimed Palestinian and Algerian revolutionaries embraced visiting Israeli negotiators with equal warmth. The malleability and fickleness of crowds trouble those who wish to think that there are durable loyalties that transcend and defy manipulations of rulers and sudden shifts of opinion. How were other Arabs to come to terms with Egypt's mind? Did Egypt speak through Abdul Nasser and Mohamed Heikal? Or was Anwar el-Sadat its authentic voice? The political gap that separated the Sadat regime from the Arab world had cultural and psychological foundations. Whatever his faults and shortcomings as a political operator, Sadat fully grasped this and exploited it: The weak country, its compromised capital, and patient, obedient peasantry would no longer fight and bleed for others. They had other options. Such, at any rate, was the president's gamble and choice.

What was the relationship between Sadat's own transgressions and Egypt's will? The other Arabs could go through the motion of distinguishing between their denunciation of Sadat and their professed respect for the Egyptian people. But the separation was difficult to make in practice. The tight control of the Egyptian media, which filter events and opinions, posed one logistical problem. But there were doubts about Egypt that the Arab professions of goodwill could not cover over, a suspicion that Sadat was not a solitary individual, that he did truly represent Egypt's inner self and her willingness to set aside the sacred struggle and accept a separate peace. Thus the Arab attempt to distinguish between Sadat as a solitary man and Egypt's will made at the Baghdad summit in November, 1978, and afterward, though understandable, is not particularly persuasive. The notion that the Egyptian problem was somehow a personal idiosyncracy of Sadat, that a different leader would have acted in a radically different way, is one of those imponderables of history. But whatever the correct interpretations, it is wishful thinking to attribute it all to the will and style of the man at the helm. Leaders may read and exploit national wounds and grievances in a particular way, but we cannot fully comprehend why they get away with what they do if we only focus on the leader. The leader may be — as Mr. Sadat put it — a "solo performer on state,"[35] but a meaningful evaluation of the theater must also take into account the audience's state of mind. It is there that gifted actors succeed or fail; the audience must appreciate and must applaud if the act is to last. To be sure, there were detractors in Egypt who doubted the wisdom of Sadat's path, and more substantial numbers who would have wanted him to do things in a different way — who were opposed to the style and extremism of Sadat's method rather than to the final goal — but overall, Tolstoy's verdict on kings may explain why Sadat was able to move all the way from the first disengagement agreement in early 1974, to the Sinai Accord in September of 1975, to his journey to Jerusalem, then to the exchange of embassies with Israel in early 1979. Sadat was simply an instrument of Egyptian history. The characters in Majib Mahfuz's sensitive fiction with whom this chapter opened wanted it this way, and it is worth restating that Mahfuz's work was written even before the October War. Some wanted to carry on as before, more were weary or dubious about the will and intentions of other Arabs, determined to find another way, to turn a corner.

Other Arabs may not agree, but there are grounds for arguing that Sadat may have been — albeit a bit too extremely and dramatically — an instrument of Arab history as well. Sadat's diplomacy dragged the Arabs, with most of them screaming and feeling defiled, into an honest encounter with the problem of Israel. He made them ask questions they had tried to avoid, face the reality of a state whose name they had previously refused to utter. The unspeakable, demonic entity was there, and a full-blown nuclear power at that, but the illusion persisted that some day the problem would vanish. As Abdallah Laroui poignantly said, it was known that "on a certain day everything would be obliterated and instantaneously reconstructed and the new inhabitants, would leave, as if by magic, the land they have despoiled; in this way will justice be dispensed to the victims, on that day when the presence of God shall again make itself felt."[36] The failure of magic to do it meant that somehow that other entity had to be accepted and mentally dealt with. The "Egyptian mission," claims Sadat's minister of state for foreign affairs, Boutros Boutros-Ghali, was to get both the Arabs and the Israelis to accept, in Sartre's terms, the existence of the other − "faire admettre l'Autre − l'état juif − par le monde arabe; d'autre part, faire admettre l'Autre − le peuple Palestinian − par les Israéliens."[37] For the Arab world Sadat may have been codifying, making de jure, making public, a reality felt deep in the psyche of the wider Arab audience: that the Arabs somehow had to find a political and existential way out of the fight, that part of them was no longer there, so to speak, that wealth had changed the ways of many of them, that the fight with Israel no longer figured in their universe as prominently, as intensely as it had before. Egypt possessed the maturity to admit these harsh facts. Bruised and battered by the world, it could admit things that more sheltered purists − in the peninsula, in Libya − could run away from. Egypt, says the perceptive Egyptian scholar-diplomat Tahseen Basheer, had lost its virginity long ago: situated at the crossroads of continents, she had been plundered and invaded and had learned the ways of the world.[38] It was her mission now to teach others that the world will not allow total schemes, that purity is other worldly. Impoverished, crowded, close to the fire, Egypt could state and do things that other Arabs were too stubborn, too provincial, and too sheltered to accept.

THE PUSH OF THE DESERT, THE PULL OF THE MEDITERRANEAN

On his way to his first meeting with King Faisal of Saudi Arabia, Secretary of State Kissinger is reported to have asked President Sadat what to expect. "Well, Dr. Henry, he'll probably preach to you about communism and the Jews."[39] The statement says something about Faisal's obsessions, but it tells a lot more about Sadat. In a way it is the cultural pretension (and reality) of a relatively occidentalized country and leadership. Sadat's statement embraces Kissinger as a fellow modern man and puts Faisal at a distance. The first two speak the language of the age; they are both rational men, players in the modern game of nations. Faisal, however, is depicted as a tribal man, a bedouin with bedouin passions and biases.

Two themes have battled one another in recent Egyptian history: the push of the desert — the reality of a poor Muslim country — and the pull of the Mediterranean. The first suggests shared destiny with other Muslim Arabs and provides the raw material with which recent pan-Arab ambitions have worked. The second theme is the product of Egypt's relatively early initiation into the modern world system, dragged as she was into the modern world economy in the mid-nineteenth century. The first was Nasser's universe; the second came to be Anwar el-Sadat's. The first path was the one that Muhammad Ali opted for early in the nineteenth century; the second was the path of his grandson, Ismael (ruled 1863 to 1879) the modernizer, the cosmopolitan man.

The yearning for the West on the part of Sadat's Egypt is a complex psychological and historical phenomenon. It can be located in today's currents and needs, in the personality of the ruler, but it has a history as well. So too does the resistance to it. The issue of a separate peace was bound to become a civilizational and cultural question, but Sadat's style and choices aggravated the crisis. Isolated from his locale, he slipped into greater dependency upon his American partner. This gave new life to cultural pretensions that had once been vanquished; it revived old fears and doubts about the powerful aliens and their ways, about the integrity of the culture and its wholeness. At the heart of the crisis lay the thorny and explosive problem of cultural dualism between an Oriental self and a modern wrapping, between a traditional culture below and more modern layers on top. Whether he meant it or not, President Sadat was to become heir to a particular legacy, lured by its temptations. Likewise with his critics at home: In brandishing what they thought to be new weapons, they discovered that the issues and the weapons were old indeed.

The roots of Egypt's cultural dualism can be found in the actions of its modernizing rulers and in the accident of its geography, situated as the country is in the path of giants. E. W. Lane's *Manners and Customs of the Modern Egyptians* (1835) gave an outsider's portrait of a traditional society and its equilibrium. A quarter century later, Lane's nephew would write in a preface to a new edition that the book could not be rewritten because the Egyptians are "yearly straying from old paths into the new ways of European civilization."[40] People had broken away from the ways of the ancestors and were being drawn into the network of an expanding Europeanbased world economy and culture.

Egypt's rulers were confronted with a challenge and a temptation: the West as model, the West as threat. What under Muhammad Ali began as a legitimate attempt to copy the ways of the West yet keep it at bay turned into total surrender under Ismael. And it is Ismael who has lately been appearing in allegorial Egyptian criticisms of Sadat. Ismael's aspirations went beyond the desire to modernize. His aspiration was, as Nadav Safran writes, "no less than the transformation of Egypt into a part of Europe." To that end, he built "operas, palaces and promenades"; he thought of himself as having a "mission civilisatrice," a drive that led him in his pursuit of an African empire.[41] Ismael forgot where he was, forgot his cultural base, the poor plot of land that had to finance his ambitions:

> His ambition and imagination startled his listeners. In this hot straitened summer of 1864 he was thinking not only of canals and railroads, but of ParisontheNile and of Ismail, Emperor of Africa. Cairo would have its *grands boulevards,* Bourse, theatres, opéra. Egypt would have its large army, a powerful fleet. Why? asked the French consul. He might also have asked, How?[42]

The dream of turning Cairo into Paris ended in Egypt's financial ruin and her occupation by Britain. But Ismael's dream managed to live on. British colonialism had served its own kind of harsh notice as to the difference between pretensions and the real thing, but some held on to the European myth. Exactly half a century after the landing of British troops in Egypt, Taha Husayn, the influential Egyptian author, educator, and minister of education in the last Wafd government (1950–1952) published a manifesto of liberal Egypt's Western identity. The book expressed the yearning of a defeated people to be accepted by a world that had dominated them, the desire to give cultural mimicry the legitimacy of authenticity by erasing the boundary between Egypt and her occupiers and asserting Egypt's oneness with the West.[43] Kipling's sharp division between East and West was no problem, Husayn assured his readers: Egypt's mind was not an Oriental mind; it was closer to Europe than it was to "China, Japan, India and the countries that surrounded them." Egypt was a Mediterranean civilization; its own illusions and backwardness prevented it from living up to its true self. "We must be able," Husayn told Egyptians, to make the European feel that "we see things as he sees them, evaluate them as he does, judge them as he does."

Egypt's Islam posed no problem for Husayn's cultural and mental geography. A secularist who had little regard for religion, a Francophile by culture, Husayn argued that Islam had not really Arabized Egypt. Just as Christianity — another "Oriental" religion — had converted Europe without orientalizing it, so too had Islam with Egypt: Islam gave Egypt its religion, but it left its Occidental core untouched.

Taha Husayn is a transitional figure between Ismael and Sadat. It is a supreme irony of recent Egyptian history that Anwar el-Sadat, who was part of traditional Egypt's revolt against the heritage of Ismael and the pretensions of the polished layers of Egyptian society, would live to be equated with Ismael, to reenact Ismael's wish (and fate?). Sadat's conversion is a riddle: Was his Westernism there all along? Had he acquired it through his second marriage to the urbane Jihan el-Sadat? Was it part of his own psychological settling of the score with Nasser, a search for a theater wherein he could outdo and go beyond Abdul Nasser, whom he came to recall as a traditional man? Was it the despair of a leader anxious for help — any help — to keep a crowded, poor society afloat? Or was he stuck with the United States and the West when he found himself cut off from other Arabs?

There is no doubt that Sadat underwent an immense psychological transformation: The man who in the early 1950s had complained to an American journalist that "the West hates the Arabs because they think that we are negroes"[44] became one of America's most popular figures; the man who once hated the West moved all the way to a full partnership with the United States, offering his society as sentry to a barbarian region in turmoil. Anwar el-Sadat, a self-defined peasant from the dusty small village Mit Abu al-Qom, had exceeded his own expectations and travelled far beyond the bounds of his world; he had become more comfortable with American television reporters and French visitors than with former colleagues and friends.

To see his poor, dusty village — as I did out of curiosity, having read his autobiography and wishing to see the cult object that his village came to be — is to come to terms with the drama and ultimately with the limits and tragedy of Sadat's epic. The personal dimension is undeniably grand: from Mit Abu al-Qom to the Nobel Peace Prize; from a lower-middle-class agrarian base in the Nile delta to the world as his theater. This has seduced and propelled Sadat. He himself speaks of it with genuine astonishment at times. In setting aside for his village the royalties of his autobiography and the stipend of the Nobel award — an estimated million dollars — he marvelled about Allah's will and the hand of fate. With disarming candor, he would recall that a hundred pounds were considered a fortune in his village.[45] He would be what every Egyptian boy playing on the banks of the Nile would dream of being. He would go places for those boys; Everyman would become king.

But there is a public tragedy in all this: the escape from one's world, the theater as substitute for action. The dream of turning his impoverished village into something like the English countryside — he insists that the houses to be built with his contribution should be painted white, for he recalls the quaint charm of the English countryside — is an escape from Egypt's troubles. That the small miracle is to be accomplished by Egypt's biggest tycoon, Uthman Ahmad Uthman, a relative of Sadat and a man whose financial dealings have become a symbol for corruption and inequity, conveys the futility of the act, an incapacity to see and solve problems. Sadat's concept of the self — all a man has to do is find his identity, the autobiography implies — and his idea of the simple village where honest men wait out history, where they accept their lot without *hiqd* (resentment) becomes a smokescreen for failure, a way of looking at troubles and pain without seeing them. That is why Cairo, with its noise and its troubles, its dissatisfied, "negativistic" intellectuals who fuel *hiqd,* has become the target of so many of Sadat's sermons. Cairo is politicized — a Nasserite legacy; goodness is in the village where life goes on as before, where people scratch out a living but do it with dignity.

The myth of the village is connected with Sadat's courtship of the West. One wonders whether the idea of Mit Abu al-Qom was not taken out and dusted off for the sake of the West, so Sadat can present himself as a peasant going beyond his world, reaching out for people and places remote. Mit Abu al-Qom has no mystique for a Saudi or a Kuwaiti or an urban Palestinian or Lebanese. When those people go to Egypt they go for the lights of Cairo, for the civility and climate of Alexandria; the rest of Egypt is unknown to them. The people who go to Mit Abu al-Qom to find Sadat's roots on the banks of the Nile are German, French, and American. Arabs would not be moved or taken in by the myth of the village. They have seen such villages and most of them come from such places — places that hold little interest for them, places that they would rather forget.

The rediscovery of Mit Abu al-Qom is part political archaeology — to find the vision of a good, steady order where politics
were the realm of the ruler, land in the hands of the landholder,
and goodness and simplicity (and toil) the lot of the peasants. It is
also part anthropology, an appeal to the West's romance with the
exotic, its love for distant, dusty villages from which ambitious
young men are propelled to great power and prominence.

The ideal of the village and the American connection keep problems away; they make it possible to escape from pan-Arab troubles,
from economic collapse; they buy time and conceal reality. Both
are manageable theaters: Sadat is a hero in his village — the local
boy made good who gives some of his wealth and prominence to his
village. The American connection provides economic protection;
it also provides a sense of psychological mobility. Egypt is a world
with strict normative, economic, and ecological limits. Sadat's discovery of America at a late stage in his life is an exciting personal
saga. The world's mightiest power — and a civilized one as well —
becomes Egypt's full partner. Libya, Syria, Iraq fade into cosmic
insignificance. Egypt and her president break out in grand style.
"Dr. Henry" was the President's friend; President Carter became
a friend and a brother. The rich, civilized power from afar will see
to it that the Egyptian economy pulls through; The United States
is a power possessing money and civilization — a reassuring contrast to neighbors that have plenty of the former but none of the
latter. Sadat's success in courting America becomes Egypt's success; his appeal to the West lends credence to Taha Husayn's contention that Egypt's mind and culture is a piece of the Occident.
Ismael played the game and lost; he cost Egypt wealth and independence. Sadat plays the same game but will, supposedly, succeed. As for independence, it is a relative thing in today's world
anyway. Besides, if Egypt had to choose between the patronage
and conditions of the United States and those of the oil states, then
surely the former is a better option: It is closer to civilization, less
offensive to dignity and pride. Ismael's loans and collapse brought
the gunboats of the West but we live in a more civilized world now.
The donors have no choice but to continue to give: Egypt's and
Sadat's weakness become sources of power; both must be propped
up if civility and order in the region are to have a chance. The collapse of the Iranian base makes the Egyptian case even more compelling: The oasis of stability must be floated if the area is not to
sink into further barbarism and disorder.

The coveted membership in that glamorous world is partly real,
for the bourgeois age did leave many things behind on Egyptian

soil, and partly an attempt to conceal and legitimate dependency. In that we see the fundamental dilemma of any liberalism removed from the core of the world system. Weak societies at the periphery of the world desperately flaunt the outward trappings of modernity, because the cosmopolitan layers intuitively feel their own isolation. On some level they realize that bourgeois civilization as process eludes them, that they may end up either with its things – in the form of machines or of "operas, palaces and promenades" – or with its outward pretensions and trappings. It is at that point that a line is crossed and the search for membership and identification with the West turns into paralyzing dependency. There is more than a sketchy historical analogy between the fate of Ismael's Egypt and the Egyptian predicament of today. An interesting account (published in 1897) of the fate of the Ismael's Mediterranean dream makes fascinating reading today:

> Egypt under his [Ismael's] sway, has, to use his own boastful phrase, entered the family of European nations – very much as a bankrupt enters Basinghall Street; but the factories, boulevards, and palaces are only so many mighty mistakes of an obstinate speculator; and the mainspring of any sympathy which he has created between the East and the West is one of debtor and creditor. He has interested Europe in Egypt, by making the European the man in possession of his country.[46]

Are there some parallels between the way dependency was faced in Ismael's Egypt and the way it was handled in 1979 when President Sadat asked the Tokyo economic summit of the major industrial countries for a foreign aid package of $18 billion? To quote *Egypt under Ismail Pacha* again:

> Ismail Pacha's submission to European control was a confession of failure, of bankruptcy, and of wrongdoing. Yet, he performed it with the air of a magnanimous prince who was accomplishing a noble deed of patriotism.[47]

In Egypt, wrote Flaubert to Louis Bouilhet in one of his letters from Cairo (December, 1849), "the European is accorded greater respect than the native, so we won't dress up completely [in native costumes] until we reach Syria." In an earlier letter to his mother from Alexandria, he had written: "One curious thing here is the respect, or rather the terror, that everyone displays in the presence of 'Franks', as they call Europeans."[48]

Others had made and continue to make similar observations: There is an awe of Westerners and things Western in Egypt. What Leonard Binder called Nasser's "protest movement" against the West[49] was on some deep level propelled by the need to defy, to say no, to assert some equality with the "Franks." It is easy to say that he overdid it, to note the absurdity of his theatrics, his compulsive search for autonomy and defiance. But nations do things in mysterious ways; they intuit their needs in ways that elude those who are ready with a judgment. The dependency on the United States in Sadat's Egypt, the mystic faith in the "Carter plan," the appeal to the industrialized countries to come to Egypt's aid, show the persistence of that propensity to depend. In their own way they offer a post facto explanation for some of Nasser's grand theatrics, for his almost neurotic obsession with independence. Egypt is yet to find that middle ground between dependence on the outside world and rebellion against it. The awe toward outsiders persists. That is why there is a legitimacy to the following query: Could it be that Sadat, the self-professed disciple of Sa'd Zaghlul — the symbol of Egyptian patriotism — managed to slay the pan-Arab myth of Abdul Nasser only to become a modern-day version of Khedive Ismael? Has the dialogue with the West and the fondness for things Western degenerated into the old dependency?

However considerable its drawbacks, the Ismael/Sadat Mediterranean temptation has all along had its adherents. Earlier I noted Taha Husayn's defense of Egypt's oneness with the West. The more recent debate about pan-Arabism triggered by the Sadat diplomacy revived the same genre of opinion.[50] Tawfiq al-Hakim's call for "neutralizing" Egypt assigned the country a role as the region's cultural center; just as Egypt was the museum of the world, she was the Middle East's cultural oasis. Politics was not Egypt's strong suit; pan-Arabism was the narcotic of the intellectuals, a catastrophe that befell Egypt and her population. The Arabs had come of age now: They had sufficient "manpower and wealth" to wage their own wars, and they need no longer burden Egypt with their problems, set on the country on a path that "paralyzes her thought, bleeds her, starves her sons."[51] Egypt had better return to its own roots, for all the sacrifices notwithstanding, leadership in the Arab world is now contested by those countries that possess wealth even though they did not "shed a drop of blood."[52] Hussein Fawzi, another Mediterranean scholar, echoed the same themes: Like Switzerland, Egypt should renounce politics and aim for neutrality — the sole "industry" of Egypt is culture, its principal mis sion is to serve as a broker for world trends. Egypt has suffered the rule of many outsiders; this "qualifies" it to be the "cultural museum" of the world, the cultural oasis of the region. Fawzi harks back to an earlier period of Egyptian history: the 1930s and 1940s, a period during which Egypt sought to deal "peacefully" with the question of Palestine until a "juvenile monarch" (Faruq) pushed it into a "losing war" and then another leader pushed it into a catastrophic confrontation that ended in the occupation of Egyptian land and the destruction and closure of the Suez Canal.[53]

Both al-Hakim and Fawzi are old men, both are nostalgic for pre-1952 Egypt, and both move between Egypt and Europe. The Arab world is *terra incognita* to them. Beneath the ivory tower of al-Hakim and Fawzi, a generation of youngsters anxiously dip into the culture and artifacts of the West. Hitherto denied access to that glamorous world, they partake of it with vengeance and at the same time travel rapidly away from the poor, pious, traditional society around them.

But the Mediterranean pull has always generated a cross-current. The language of opposition may have differed from time to time, but there is a common denominator: Islam, Arabism, authenticity. The tragedy of Ismael's world view and later, of liberal nationalism, was its incapacity to stay at home with its own world, to keep a safe and respectable distance from the West. This may have something to do with the poor resource base, but there is a proneness to cultural dependency as well. What begins as a dialogue with the West ends in embrace and surrender. Then the legitimacy vanishes, and the adherents are exposed as collaborators. The need to appear modern to a Western audience erodes the base at home; the voice of authenticity reemerges to redeem self and pride. Ismael's surrender gave rise to the revolt of the soldier/peasant Ahmad Urabi in 1882. The failure of liberal nationalism and the incapacity of the generation of Taha Husayn to build an autonomous liberal path brought about the revolt of 1952 – a local breed hostile to Europe and to the vision of Taha Husayn but still distant enough from the fundamentalism of the Muslim Brotherhood, from the chaos engulfing Egypt. Their revolt came, as Safran writes, in the nick of time to spare Egypt the dire consequences of chaos and to stem the tide of fundamentalism.[54] The men who accomplished the revolution were in their own way heirs to the nationalist movement – less pretentious than the cosmopolitan liberals, more of this world than the Brotherhood.

When Taha Husayn wrote his liberal manifesto, another Egyptian, Sayyid Qutb, a brilliant thinker and activist of the Muslim

Brotherhood, gave the answer of authenticity and the native culture to Husayn's pretensions. Taha Husayn's division of the world
into East and West struck Sayyid Qutb as a fraudulent and incom-
plete division. Husayn, he said, had forgotten a whole world that
had its own vision and integrity: the world of Islam. It was to that
world that Egypt belonged, and all else would end in failure.[55]

Sayyid Qutb is no longer around; his activism cost him his life
during the Nasser years. But the view that inspired him remains:
It moves scores of pious young men and women at the nation's universities; it provides an answer to the complicated problems of a
stalemated society. As always, its message is faith and integrity, its
material the failure of the dominant order on the battlefield, in
solving the problems of identity, in economic matters. New problems – peace, economic crises, the corruption of public officials
– are easily accommodated into its flexible container. Its pamphlets and magazines – some underground, some tolerated –
offer a contrast to the banality and hypocrisy of the official media.
Its tracts offer some easy solutions, faith instead of detail, but they
also tell the truth about treaties, diplomacy, the corruption of officials.

The fundamentalist call has resonance because it invites men to
participate – and here again there is a contrast to an official political culture that reduces citizens to spectators and asks them to
leave things to the rulers. At a time when people are confused and
lost and the future is uncertain, it connects them to a tradition
that reduces their bewilderment.

The fundamentalist stand against President Sadat's diplomacy is
part of a larger tapestry. It issued from a deep-rooted tradition.
The Muslim Brotherhood's opposition to Camp David was
phrased in familiar idiom: the struggle of the Prophet, the integrity of Islam, the need for sacrifice, the clash between the world of
Islam and the Jews, who will "never abandon their belief that they
are God's chosen people." Sadat's whole design was a false one: It
accepts a "Middle Eastern order" – the Middle East is a repugnant term to Muslim sensibilities because it defines the Muslim
world in relation to the West – "under Jewish hegemony." One
cannot negotiate with the intruder and surrender historical
rights; some conflicts cannot be wished away. Egypt was invaded
before and it must again resort to resistance. All the rulers have to
do is abandon their "fancy palaces," their expensive cars, and their
pretensions. Islam taught men to struggle and die for worthwhile
causes, and the believers must rediscover the will to perservere,
the capacity for patience.[56]

Muslim fundamentalism may never carry the day in Egypt. Perhaps the society has gone beyond the puritanism of the fundamentalists and reached the point of no return. The Egyptians are sophisticated people (a cliché, to sure, but true nonetheless): They
know that the task at hand is to keep their world from falling
apart, to keep their society functioning. Besides, they know the
history of the Muslim Brotherhood. They saw the frenzy of its
early idealism degenerate, as the 1940s came to a close, into terror
and nihilism. They recall the fate of the Brotherhood's "Supreme
Guide," Hassan al-Banna, living and dying by a code of violence
and toward the very end of his life denouncing his own followers
– most likely to save his own skin – as "neither brothers, nor
Muslims." They recall the brotherhood's collaboration with the
monarchy, its curious mixture of reactionary politics and pious
sermons.[57]

Short of the fire of the Brotherhood, even Qaddafi's relatively
mild austere utopia would not stick on the bourgeois soil of Egypt.
Cairo's professional women have long broken with the norms en-
forced in other Muslim societies. Egypt has the West under its
skin. That is why Sadat – and Mrs. Sadat – could propose and
pass legislation favoring women's rights at a time of seemingly fundamentalist reassertion all over the region.

There is an instinctive Egyptian dread of great crusades, a preference for those people and ideas who somehow steer a path amidst
rival and extreme utopias. The Egyptian social predicament has
been deep enough in this century to encourage millenarians and
radicals of all sorts: fascists, Muslim fundamentalists, wild-eyed
radicals. They had in common what all such movements possess:
their belief in another world, in short, what Crane Brinton would
call the "revolutionary ideal."[58] All received a hearing, but caution
ultimately prevailed: Fascism found an expression in the Young
Egypt party, which was a parody of the fascist movement that
swept Europe in the 1930s and 1940s; the Muslim Brotherhood
thrived at a time of crisis and continues to survive at the present.
The Communists made their appearance on the scene with the establishment of a small group in Alexandria as early as 1921; and
their fortunes were subject to the wild changes that such movements have suffered, but they remained "for most of the time a
small coterie of squabbling and secretive theoreticians."[59] The
dominant instinct was for the center: This is what sustained the
more-or-less liberal experiment of bourgeois nationalism (1919 –
1952) and what inspired the revolution that stepped in to arrest
the drift toward breakdown and extreme solutions. And this is the

instinct that continues to guide the Egyptian ship on its ever-hazardous journey. The dialectic (if you will) between the radical temptation and the world as it is has generally favored the latter. This phenomenon is perceptively illuminated by the Egyptian intellectual Ghali Shukri in a brilliant set of reflections and essays on Egyptian social and political thought entitled *Mudhakkirat Thaqafa Tahtadir* (Memoirs of a Dying Culture). The Egyptian people, he observes, have always been deeply religious; this gave the Brotherhood room for maneuver and material with which to tap passions and to mobilize, but the Brotherhood failed because its reactionary extreme call "did not answer the need of a people yearning for progress." Likewise, Egyptian patriotism fed the Young Egypt party's fascist tendencies, but this extreme line also failed to mobilize a people who have synthesized "in their blood" many civilizations and religions. Egypt remained most hospitable to those who offered "peaceful, moderate ways."[60] This is not the kind of tale that would grip those who see societies driven by the purity of saints and the fire of revolutionaries, but this has been Egypt's tale.

Thus the importance of Muslim fundamentalism is not measured best in terms of its capacity to capture political power. Its power may lie in its ability to destabilize a regime, to help bring it down by denying it the religious cover that remains an important source of political power. Here the 1952 revolution is instructive. The Muslim Brotherhood helped topple the monarchy, but it became the victim and target of the new regime. Fundamentalism may supply fervor, some of the committed manpower, and the willingness to take the risks of political action. Other types — more capable of making compromises, less likely to frighten modernized young men and women — would inherit the postrevolutionary world.

This is where Muslim fundamentalism intersects with the surviving remnants of Nasserism and Arabism in Egypt. While in power, Abdul Nasser was brutal in his persecution of the active, militant Brotherhood. But Nasser's heirs and the Brotherhood share one thing in common: They are part of the indigenous path. Faced with one another, they discover all the things that separate them; faced with the adherents of the Mediterranean path, they can see what they have in common. The fundamentalists see in the Mediterranean path a betrayal of Islam and the Nasserites object on more secular, nationalist grounds, but both believe that the Mediterranean temptation is a mirage. For all his faults, Abdul Nasser remained at home in Egypt. To be sure, his ambitions exceeded his country's means; he made more than his share of errors, but he was never a mimic. He lived and entertained simply; he kept his wife away from the spotlight. These images have power in a Muslim society. Gaps in power between ruler and ruled are expected and tolerated; gaps in culture have a way of compromising the ruler or suggesting that he left his world behind in search of the lights and the glamor of the West. Ayatollah Khomeini's indictment of the shah was caused not so much by the shah's excessive power; it was his alienness, his distance from popular culture and religion. Heikal's Nasser — a simple man with a taste for simple, modest things — taps the same sentiments: The implication is that Abdul Nasser never strayed from Egypt and that Sadat did.

The Egyptian Nasserites' view — like that of Sadat — proceeds from the centrality and weight of Cairo. But they have a different Cairo in mind. As Heikal puts it in his book-length discourse on the Sadat initiative, the Cairo that decides on matters of war and peace is the one that embodies the "pan-Arab idea, current, historical movement."[61] Cairo, the Capital of the Egyptian state, is a diminished entity. This is why Heikal faults Sadat's policy: It diminished Egypt and turned the country into a poor, vulnerable state on the banks of the Nile; amputated, cut off from the Arab world, it stood vulnerable and exposed. The old European dream of isolating Egypt from the rest of the Arab world was accomplished. This left the Arab world confused and without its balance but it left Egypt prey to the schemes and offers of others.

How did this come to pass? In the Nasserite view expressed by Heikal, the Egyptian leadership (presumably Nasser and Heikal themselves) should have explained to the population that Egypt was a party to the Arab – Israeli conflict, that Egypt was not fighting others' wars, and that there were serious geopolitical issues involved. Second, Nasser and Nasserism had taken Egypt's Arabism for granted. That, says Heikal in retrospect, was an error. Where a separate national identity existed, as it did in Egypt, there should have been a more vigorous mass-based Arabization of Egypt. Third, the lack of a fair inter-Arab division of labor created resentment and disillusionment in the confrontation states. Other reasons had to do with the harsh treatment by other Arabs after 1967 and with the continual hammering by other Arabs at the worth of the Egyptian experiment. This helped foster despair in Egypt, and the Sadat diplomacy was the product of such despair. If nothing made sense, if Egypt's revolution had been inauthentic (as the Arab left asserted), if its socialism was a failed state capitalism, then why not seek the safety of peace — any peace, on any terms?

But this too shall pass, the Nasserites maintain. The Mediterranean temptation will blow over, and Egypt will be reclaimed by its authentic habitat. Nasser's three circles — the Arab, the Islamic, the African — will prevail once again. Their hope evokes an image of Egypt larger than the riverbed it inhabits, and in the aftermath of the Shah's collapse their view rests on faith in the ability of the culture and geography to assert themselves. Tawfiq al-Hakim and Hussein Fawzi's apolitical utopia — the Switzerland example, the neutralization of Egypt — drew fire from a wide range of thinkers. The critics' answers were long, reasoned, and passionate: All rejected the Mediterranean option, all said that it was not worthy of a self-respecting nation. Bint al-Shati (the penname of a distinguished woman writer) recalled Lebanon's dream and fate: The Lebanese too wanted to be safe hotelkeepers, a neutral Mediterranean nation. Lebanon's collapse was proof that nations that play with their identities and deviate from their habitats play with fire.[62] Others warned that Egypt could not go it alone and lamented the incapacity of the Egyptian pendulum to stop in the middle — cycles of pan-Arabism alternate with isolationist periods; love affairs with the West are followed by calls to revolt and authenticity. Some threw into the debate harsh geopolitical realities. To them the push into the Arab system was not the whim of a charismatic leader but something decreed by the constants of geography: "The destiny of Egypt," observed one of the participants, "has always been linked to that of Palestine in particular and Syria in general. The defense of Egypt and the Canal begins in Palestine . . . It is clear that whoever occupied one of the two countries [Syria and Egypt] instinctively proceeded in the direction of the other as the Crusaders did in one direction and Napoleon from the other. The most recent examples were the British who proceeded from Egypt in the direction of Palestine and Jordan, matched in the other direction by the contemporary Israeli example."[63] Arabism, said the journalist Ahmad Baha'a al-Din, was not a garb to be donned in 1956 and taken off in 1967, donned in 1973 and taken off in 1977; the battles waged by Egypt were not waged for the sake of others. At stake were Egyptian interests and Egyptian security.[64]

Beyond the debates of scribes, a similar set of concerns were put to President Sadat in an important message submitted by some of the five surviving members of the Revolutionary Command Council — the original leading free officers who accomplished the 1952 coup d'etat. The message signed by Hussein al-Shafalai, Zakaria Muheiddein, Abdul Latif al-Baghdadi, and Kamal al-Din Hussein had none of the arguments familiar to the hazier advocates of pan-Arabism. The case it made against President Sadat's diplomacy and his separate peace questioned whether an Egypt cut off from the Arab system would be able to survive; it expressed the historic fear of isolation: "We cannot imagine a bright future for Egypt in isolation from the Arab nations. The isolation of Egypt from the Arab nation had been the dream of European colonialism . . . The security enjoyed by Egypt in the shadow of this agreement [the Camp David Accords] is akin to the security felt by a lamb in the midst of a pack of wolves."[65]

EGYPT AS MIRROR, AS STATE

I want to return to where I began: Egypt's meaning to other Arabs and Egypt's struggle with herself. Egypt is the place where Arab history comes into focus. The way other Arabs have recently turned away from Egypt indicates the depth of the Arab predicament in the modern world. Arabs look at Egypt and they do not like what they see — it is not revolutionary enough, or religious and austere enough, or militant enough. There is in what they say a judgment on things Egyptian, but there is a wider judgment about the state of Arab civilization as well.

The Arab world has become fragmented, and the Arabs have desperately tried to ignore their fragmentation. It was Egypt that provided the harsh confirmation of Arab disintegration that so many had tried to avoid. Egypt's leader was more daring in his break with pan-Arabism than anyone else, and he did it without due regard to formalities and appearances. Egypt's intellectuals were the ones who were most willing to voice their doubts about Arabism. Others surely entertained such doubts, but they kept them to themselves. Egypt was the biggest piece, and its break — made in full daylight and symbolized by Sadat's short flight to Jerusalem — challenged the dogma of unity. There was bloodshed in Lebanon, poverty and treason in Egypt, wealth in the oil states, and Algeria was far away. The Arabs wanted to persist in their unionist myths. The intellectuals wanted to engage in the same polemics; the leaders — at least some of them — had spoken the language of Arabism long enough that it was difficult for them to

speak a new idiom. Egypt forced on all of them an encounter with
their own fragmentation.

Mr. Sadat's diplomacy was the most dramatic and objectively
the most important illustration of the weakness of pan-Arabism, if
only because Egypt had been, as Heikal rightly states, "the main-
stay of the Arab system."[66] Throughout the preceding decade,
however, there had been other "revolts," other "separatist" attacks
against the monolithic pan-Arab doctrine. Those must be recalled
for it is only then that the Sadat diplomacy can be correctly placed
in Arab politics.

The Palestinians launched the first post-1967 attack against pan-
Arabism; given their predicament, their economic and political dependence upon the Arab states, their lack of a territorial base,
theirs had to be a different kind of attack. But there was no doubt
that those who rallied around Yasser Arafat and George Habash in
the aftermath of the Six Day War had given up on pan-Arabism,
the first group in the name of Palestinian nationalism, the second in
the name of social revolution. The duel that raged between the
Palestinians and the Nasserites from early 1968 until Nasser's
death in 1970 was in essence a fight about the independent rights of
Palestinian nationalism: If the Arab states could not protect themselves against Israel, let alone do something for the Palestinians,
then the latter were to construct their own independent politics.
And in the final analysis it was Arafat's brand of nationalism, with
its pledge of nonintervention in the internal affairs of Arab countries, that found its way into the organized Arab state system,
rather than George Habash's revolution. Arafat's narrow focus on
Palestinian nationalism and his avoidance of social and ideological
issues were in keeping with the new tenor of Arab politics. That is
why Arafat's course found a reasonable measure of support in
Riyadh. In Arafat's strict Palestinian nationalism there was an ac-
ceptance of reason of state. This is not applicable to the two sanc-
tuaries of Jordan and Lebanon, which explains the two civil wars
in which the Palestinians came to be involved.

The embrace on the part of the Palestinians, made public in
1974, of the idea of a national authority over any inch of liberated
land confirmed the shift that had taken place in Palestinian and
wider Arab thinking since 1967 — the state as a reality had
triumphed; the wider metaphysical adherence to pan-Arabism was
set aside. An intellectual episode that took place in the aftermath
of the Six Day War illustrates the shift. When the Egyptian writer
Ahmad Baha'a al-Din floated a suggestion for a Palestinian state in

late 1967, his call touched off a fierce intellectual debate. Palestine, said one of his many critics, was not a *watan* (homeland), but a piece of homeland. The suggestion of a Palestinian state, argued another, the Palestinian scholar Walid Khalidi, was premature. Priority should be given to "eradicating the consequences of the June 5 aggression." It was the pan-Arab case that had primacy.[67] A decade later, Khalidi was making a plea for a sovereign Palestinian state on the West Bank Gaza.[68] The Jordanian civil war of September 1970, the Lebanese drama of 1975–1977, and the grim Palestinian encounter with Syrian armor in 1976 that had taken its place in Palestinian folklore and memory had driven home to Palestinians why men need states in the modern world and that their place in the Arab world had repeatedly exposed them to the power of others.

Another crack in the pan-Arab edifice was the virtual end of the Ba'th party. A shell called the Ba'th remains, and it claims power in both Syria and Iraq, but President Asad is probably the first leader in modern Syrian history to make peace with Syria's national situation and to accept the limitations of geography and resources. Since the end of World War I a national concensus of sorts developed in Syria that Syria's mission transcends her boundaries and that within those boundaries she is an amputated state. The French severed one part of Greater Syria in 1920 and appended it to Lebanon. Then came the establishment of Transjordan, and in 1939–1940 Syria lost Alexandretta to Turkey. The establishment of Israel in 1948 was in territory that Syria existentially thought of as southern Syria, and finally in 1967 there was the loss of the Golan.

In the post–World War II years, Syria was home to the Ba'th, the pan-Arab party that took seriously its mission of bringing about the one Arab nation. The Ba'thists had stout lungs and plenty of rhetoric – for them Syria was a base, but the dream was bigger than Syria. Hafez Asad was cut of a different cloth; a cautious member of a minority sect, he harbored no illusions about Arab unity. He put his predecessors' entire tradition behind him, accepted a reconciliation with King Husein, and abandoned the infantile Ba'thist notion of bringing Egypt into the pan-Arab fold and making her do the pan-Arabists' bidding.

In an otherwise across-the-board break with the universalism of pan-Arabism, it was only the young group of officers who came to power in Libya in September, 1969, who would raise the old banner in the decade that followed the 1967 defeat. Libya, which had been insulated from the Arab world, was to go through then the same stage that the Nasserites and Ba'thists had gone through in the preceding decade. Qaddafi and his fellow officers were to repeat the slogans that others had tired of; they too were to see the Arab world as one and earnestly to push the cause of unity. The principal difference between them and earlier unionists was that they combined, perhaps for the first time, two forces that had generally been at odds in recent Arab history: oil and pan-Arabism. Coming from Egypt and Syria, the unionist movement had been a claim by poor states for the collective wealth of the Arab world. In the Libyan there was the exception: an affluent society wanting to unite with its poorer neighbors.

Determined to realize the old dream, Qaddafi sought unity with such an odd ally as Bourguiba's Tunisia, but it was Egypt that was the focus of his aspirations. And for four years, he urged unity upon both Nasser and Sadat, although one suspects that the offers were made in a different spirit: He offered Libya to Nasser, whereas he wanted to steal Egypt from Sadat.

In both the Tunisian and Egyptian cases, Qaddafi was urging unity upon two older men for whom he had little if any regard — much older men than himself whom he thought he could eventually push aside. Qaddafi's attitude toward Bourguiba can be guessed at: Qaddafi is a Muslim Arab soldier through and through. Bourguiba can only seem like a compromised francophile, a symbol of a bygone age in which Arabs accepted the supremacy of the West and aped its ways. As for the pre-October 1973 Sadat, Qaddafi could hardly be blamed for the low opinion he held of him. That was a more-or-less universal judgement. During that transitional and difficult period, Sadat lacked legitimacy, and many of Nasser's followers within and outside Egypt came to think of Qaddafi as the spiritual son and true heir of Nasser. As it turned out, the source of Qaddafi's appeal lay more in Sadat's seeming ineptitude than in anything that Qaddafi himself had done. And so, when Sadat finally made good on his promise to break the military stalemate, the Qaddafi appeal came to an end. The October War might not have been the glorious achievement that Sadat made it out to be, but it was nonetheless an achievement. Egypt was once again a country with a leader, and thus Qaddafi's bid for unity could be pushed aside. Reenacting the past had had its day, and it was now time for the new realities to unfold.

Since their seizure of power in 1969, Qaddafi and his fellow officers have gradually come to see the differences among Arabs that had previously eluded them. The contrived boundaries had a reality after all; they ought to know that, for their own rather strict immigration policies contradict their talk of pan-Arabism. In the Arab world as elsewhere, the state is the dominant politicoeconomic reality: It protects the wealth of a people from outside claims; it separates them from others who are claimed, protected, and ruled over by other states.

Neither the fire and passion of the Libyan revolution nor its money could turn history around and revive an exhausted idea. Here and there, a few writers and publicists — not to mention some troublemakers — prospered on Libyan money, repeating Qaddafi's slogans about his Third Theory or carrying out Qaddafi's wishes in Beirut and Cairo. But this was not to be Qaddafi's era. He was an anachronism: what he said and thought in the 1970s other Arabs had experienced and lived through in the 1950s and 1960s. More neutral judges may not think that he is "al walad al majnun" (the crazy boy), as Sadat says he is, but this much can be said: Qaddafi's arena is now Libya; his pan-Arab dreams have aborted. Qaddafi's conviction that the Arabs are one nation is no longer shared by a critical segment of Arabs — the students and the youth — who once gave pan-Arabism power in Arab life.

A social scientist at Kuwait University has supplied us with important evidence that substantiates the demise of pan-Arabism and suggests the shape of things to come. He administered a questionnaire to nearly five hundred undergraduates at Kuwait University with the aim of ascertaining their views on pan-Arabism, family, state, and religion. His sample included students from practically all Arab countries. What he found was a remarkable assertion of Islamic sentiment and an assertion of patriotism associated with particular Arab states. In other words, the vacuum left behind after the demise of pan-Arabism is being filled by religious belief on one level and loyalty to the state on another. As for pan-Arabism, the data led the researcher to conclude that discussion of "one Arab nation" and "Arab brotherhood" are myth and exhausted slogans."[69] There is no longer a collective Arab crisis, and there is no use pretending that it exists. The unevenness in the distribution of wealth — a gap of forty to one in per capita income separates the wealthiest Arab states from the poorest — makes a mockery of the idea of human brotherhood. The horizons open to some men and states in the Arab world exceed the imagination of others. Shall we then insist on still seeing the unity of a people because there are roots in common texts and claims to brotherhood? We know the themes and memories that lent unity to the Arabs' consciousness and history: one language, the classical golden age of

Islam, the universalism of the Ottoman Empire, the yearning for independence, the trauma of being initiated into an international system in which they were not full participants but mere stakes, the Palestine defeat, the Six Day War, and finally, October 1973. The memories and the bonds remain, but the unevenness in the distribution of wealth and the realities of the state system — the harsh logic of raison d'etat — have done their deed.

The boundaries of Arab states have been around now for nearly six decades. It is not their existence that is novel but the power of the state (inasmuch as that power exists in today's state system) to keep pan-Arab claims at bay and to claim the loyalty of those within. The boundaries are no longer as "illusory and permeable"[70] as they were once thought to be. The states that lie within them are less shy about asserting their rights, more normal in the claims they make. The Arabs who once seemed whole, both to themselves and to others, suddenly look as diverse as they were all along. Egypt's defection was neither the will of an isolated man nor the weakness of a particularly craven country anxious to welcome the West and bid farewell to a sacred myth. The pan-Arab idea that dominated the political consciousness of modern Arabs has become a hollow claim. In an earlier decade, loyalty to a particular state in the Arab world was, as historian Bernard Lewis reminds us, "tacit [and] even surreptitious," and Arab unity was "the sole publicly acceptable objective of statesmen and ideologues alike."[71] Now political thought is more daring in its defiance of the myth, more willing to acknowledge that the Arab states have gone their separate ways.

How a political doctrine seizes people's imagination is a mysterious thing; in our age we do not quarrel with the phenomenon, for we have seen it over and over again. We may wish it to be otherwise, we may want people to be more discriminating, but we accept it as a fact of life that ideas — logical or not, justified or not — grip people and are in turn gripped by them in their struggles. Greatly as we may quarrel with the rationality or objectivity of political ideas, they defy logic and create their own realities. Then they play themselves out: They either create a world in their image to be later shackled by routine problems not anticipated by those who spun the myth, or they live past their time and cease to be sufficiently gripping and moving. Or they vanish and leave behind them a trail of errors, suffering, and devastation.

Prior to the emergence of Nasser as a pan-Arab savior, the doctrine of pan-Arabism had been the realm of publicists, intellec-

tuals, and a few officers — in other words, it had been an elite endeavor. Nasser took the theories and the emotions to the masses,
and in so doing, he gave pan-Arabism its moment in the sun and
then its tragic end in 1967. It does not matter in retrospect how he
stumbled onto the idea: The once-shy officer, uneasy around
crowds, might have been a peculiar candidate for leadership of the
movement; Cairo might have been a peculiar capital, for there
were many in Damascus and Baghdad who felt that Cairo was a
latecomer to pan-Arab politics, an illegitimate center. But that
was the turn that history took, and the idea held Nasser as much as
he tried to hold and direct it; it made him plunge into the explosive, unpredictable terrain of Syrian politics for an unsuccessful
union with Syria; it took him to Yemen for a small-scale Vietnam of
his own, into a society about which he knew next to nothing and
into a war which his impoverished society could not afford. Finally, it dragged him into the tragic event of his life and career in
1967. Along the way, the pan-Arab quest turned him into a hero
in Libya and Lebanon, Saudi Arabia and Syria, and pitted him into
a sustained struggle with monarchies and fellow radicals as well as
with Western powers committed to upholding the territorial division of the Arab world against the pan-Arabists' designs.

The circumstances that produced the ebb of Nasserist charisma
and pan-Arabism may be *sui generis*: With defeat in 1967, charisma turned to ashes and the conservative oil states made their financial help contingent upon a new style and kind of politics. But
there is a broader phenomenon here, and the end of Nasserism is a
piece of a bigger puzzle; it is the end of that stage of Third World
history represented by men like Nasser, Nehru, Sukarno, Nkrumah. These men were dreamers who sought what one of them,
Nkrumah, described as the "kingdom of politics." They sought in
politics answers to questions of identity and self-worth and dab-
bled in dreams and intangibles. But their kind of politics was bound
to come to an end, for the nationalist fervor that they embodied
can triumph for a moment but cannot last forever.

The exhaustion of the nationalist fervor generally signals the
coming to the fore of economic issues and demands, of problems
that do not lend themselves to solo performances, to the magic
touch of charisma, to the spectacular and psychologically gratifying performance of a Nasser, a Nkrumah, to the theatrics of a
Sukarno, to the flair of a Nehru. Less colorful leaders whose links
to the nationalist struggle are often tenuous are the ones who have
to satisfy the new needs. The romantic phase of nationalism is then

over – words and symbols lose some of their power as societies begin the infinitely more difficult search for ways of putting a domestic order together.

Egypt's diplomacy served a harsh notice on the panArab myth, but others had broken with it in their own way; the world had changed and nationalist ideas as such had become somewhat banal and insufficient. The storm over Sadat's policy was a fight to keep the myth alive.

If the Sadat diplomacy was a revolt, an exit by a poor society, the wealthy Arab states had exited in their own way. Great wealth had practically Northernized some Arab states – in material standards but not in culture, to be sure. Distrustful (as they should be) of the poor, embittered world around them, their wealth had knit them into the Westernbased international economic system. The new age expected by those who pinned inflated hopes on Arab wealth was not to come: Wealth only heightened the need by the wealthy states to separate themselves, to limit the expectations and demands of others. Neither the world view nor the mechanisms existed that could create that public project that had tantalized the imaginations of those among the Arabs who saw the need for economic integration, who could argue on perfectly defensible economic grounds that separate Arab states were too small to stand on their own, or to provide for economies of scale. About the same time that Egypt was breaking with the monolithic Arab camp (the gladiators of the Arab world abandoning their role), Arab wealth was asserting its own independence, finding its own way into the world. Consider the following investment statistics of oil wealth.

> The OPEC countries have behaved like other prudent investors in disposing of their financial surpluses; that is, they have invested almost exclusively in low risk, high yield assets such as government securities in the hard currency countries, in stocks and bonds offered by Western corporations, and in deposits with the 15 or so largest multinational banks. Thus, according to the U.S. Treasury estimates, of a total of approximately $133 billion in financial assets accumulated by OPEC in the period 1974–76, that can be accounted for, an estimated $48 billion was invested in government paper, portfolio and long term direct investments in the industrial countries; another $9.75 billion was loaned to international organizations; and by far the largest amount, $49 billion, or 37 percent of the total, was

deposited with private commercial banks, mostly in New York and London. Only $16 billion, or 12 percent of the total OPEC surpluses, went directly to the developing countries, mostly in the form of grants to Moslem countries.[72]

The average citizen in Cairo, Damascus, or elsewhere in the Arab world may not have been well informed about the investment details, but he or she knew about the ways of the wealthy, knew that they had become a separate breed. Egypt's poverty at the height of Arab wealth epitomized the limits and, for many, the selfishness of Arab wealth. In Egypt's turn to the West, other Arabs could see how evanescent was the idea that the Arab world had become an autonomous center of power. Other Arab capitals — Baghdad and Damascus — were more discreet in their dealings with the West, more inaccessible and remote. The oil states could deal with the West from a position of power and affluence — or so they could think. Egypt lacked the cultural distance, the militant pride of Baghdad and Damascus; it lacked the money of the West. Egypt was all too willing to embrace and surrender. But here too there was an undercurrent of opinion in the Arab world that sensed that Egypt's and Sadat's surrenders were not unique and isolated acts, that other Arab states had thrown in their lot with the West as well, that that impenetrable core of self and authenticity had long been violated, that Sadat's only sin was really a matter of style. Other Arab leaders and states were careful or rich or nervous enough to conceal their independence upon the West — Sadat was too flamboyant, too poor, and politically secure enough to do things in a different way. But surely, many Arabs reasoned, those living in glass houses should not go about hurling rocks at others. The profound truth of Egypt's defection was not to be found in the utterances and self-righteous denunciations of Arab summits but in a column written by a Saudi journalist on the occasion of the exchange of embassies between Egypt and Israel. The column took the form of an ode to an Egypt. The column's writer, Fatna Shaker, writes with a straightforward and refreshing honesty, a seeming desire to get to the core of things. "I look for you, oh Egypt," she wrote, "for your depths, trying to find a mere echo of your wishes, something that tells me what you really feel about what goes on in your land . . . I looked for you during the "wedding celebrations" and wondered how you were . . . I yearn for your water and land but your features have changed on me; they are no longer the ones I knew as a child and a youth . . . The raising of the Israeli flag on your land has inflicted a deep wound . . . But you do not bear the sole responsibility . . . All of us, the other Arabs, cannot feign innocence."[73]

In their disillusionment with Egypt, the Arabs expressed their disillusionment with the present. The notion that the "long winter of the Arabs"[74] had come to a close was illusion. Egypt provided the serious and somber reminder that all was not well, that things were falling apart. This is something for other Arabs to settle: Egypt cannot be the laboratory for others' experiments; it cannot be bigger than itself, for in many ways – Heikal notwithstanding – Egypt remains a hemmed-in riverbed on the banks of the Nile.

This cuts both ways, for knowledge of its limitations brings Egypt into a more honest encounter with its problems and responsibilities. Egypt's revolt against Arabism – its search for itself, the vision of a great imagined past – is in part frustration and scapegoating. It is an escape from what a society has to do, from the serious task of putting together a shattered world, reviving a desperate economy, injecting a sluggish bureaucracy with mission, purpose and skills. The great imagined past is a mirage; it can supply inspiration in moments of doubt, but it can become a narcotic, a way of avoiding coming to terms with the society's troubles, of ignoring its stalemate. The July 23 revolution of 1952 is a faded memory. The story of how the young officers overthrew the monarchy has been told over and over again, embellished, and distorted. Once upon a time it was an exciting tale, but it has become routine. It survives as a tired, overworked piece of symbolism, it has become an incantation that no longer grips and moves.

Sadat's symbols – the community of love, the country as family, himself as the "eldest of the Egyptian family" – serve the same narcotic purpose: escape, a fake harmony of interests, a curious avoidance of politics. The myth of the family serves to freeze the society. That is why Sadat formed and then dissolved political parties: Opposition was tolerated so long as it did not really oppose. Sadat's language – "my army," "my party," "my sons," "my opposition" (to refer to an opposition party that he himself set up) – reveals Egypt's predicament and stalemate. Sadat does not seem able to move the society – the best he can do is to stay on top, more like royalty than an active executive. He is beyond politics, beyond criticisms.

In the midst of disorder and breakdown, he maintains coolness and serenity and peddles dreams of prosperity and visions of a static order: *Misr* (Egypt) as the oasis, *al zaim* (the leader) as the focus. Sycophants who flatter, who play by the rules and conceal

reality, enjoy access and power. Those who oppose do so by with-
holding their cooperation, but they deny the country their energy.
The machinery of the state is powerful enough to stifle opposition,
but it is too weak to do anything about Egypt's lethargic bureaucracy, to solve the country's crises, to check population growth or
the urban nightmare. The stalemated society (Crozier's and Hoffmann's writings on France apply even more poignantly here)[75] is
given a high moral status. Nasser tried to move forward and in so
doing upset the balance of the country; Sadat will keep that balance intact: no prisons, no great crusades, no ambitious pushy bureaucrats, but no work, either. There is a tacit agreement to ignore troubles and to transcend politics. Troublemakers are
expelled from parliament, denied access to the media, disowned by
the Egyptian family.[69] Once lively organs have become safe and
banal. The leftist monthly Al-Talia now deals with matters of science and outer space – fitting subjects for a civilized country.
Ruz al Yussef, which has a long history of hard-hitting journalism,
is pacified. One of its issues carried an astrologer's predictions for
1979: There will be peace and prosperity in the area; the shah of
Iran will survive in power; more Arab countries will follow
Egypt's leadership; massive oil discoveries will turn Egypt into a
wealthy country; more civilized countries will come to Egypt's aid
and give her love and recognition. This was a serious item –
wishes substituting for analysis, dreams for work.

Meanwhile, some of the more gifted and sensitive of the country's youth have been responding in their way to the politicoeconomic decline by means of emigration, what Albert Hirschmann
would call the phenomenon of exit.[77] In one survey of university
students, nearly 85 percent expressed a desire to leave Egypt upon
graduation.[78] In Egypt as elsewhere, emigration obtains a measure
of stability by removing from the system potential dissidents, but it
also removes those who would have been likely to contribute to the
public interest.

Traditionally Egypt was a society whose inhabitants were reluc-
tant to venture to other lands. It possessed the stability of an
agrarian order where people stayed, at home, in their minds and
values as well as their bodies. Writing in 1835, E. W. Lane described the reluctance of Egyptians to leave their native land:

> Love of their country and more especially of home is a
> characteristic of the modern Egyptians. In general they
> have a great dread of quitting their native land. I have
> heard of several determining to visit a foreign country for

the sake of considerable advantages in prospect; but when the time of their intended departure drew near, their resolution failed them.[79]

More than a century after Lane had made that observation, Jean and Simone Lacouture confirmed it.[80] But now the "dread" of quitting the native land has turned into a near exodus. The private gains are easy to document, the private incentives easy to understand. But surely there is a public price. The stability that rulers covet has an advantage, but societies can stagnate and die even if regimes manage to hang on to political power. The Egyptian revolution, observed Lewis Awad in an important assessment of Nasserism, has "aged": It needs a new social contract with the society, a new vision.[81] It will not do to remind younger men and women of the evils from which the revolution saved them, of the record of the ancien régime.

Nor will it do to escape into the realm of foreign policy. Geopolitics can be a ruler's escape, all the more so when the ruler has a poor society to run, when his horizons and ambitions exceed his society's limits. Something about Egypt has always driven its rulers to entertain ambitions that end up breaking the back of their society. This was true of Muhammad Ali, who laid the foundations of a modern society and then set out to establish an imperial order only to be broken by the European powers. It was particularly true of Ismael, who wanted to create in Africa the empire that had eluded Muhammad Ali in Asia — all that at a time when he was losing control of his own realm. It was also true of Faruq, who entertained hegemonic ambitions of his own and whose rivalry with the Hashemites goes a long way toward explaining much of what he did in inter-Arab matters. Then there was Abdul Nasser and his drama. The deep structure of his pan-Arabism might have been a desire to escape from the limits of his country: as Awad puts it, to escape from coming face to face with the "wretched millions." Thus pan-Arabism and Arab socialism were a

> way of avoiding the barefoot peasants and the desperate laborers and the millions who belong to neither countryside nor city, just exactly as the Egyptian teacher escapes from teaching the children of the peasantry and the working class because it is not as lucrative as teaching the children of the Kuwaitis, Saudis, Libyans, Algerians, etc. . . .[82]

Sadat has followed the same tradition, and at the root of his policy can be discerned the same desire for escape, that same national

situation (perhaps it is the combination of internal stability and external vulnerability) that drives the man at the helm of the Egyptian polity to forget where he is, to entertain dreams that his society cannot sustain. In 1978 Sadat boasted and complained (in
that unique Sadat style) that a power vacuum in the region was
forcing him to "act like a superpower."[83] By that time, and steadily
thereafter, the head of the Egyptian state became committed to
keeping order as far away as Zaire and Afghanistan: In the aftermath of the shah's collapse, the role that Sadat had coveted as a
regional power was his. Of the two previous pillars of American
influence, Iran and Saudi Arabia, one had faltered and one had
dropped out, and Sadat could argue that his country offered a
more reliable base, that he could stem the chaos and the disorder of
a region that seemed to be falling apart all around him. His was a
society more obedient to its "leader" than was Iran, more populous
and daring, more open to the outside world than was Saudi
Arabia.

Once again the dialogue with the outside world had turned to
an embrace, and Egypt had swung from leading the protest movement against the West to being its sentry. The same Egyptian talent, the same eloquence and resourceful media that once condemned foreign pacts and security doctrines, was now hounding
those who failed to stand up to Soviet adventurism, who were too
squeamish to identify themselves with American power and American interests. The zeal with which Cairo once condemned the Ei-
senhower doctrine and the "pactomania" of John Foster Dulles
now went into promoting the Carter doctrine and the legitimacy
of an American military presence. Cairo and Baghdad had, as it
were, reversed roles: In the 1950s it was the former that urged
nonalignment and the latter that wanted to do the West's bidding,
to use the power of allies from afar to crush local rivals. Now it
was Cairo that wanted the presence, the patronage, and the power
of distant allies. America's security predicament gave the Egyptian
leader the latitude and maneuverability he wanted. The United
States was willing to abandon its previous reserve, to offer Sadat
the role and the help he wanted.

> In late 1979, with the attack on Mecca, the seizure of the
> U.S. embassy in Tehran, the Soviet invasion of Afghanis-
> tan, the Administration's attitude towards the Middle
> East took on a distinctly more militant and military tone.
> American policy towards Egypt lost most of the little re-
> serve it had had earlier in the year. Those Americans

searching out for friends in the troubled Middle East — as Americans are wont to search out "friends" — naturally and sometimes enthusiastically set their eyes upon Sadat's Egypt. Playing to the American public in his opposition to the Soviets, the Iranian revolutionaries, and the Saudi fundamentalists, Sadat put his regime on the side of the angels with his invitations to play host to the Shah.[84]

For Egypt the threat is at home. The tendency of the Egyptian state to go beyond its society and leave it behind is a trap and a mirage: states can never outgrow the world that anchors them and gives them the power and the material with which to meet other states and other people. Sooner or later the base below makes its demands, imposes its limits, serves its own warrant on the dreams of rulers and the illusions of bureaucracies.

Mediterranean European Egypt is no help either. Lawrence Durrell's Alexandria is gone; even he could not find it on a recent nostalgic trip. What are there are large, decaying cities and poor villages — not just Mit Abu al-Qom that could be redeemed with an individual contribution, but all of them. Without the human energy to accomplish tasks, civilization becomes a fraudulent wrapping, a pathetic act of mimicry. Cut off from its roots, alienated from its locale, civilization turns into a nauseating pretension. Then it awaits its death, as less sophisticated, less polished people — claiming authenticity, more connected to the earth — push it into its grave.

3

Fractured Tradition
The Claims of Authenticity, the Realities of Dependence

∽∽∽∽∽∽∽∽∽∽∽∽∽∽∽∽∽∽∽∽∽∽∽∽∽∽∽∽∽∽∽∽

Out of the past we make a future.

Thomas Hobbes, *Behemoth,* VI

∽

The destructive distortions of the tradition were all caused by men who had experienced something new which they tried almost instantaneously to overcome and resolve into something old.

Hannah Arendt, *Between Past and Future*
(New York: Viking, 1961), p. 29.

∽

Is this a dream?
Is there a voyage called return?

Adonis, *The Blood of Adonis*
(Pittsburgh: University of
Pittsburgh Press, 1971), p. 32.

∽

THE ARAB PREDICAMENT

HISTORY SERVES MANY A HARSH NOTICE on civilizations and social orders. There is a temptation to reenact the past, to go back to things one knows and feels comfortable with. But the past is of course punctured; it cannot be regained. There is a profound difference between the real thing that once existed and had its own logic and legitimacy and a conscious, contrived insistence on the wisdom of the past, on its capacity to contain people's lives and explain their needs.

The Chinese revolutionaries, observes Joseph Levenson, accomplished a revolution "against the world to join the world, against the past to keep it theirs, but past."[1] China's success contrasts with the failure of the Arab order. There has been an incapacity to rebel thoroughly against the outside world, and thus to join it, or against the past, and thus to see it for what it is and keep it at bay. To be sure, there is plenty of resentment against a world that has been largely seen as unfair and treacherous, but there is also a great deal of buying into the modern international system. But there is a world of difference between resentment and rebellion, between buying into the ideas and labor of others and actively participating in the world. There has also been a mountain of words about slaying the past. Such was the promise of Abdul Nasser's generation, and surely it was the claim of post-1967 radicals who had vowed to succeed where their predecessors had failed.

But a decade after the new revolutionaries had their chance, and after a major so-called victory over the West in October, 1973, there was overwhelming evidence that the Arab world had come full circle. The vocabulary and concern of Arab politics and the drums to which people were marching showed the remarkable tenacity of the past. Both the Arabs themselves and those who interpreted them were suddenly saying that the Arab world was after all the Arab world — moved by its ancient passion, entangled in its old snares, afflicted with the old doubts and predicaments. Underneath it all, the Sunnis and Shiites in Iraq were after all Sunnis and Shiites; no ideological pretension of any kind would bridge that gap. Indeed, things were regressing. The most authoritative study of modern Iraq depicts a pattern of retreat. The ruling Ba'th party, which until 1963 had the characteristic "of a genuine partnership between Sunni and Shia 'poor-Arab' youth," had by 1968 become the almost exclusive preserve of the ruling Sunni stratum.[2] Ideological pretensions were equally irrelevant to the Syrian case. The base of Syrian politics was still communal, and the most important hard fact about Syrian politics was the political ascendancy of young countryside Alawites who went into the army and then managed to grab the power of the state. Likewise, the Lebanese civil war that started out with all kinds of ideological claims finally degenerated into a ghastly communal fight. The identification card, which designated not only one's religion but also one's sect, was the final arbiter, the pretensions of ideology were set aside and people presumably were seen for what they really were. Finally, in inter-Arab politics as a whole, it was not the radical nationalists of a decade before who seemed to be setting the tone of Arab politics, but the rulers of Saudi Arabia. Mohamed Heikal, once the propagator of Nasserite ideology, now told his readers that the Arab world had entered the "Saudi era" and that power had passed from the "charismatic revolutionary" state of Abdul Nasser to the "traditional" Saudi state. Radical nationalism was the pillar of the Nasserite order; Islam is the presumed pillar of the Saudi one.

The idea that ideology revolutionizes the world and blows away ancient feuds and weaknesses may or may not be empirically valid, but it has become a dictum of our age. When it is subscribed to, it can magnify the futility that societies experience as they discover those stubborn traits that simply refuse to go away. Then men begin to think that they have labored in vain, that their deeds are like footprints in the sand. Is not the resurgence of Islam that is said to be sweeping the region proof that generations of nationalists, liberal and Marxist ideologues alike, have failed to leave any real sign of their presence?

In the aftermath of Iran's upheaval, the resurgence of Islam has become a grande idée of sorts that explains all. Yesterday's grande idée was the withering away of tradition, the triumph of that great universal solvent, modernization. In yesterday's imagery, societies were to leap, as if by magic, historical stages; they would move instantaneously from traditional society to the rational-bureaucratic stage. In today's evocative imagery, the return of Islam is akin to a desert wind sweeping progress in its way, forcing people back into the world of their ancestors. But today's grande idée may fail us as completely as yesterday's did. The hopes of those among the faithful who sense that a civilization broken and defeated several centuries ago is on the verge of resurrection and the fears of those who see in Islam's reassertion some great revolt against modernity are both mistaken. We must know the real struggles and concerns that people and societies are engaged in if we are to understand why they brandish the weapons they do and why they turn to a particular set of symbols.

What is behind the resurgence of Islam? How much is genuinely felt and how much is mere pretension by people and societies in desperate need of ideological cover to divert attention (their own and others') from excessive wealth or from acute dependency on the very infidels they denounce? What does this "desert wind" consist in besides the closing of beauty parlors, the banning of music, the enforcing of strict dress codes, and the usual incantations against atheistic Marxists? What is the prospect for the *turath* (heritage) proclaimed and defended by the Saudi state in Arab politics? If the *turath* is to win by default (as I will contend here), what is to be the fate of competing options and how did they play themselves out in the aftermath of the June 1967 defeat?

Let us consider an essential distinction made in Joseph Levenson's study of China between *tradition* as a primary, genuine commitment and *traditionalism* as a conscious system of defense. What Levenson said of Confucianism applies to Islam's reassertion and runs through this analysis:

> When Confucian traditionalism comes to be accepted not from a confidence in its universal validity but from a *traditionalistic* compulsion to profess that confidence, Confucianism is transformed from a primary philosophical commitment to a secondary romantic one, and traditionalism from a philosophical principle to a psychological device.[3]

The "withering away" and "return" of traditions are simple images that glide past troubles and realities and miss the way by which and the reasons for which people turn to particular symbols at given moments. The apparent victories of traditions are more often a sign of their decay than their flowering. Traditions are most insistent and loud at the time when they rupture, when patience wears thin, when people no longer really believe, when the webs of meaning and significance have blown away, leaving a society a mere parody of itself:

> The end of tradition does not necessarily mean that traditional concepts have lost their power over the minds of men. On the contrary, it sometimes seems that this power of wellworn notions and categories becomes more tyrannical as the tradition loses its living force and as the memory of its beginning recedes; it may even reveal its full coercive force only after its end has come and men no longer even rebel against it.[4]

Thus the seeming contradiction between the reassertion of Islamic fundamentalism — all the tradition mongering of the Saudi

era, all the insistent talk about authenticity – and the unprecedented integration of the Arab world into the world economy and
the extensive political and cultural advances of the United States
into the region is no contradiction at all. The two phenomena are
twins. There comes a time in the life of nations when the outside
world intrudes, when it appears with all its threats and temptations. People either respond to it coherently and competently or
they lose their bearings. And if they do the latter, they need all
kinds of psychological devices: They stress their uniqueness and
the great achievements of their ancestors all the more as they surrender to others more powerful and more glamorous than themselves. Reassertion and chauvinism alternate with self-doubt and
mimicry. This creates its own vicious circle. The failure of claims
and movements, the troubles of a reigning order trying to have it
both ways – to insist on its autonomy at the same time that it
trades it for what the outside world has to offer – send everyone
scurrying for cover. The rulers create fake victories, the citizenry
tend to their private matters, and the intelligentsia and politically
sensitive either give up or escape into metaphysics and absolutism.
Imagined revolutions and breakthroughs follow one another. Salvation is proclaimed, then there is a feeling of disappointment after
the dust settles and people discover that the whole rotten thing
starts all over again. Authenticity becomes a refuge when practical
politics fails to deliver concrete solutions to foreign weakness, to
domestic breakdown, to cultural seduction. The connection between the Arab *thawra* (revolution) of the post-1967 years to the
Saudi era of a decade later, from the Marxist–Leninist tracts to
the fundamentalist exhortations, is not as tenuous as it at first
seems. One leads to the other. Both are made of the same material:
the desire for a quick fix, that brief moment of elation when all appears resolved before things come tumbling down. Thus "return"
and "restoration" must both be situated in their proper context:
first in terms of the failure of what passed for revolution, and then
in the troubles of the dominant Arab order that waged the October War and then went on, after vanquishing old foes and exorcising old ghosts, to confront different and more deadly dilemmas.

THE "REVOLUTION" CONTAINED

The outcome of the Six Day War was a textbook case of a revolutionary situation, with all its standard ingredients: military defeat,
internal exhaustion, the disaffection of intellectuals, a generation

gap that was rapidly turning into an abyss, scathing critiques of the most sacred facets of a culture's life. That, at any rate, was the view of those who pinned their hopes on the new revolution – the Palestinian movement – and who broke with Nasserism and the Ba'th. George Habash's own transformation from the pan-Arabism of the Nasser years reflected the new drift. Historically, Arab nationalism had been confined to the political realm; it had not been particularly concerned with socioeconomic questions. Albert Hourani's survey of the "liberal age" in the Arab world had noted the "indifference" of liberal nationalism to social reform and economic justice. This he attributed partly to the "liberal atmosphere of the time," which stressed national independence over all other matters and partly to the fact that "most of the leaders and spokesmen of the nationalist movement either belonged to families of standing and wealth or had raised themselves into that class by their own efforts."[5] Both Nasserism and the Ba'th had presumably tried to do just that. Both had insisted that nationalism without social improvement was reactionary and insensitive; both had pledged their allegiance to a brand of nationalism that incorporated radical reform and socialism. In the light of the June defeat, a younger generation was to dig deeper into the political tradition and the social structure. It was to see in the ideas and deeds of the heroes of the 1950s and 1960s the dead hand of the past. A flood of new writings – some indigenous, some the standard revolutionary tracts of Debray, Fanon, Mao, Guevara – opened up new horizons. They gave a revolutionary tone to political discourse; they underscored the gap between the young and the dominant order.

But revolutions cannot hover in the air. They require concrete channels, and the channel for the Arab revolution was to be the Palestinian movement. Where it had once been believed that the Arab states would liberate Palestine, it was now expected that the Palestinian struggle would topple the Arab order. Thus, when a group of young intellectuals was invited to reassess the Egyptian revolution on its seventeenth anniversary, they performed an autopsy. With the exception of Nadim Bitar, a faithful Nasserite who insisted that Abdul Nasser still represented the best of alternatives, all were convinced that Nasser's great deeds were behind him and that his revolution had been shackled by bureaucracy and tarnished by defeat. For the young philosopher and activist Sadeq al-Azm, the Palestinian revolution promised a new theory and practice. For the writer Adonis, the new "revolutionary moment" was the moment of the Palestinians. Other "Arab revolutions" –

and the quotation marks are Adonis's — were real and living revolutions to the extent that they followed the lead of the Palestinians. A publicist for the Palestinian movement saw the whole Arab order at the mercy of the Palestinians.[6] Three months before the carnage of Amman culminated in the victory of King Husein's army and of so-called tradition, the radical intelligentsia were convinced that the Palestinian movement was well on its way to becoming a total Arab revolution.

This revolutionary moment lasted for three years. Looking back with the benefit of hindsight, one can see the overwhelming odds against its success; one can dismiss George Habash's designation of the four enemies of the revolution — Zionism, imperialism, "Arab reaction" (Jordan and Saudi Arabia), and "Arab bourgeois regimes" (Cairo and Damascus) — as the kind of messianic stuff from which revolutionary bubbles and aspirations are made. But to do so would be to overlook the vulnerability of the Arab order at the time. There were deep domestic troubles in Egypt; the lines were drawn in Jordan, and to a lesser extent in Lebanon, between the regimes and growing Palestinian activism that intersected with local grievances; there was despair throughout the Arab world, and people were vulnerable to any remedy, any banner. Moreover, two regimes (Egypt and Jordan) were trying to negotiate a diplomatic settlement and at the same time to cover their tracks, for they had little to bargain with and their ineffectual diplomacy lacked the appeal and the fire of Palestinian deeds.

The outside world intruded into this fight. This was a time when the belief in Third World revolutions, in guns and pamphlets, had a vast radical constituency in the West. Distant lands seething with contradictions and unrest were, after all, part of the revolt against the banality and imperialism of the Western radicals' countries. The future of the world, Western radicals were convinced, would be decided in remote Third World countries. As a French former Maoist recalls it, "Everything seemed possible, beginning with a return to the pure sources of the revolutionary ideal, at the wellsprings of the Third World, with a great strategic detour through countries whose outcasts rose up with empty bellies, guns flowering from their hands. Thus, we invented our own Third World . . . One need only recall our passionate discussions to realize that each epoch nourishes its own hopes of imaginary lands."[7] And because the world is what it is, images and convictions spun in the West (including those about the non-West) filter down to other lands and people begin to see themselves and their own situation in the images of others. This the radical left has always noted as part of its indictment of the asymmetry of the world system. It neglects to note, however, that the same thing happens in radical circles. There, too, there are centers and peripheries. The images about "revolutions in the revolutions" and "decadent feudal orders" filter down to poorer societies and are consumed by others. But the West's Third World was more revolutionary than the real Third World. In the Arab world, as in other regions, there was always the propensity (revealed in the 1967–1973 interlude) for people to forget where they were and to see themselves and their situation through the print and footage of the Western media.

The decisive duel between the dominant Arab order and the Palestinians was fought in Jordan. In Jordan (and later in Lebanon with the Syrian intervention against the Palestinians) the dominant order would demonstrate not only the superiority of its firepower but also the weakness of theory disconnected from the hard facts of political life. No revolutionary tract had an analysis of the bedouins who comprised the base of King Husein's army. The disembodied "revolutionary masses" discussed in the pamphlets were one thing, Jordan's realities were another.

Some time after Jordan's civil war ended, a leading member of the Palestinian movement conceded that many in the leadership did not really know Jordanian society, that they did not understand the seamy side of the regime, the hold of the king on his army, or the political and cultural significance of his Sharifian descent. The theorists were convinced that Husein's army would refuse to fight the Palestinians. But the men who fought for the king were mostly illiterates or barely able to read. They were beyond the reach of the radicals' pamphlets. For them the fight was between the king – their chieftain, their financial provider, a man who claims descent from the Prophet – and atheistic troublemakers, townsmen with alien and offensive ways.[8] Belief was pitted against unbelief. Islam was once again a pillar of political authority.

The capacity of the sultan to have God on his side is a recurring Islamic phenomenon. In the confrontation between Habash's Marxism and King Husein's army, the weight of tradition was on the king's side. Consider the following examples. In an issue of Al Aqsa, the magazine of the Jordanian armed forces, a soldier asks God to grant Husein victory "over Zionism and the unbelievers." When the headquarters of a radical Palestinian magazine were destroyed in the fighting, Radio Amman told its listeners that a "vindictive hired voice" had been silenced: "One that had tried to poison many thoughts and tried to disconnect you from your past,

your traditions and religion." In yet another statement, the Palestinian movement was said to have "surrendered to Satan"; the soldiers were assigned to kill the Palestinians and pray for them at the
same time. This was powerful local idiom that would stick, not
metaphysical argument. More poignant still was the following
short story disseminated to the Jordanian army. Its main characters were a "tough" bedouin soldier and an elegant "effeminate"
young man from the Palestinian movement. The latter interrupts
the soldier's prayer to talk with him about "revolutionary matters." This is their exchange:

> The soldier praying, "Praise be to Allah, lord of the world,
> the merciful and the compassionate."
>
> The young man interrupts: "Haven't you heard Marx say-
> ing . . . "
>
> The voice of the soldier (now rising): "Thee we worship,
> Thee we ask for help . . . "
>
> The young man again: "But Engels said . . . "
>
> The soldier still reciting: "Say I seek refuge in the Lord of
> mankind . . . "
>
> The young man: "Forget about such things; religion is the
> opiate of the people . . . "
>
> The soldier, continuing his prayer " — from the evils of
> the sneaking whisperer . . . "
>
> The young man; "Counter-revolution is the one . . . "

This time, the soldier turns around and threatens the urban youth,
who of course runs away. The soldier returns to his prayer, raises
his hands toward heaven and pleads: "Oh Lord, give victory to
Husein and his soldiers . . . the soldiers of Muhammad against
Zionism, Zionists, and the unbelievers."[9]

Husein's soldiers were the soldiers of Islam; their enemies were
revolutionary outsiders, men who had gone beyond the bounds of
the community and its ways. The king had prepared for his fight.
Once the carnage began, he was in no hurry to stop it. The fight
was on and it was a fight for Jordan. Prior to the eruption of the
fighting, Husein had said that when the Hashemites came to
Amman it was only a small village, and if the time came when he
had to leave, he would leave Amman the way it was when his forefathers arrived. Slogans like "all authority to the Resistance" had
had their day; Husein was to be the final victor. But some men do
not easily change or learn from history. One of the more extreme

{ 145 }

of the Palestinian movements, the Popular Democratic Front for the Liberation of Palestine led by Nayef Hawatmeh, attributed the defeat to the absence of revolutionary theory. No revolution could be accomplished, it profoundly proclaimed, without revolutionary theory. More sophisticated analyses came from another group. The devastation of the Arab regimes after 1967 had given the Palestinian movement some room for maneuver, but the regimes were now reasserting their control. The Arab states needed heroic deeds after 1967 and the Palestinians were able and willing to provide these deeds. Sooner or later, however, the Arab state system had to strip the Palestinians of their delusions. This they did in Jordan in September, 1970. Six years later, the Syrian army would administer the same lesson in Lebanon.[10]

In the heat of the Lebanese civil war as well there was a feeling that the dominant order could be overthrown, that there were new possibilities. "We feel," said George Habash in mid-1976, "that the reactionary, bourgeois, confessional regime has collapsed and that the Lebanese national movement would make a big mistake if it allowed this regime to be resurrected and reconstructed on a reformist basis. The Lebanese National Movement has a chance to insist on a new Lebanon — a democratic, nationalist, secular Lebanon." But the old Lebanon, although transformed, survived the civil war. The old men who ran things — be they on the right, such as former presidents Camille Chamoun and Suleiman Franjieh and the leader of the Phalangists, Pierre Gemayyel, or on the left, such as Kamal Junblatt — had sons, and to their sons passed their power and the old ways of doing things. Aptly enough, as though to forecast the turn of events in Iran, the fight in Shi'a Southern Lebanon between the old feudal boss Kamel Assad and the left ended in victory for neither. Power passed to Imam Musa al-Sadr, a young Shi'a Mujtahid of the Khomeini variety. In Lebanon, the dominant order remained. The Syrians upheld it and made the Saudis finance their "stabilization" effort. The fight in Lebanon was less dangerous, less loaded with socioeconomic meaning than the radicals assumed.

The real struggle between the old order and the radicals had dominated the 1967–1973 interlude. The old order had prevailed both in Jordan and of course in October, 1973. Whatever the military judgment on the October War, there can be no doubt that the war bought time and helped defuse the frustrations and the radicalism. Writing in early 1973, Arnold Hottinger, a careful analyst of Arab politics, caught the radical mood of the time when he stated that the Arab society that might emerge from the turmoil "might well resemble present day China more than any society known to us."[12] The Chinese analogy was far fetched, but the mood was bleak enough to suggest the comparison. Thanks to the October War, however, Arab politics took a new turn, and the order put together by the Egyptians, the Syrians, and the Saudis was able to contain and outflank the radicals. The fact that the Arabs were unable to maintain a united political front was a problem for the future. It was to be a quarrel about tactics rather than over fundamental socioeconomic issues. By the time this problem arose, "the revolution" had been aborted and the order given a breathing spell.

One need not engage in excessive psychologizing of politics to note that nothing less than patricide was at stake in the early fight between the dominant order and the radicals. Nasser and the Ba'th had flirted with some new ideas, but there existed then a basic continuity with the past when compared to what the young were doing and saying after 1967. The shift from the notorious Ahmad al-Shuqairi to George Habash was a qualitative one. Al-Shuqairi, a sycophant and a braggart, was part of an old culture of defeat and compromise. He spoke the old language and was too much a creature of Arab courts, having served the Saudis and the Syrians as an ambassador to the UN, later shifting his allegiance to Abdul Nasser, who rewarded him with chairmanship of the PLO. Habash represented a discontinuity. He was a public man, ideologically committed, whose path to power came through the cell and the street. By the logic of the old world around him, Habash, a physician, could have gone on to mind his own business, (all the more so because he was a Christian), tend to his private matters, and, like other members of his profession, accumulate a fortune. His choice was a break with the ways of the elders: To go beyond personal safety and success and opt for the risks of public politics was to inject into that world a sense of new possibilities.

Then there was the impact of a political and intellectual renaissance of sorts. The young radicals dragged the Arab world out of its provincialism, out of its obsessive concern with the tired themes of its own history into the full light of world events and currents. They connected the Arab world's dilemmas with the dilemmas and successes of others. That it was all done in too mechanistic and imitative a fashion was not seen at that moment. That realization began to sink in after Jordan, when even the most diehard believers had to concede that the battle with the culture's ways had been lost, that the world of the elders had eluded and outwaited them and bounced back with seemingly new vitality.

{ 147 }

As though to convey the parallels between the defeat of the Palestinians in 1970 and the Arab defeat of 1967, it fell to the young radical scholar Sadeq al-Azm to do the same kind of autopsy on the Palestinians as he had earlier performed on Nasserism in his book *Self-Criticism After the Defeat*. September, 1970, in Jordan, wrote al-Azm in a new wave of revisionism, was to the Palestinian movement what June, 1967, was to the pan-Arabist movement. The Palestinian movement had been but a natural extension of the earlier movement, a branch of it. The characteristics that crippled the earlier movement found their way to its offshoot.[13] Palestinian leaders too were more anxious to "strut on the world stage," to give press conferences, to flaunt their weaponry, to put forth easy arguments, than to undertake the patient work of reconstituting a Palestinian nation in exile, doing the steady and painful work that social revolutions entail. If the leaders of the Palestinian movement were giving an average of one-and-one-half press interviews a day — as was reported in a detailed and unpretentious analysis by a member of the Executive Committee of the Palestine Liberation Organization between 1969 and 1971 — was this not proof that people had remained braggarts, that the old world had survived?[14]

Of course the expectation that a brief and spectacular push against a dominant political and cultural tradition would sweep away the past was sheer illusion; like all illusion, it had disappointment written into it. But such was the expectation after 1967, and the disappointment was quick to follow. The same young men and women who had embraced the Palestinian movement became its relentless critics, and Azm's revisionism was but a manifestation of the general disillusionment. The new revolution, like the old Nasserite one, he observed, had exaggerated its achievements; it too had peddled its myths and made the Arab masses live on illusions. Indeed its moment of success was due to the fact that it "renewed and nurtured the old illusions that the masses had been used to and had survived on for a long time." Was not Arafat's statement that he did not expect King Husein to hit with all his might akin to Nasser's statement after the June defeat that he had expected Israel's attack to come from the east and the north but that instead it came from the west? Was not the growth of bureaucratization and profiteering a reaffirmation of an old cultural theme — the gun serving as a way of exorcising self-doubts and hoarding resources? In drowning the Palestinian movement in words, was the culture doing what came most naturally to it: spinning its wheels, turning everything into a forum for oratory, making and remaking the world with phrases but leaving the substance unchanged?[15]

To the extent that the Palestinian movement represented and embodied the post-1967 Arab revolution, its troubles burst the revolutionary bubble of the post-1967 years. There would be no easy way out; the panacea of a people's war of national liberation was but a brief illusion. It thrived so long as the Arab regimes seemed castrated and so long as the youthful energy tapped by a new wave of thought and practice had the daring and energy to push for a new world. By the time the Arab armies went into action in October, 1973, and the reactionary oil states deployed the oil weapon, the old world had made a stand of its own; it promised its own dawn of a new age.

THE DOMINANT ORDER'S BRIEF TRIUMPH

The revolution, then, eluded the Arab order, and people were left searching for an explanation of its failure. Nostalgia would have it that the battle was almost won. The political climate of a particular period and the real — as opposed to the perceived — balance of power among contending forces is difficult, if not impossible, to determine. Perhaps the Arab order was as weak as its challengers believed. On the other hand, the power of the challengers may have been ephemeral, their momentum more of a mood than a concrete reality. A greater number of obstacles stood in the way of the Arab radicals than was generally believed at the time.

For one, the Arab—Israeli conflict itself, on which the radicals depended as a catalyst of revolutionary upheaval, was in reality a conservatizing force. Hard as the radicals tried to turn that war into a war of national liberation, hard as they tried to draw parallels with Algeria's anticolonial war or China's revolution, the Arab—Israeli conflict was an interstate duel — and all the more so because the power of the Palestinians was located outside the occupied territories. The two Arab—Israeli wars of the post-1967 years — Nasser's war of attrition and the October War — served effectively as sponges: They absorbed frustrations and they demonstrated that the initiative still lay with the dominant order. The October War, in particular, satisfied the popular need for revenge against Israel for the wounds and humiliations of June, 1967. If the Arabs wanted a new world, a new place in the sun, it was offered to them by President Sadat and King Faisal. The victory of October, 1973, posed a difficult dilemma for the Arab radicals. It was risky to question the achievements of October (and that goes a long way toward explaining Qaddafi's eclipse in inter-Arab politics, for he dismissed the October War as a "comic affair") and self-defeating to pay homage to those who pulled it off.

Inasmuch as the October War became a great historical event in Arab history – it symbolized, wrote an Egyptian, the return of the Arab to his proper place in history, the first Arab military victory after centuries of defeat – there was very little to be gained from belittling what the dominant regimes had accomplished.[16] When all appeared lost it was the dominant order that supplied the answers: crossed the Suez Canal when it was believed that it would be unable to do so; brought about one of the most massive shifts of wealth known in the history of the modern world system; promised and for a while seemed to succeed in delivering a brighter world. Under these circumstances, it was natural enough to dismiss the talk about social revolution. Given a choice, and the dominant order did supply one, people simply chose, as Edmund Burke would have put it, to be "good patriots," and "a good patriot and true politician considers how he shall make most of the existing materials of his country . . . Everything else is vague in conception, perilous in the execution."[17]

The "perilous" schemes of the revolutionaries and their "vague" conceptions were shunned in favor of the known world, and the choice was made that much easier because of prosperity that the new order promised. In the Palestinian movement itself, the final word belonged not to George Habash and the Marxists but to Yasser Arafat and the believers in Palestinian nationalism. The latter were part of the old world, they read the old texts, they were at home with the dominant tradition. Their demand was a limited one – statehood – and it was a demand that the Arab system of states could pay homage to. Thus the Palestinian movement was absorbed into the dominant order – taken into summit conferences, subsidized by the oil states, lent the prestige of Arab diplomatic power. In return, the Palestinian movement had to tame its own radicals, keep *al mabadi' al mustwarda* (the imported doctrines) at bay, accept the rules of the game, abide by the dominant tradition.

The institutionalization of the Palestinian movement had been the consistent demand of the Arab states. Early in the post-1967 years, it was repeatedly made by Nasser and his spokesman Mohamed Heikal; it was even endorsed (at least as long as Nasser lived) by Qaddafi, who asked in early 1970 that the Palestinian movement be transformed into a Palestinian government. This all along was the demand of the oil states that wanted a responsible Palestinian movement. The Rabat Resolution of 1974, which desig-

nated the PLO as the "sole, legitimate representative" of the Palestinian people, consummated the deal between the Arab order of
states and the Palestinian movement. It was a deal concluded at the
height of the dominant order's power. The Arab states had an embarrassment of material and diplomatic riches, or so it seemed at
the time. It was time to be benevolent, so they conferred upon the
Palestinians what one observer described as a "metaphysical" right
to the West Bank and Gaza.[18]

Remaking the social order and settling the local grievances of the
Arab world were no longer proper Palestinian concerns. The Syrian intervention in Lebanon in June, 1976, drove home this point.
Hafez Asad was bent on decoupling the Palestinian movement from
the Lebanese National Movement and the aims of its leader, Kamal
Junblatt. In justifying his intervention in Lebanon, Asad would
claim that the Palestinian movement had strayed from its proper
objectives. In this statement can be seen the difficulty of sneaking
radical politics through the back door of Palestinian nationalism.

Vulnerable on its flanks since 1967, the Arab order would not be
brought down either by George Habash and Nayef Hawatmeh from
the left or Qaddafi from the right. Restoration was as much a possibility as was revolution. The young radicals were convinced that
the old order was bankrupt, that its leadership was discredited,
that its symbols were battered. In all that they were probably
right; but they drew the wrong conclusions about the inevitability
of the dominant order's collapse. An exhausted world can still
hang on long after it loses its vitality; it can cover up its weaknesses
and pull off semivictories; it can rely on the built-in human preference for normalcy, play for time, and then reassert itself. That is
what the men in power did with and after October, 1973.

This time it was the dominant order's turn to strut on the world
stage. The Arab world had turned the tables on the West. After a
long period of decline, there was talk of renewal in the air. Anwar
el-Sadat's boastful statement that the Arab world had become the
world's sixth power appealed to the historic desire for revenge
against the West. To the politically conscious among the Arabs, it
appeared that the Arab world had finally managed to find its place
in the sun. For a culture that had sustained itself through a long
stretch of frustrations and setbacks by dreams of sudden resurrection, it all seemed to make sense and to conform to a cyclical vision
of history. This vision witnesses individual careers and whole social orders rise and fall in a way that mysteriously humbles the
mighty and redresses the grievances of the weak. In this confrontation, the West, which had always seemed threatening and reso-

lute, was full of its own squabbles, unsure of its power and purpose. The arrogance of the West had clearly come up against all
sorts of limits — its own self-doubts and the resistance of others —
and it was increasingly obvious to those who had traditionally stood in awe of Western power that there were cracks in the
edifice.

The so-called decline of the West may or may not have been an
objective reality, but for people and societies long at the receiving
end of Western power, October 1973 was a turning point. The
wounds inflicted by the West had left deep scars everywhere, and
non-Westerners were quick to see the dawn of a new age. The
weapons, ideas, and diplomatic skill with which one segment of the
world had erected a world system in its own image were now available to hitherto dispossessed groups and nations. In the Arabs' petropower, in India's nuclear explosion, and in the power of the
new majority at the UN non-Westerners saw the beginning of a
new world.

Even the friends and clients of the West were now compelled to
assert their defiance and autonomy. Marcos of the Philippines became openly contemptuous of Western democracy; his "New Society" became more bluntly authoritarian. In the shah of Iran's interview with the Italian journalist Oriana Fallaci, the West was
portrayed as a row of vulnerable dominoes. Power and the future
belonged to the shah's quest to marry the power of Western technology to the ways of Persian kingship.[19] Yet another client of the
West, Mobutu, of Zaire, said he was seeking a future based on the
ways of the ancestors, on the wisdom of the bush. He offered his
society a philosophy of authenticity, Mobutuism, as an answer to
both Western democracy and Marxism. In the shedding of his
Christian name for a native one, the local culture of Zaire was presumably reasserting its worth.

But the stage on which the protagonists — the Third World and
the West — met and the circumstances of their new encounter
were prone to distort the results. This would be seen a few years
later when the challenge of the Third World seemed to lose much
of its initiative. By then the Arab world, which had led the rebellion, was itself in deep trouble; the shah of Iran's dreams were
dashed at home, where all battles and claims begin and end; and
Mobutuism could be seen for what it was all along: a cover for collaboration, a bit of glamor and theater sprinkled on top of a world
of mismanagement and corruption that culminated in International Monetary Fund (IMF) advisors in virtual control of Zaire's
economy. There is, when all is said and done, a difference between

pretension to power and the real thing. The underlying weaknesses of the Arab and Third World states eventually came to the
surface. But in the immediate aftermath of October, 1973, the impression was one of dazzling success.

In the Arab world, power in the post-October 1973 period belonged to a new group:

> For a generation the men who directed the course of events
> in the Arab world had been ideologists or officers from the
> armed forces — or sometimes officers who turned into ide-
> ologists or ideologists who tried to behave as if they were
> officers. Such were Sadat, Assad, Ghadaffi, Boumedienne,
> Michel Aflaq, Sadam Hussein and many others. Many of
> these were still there, but they were now being joined by
> the first instalment of a new breed of power brokers, the
> middlemen, the arms dealers, the wealthy merchants who
> flitted between East and West, between royal palaces and
> the offices of oil companies — men like Kamal Adham,
> Mahdi Tajjir, Adnan Khashoggi and others — and by roy-
> alty itself, for who in the Arab world now exercised more
> power than Prince Fahd or Prince Sultan of Saudi Arabia?
> Could not individuals such as these, it was argued, achieve
> more for the Arabs than mass movements and radical revo-
> lutions?

> It is not surprising if in this changed atmosphere men and
> women in Egypt and Syria felt that the time had come for
> them too, to see some improvement in their material cir-
> cumstances. They had known hardship; now they looked
> for their reward — for more to eat and for better houses to
> live in. Of course money would have to be found to pay for
> this, but who would dare to suggest that the Arabs were
> short of money? It was being said that the Arabs possessed
> the power to bring the rest of the world to starvation;
> surely they must have the power to feed themselves? So
> eyes turned to the oil-producing countries. Oilfields began
> to loom far bigger in the public mind than battlefields;
> *tharwa* (riches), it was said, had begun to take over from
> *Thawra* (revolution).[20]

But the new leaders really represented a variation on an old
theme. In a crossroads civilization the triumph of the merchant is
hardly surprising. The defeat of the officer-ideologues who dominated Arab politics in the 1950s and 1960s left a political vacuum
that the new men, and, behind them, petropower, were now aim-

ing to fill. The new men could draw comfort from the defeat of their adversaries in Cairo and Damascus. The "open-door economy" of Egypt, proclaimed with great fanfare in 1974, and the much less trumpeted but no less real and similar shift in the Syrian economy, could be taken as proof of the supremacy of conservative ways. Those who managed state enterprises during the more-or-less radical interlude of Nasserism and the Ba'th were anxious to make the shift to the private sector, to pay homage to the sanctity of property, to accept time-honored traditions and class arrangements. Furthermore, many of the younger radicals who had been even more audacious, more indifferent to the ways of the culture, were turning up, as one Syrian scholar puts it, "in the Gulf area and the Arabian Peninsula in business suits taking advantage of the 'Black Gold Rush.'"[21]

The deep structure of all this was a reaffirmation of the old order. People may rebel, but they ultimately make their peace. In a conservative world where people are not likely to risk rebellion, where parents and extended families put up all sorts of barriers to rebellion, this was a verdict that the old ways were still the only possible ones. The world of the fathers, so to speak, had won out.

Authenticity, or what passed for it, had triumphed. The victory of the people of the desert was a victory for those who seemingly had remained themselves. The bourgeois, cosmopolitan capitals that had defiled themselves (such as Beirut), and those that had surrendered to imported doctrines (such as Cairo and Damascus), had lost out. In the ruin of Beirut, the Saudis would see the failure of societies that allowed individuals to do what they wished; in the troubles of Nasser and the Ba'th there was an indictment of those who dared turn things upside down. This was a vindication of the cultural and political superiority of some imagined pure tradition.

Several centuries ago, the great North African historian Ibn Khaldun depicted the struggle between the bedouins and the cities as the key to the rise and fall of dynasties and empires. In a new variation on Khaldun's theme, the Arab cities were in decline while the bedouins (both the radicals like Qaddafi and the conservatives in the peninsula) were on the ascendancy. Although no deliberate effort had brought about this remarkable historical shift, the military effort of Egypt and Syria had paved the way for the new order. Oil prices were raised under the cover of the October War; the decision had taken place under peculiar global circumstances, and the shah of Iran was as responsible as anyone for the dramatic increase in prices.

All that was easy enough to ignore and in a way was academic and irrelevant. The shift had taken place and the new success were all the more startling when compared to the failure of what had passed for radicalism and socialism. There was not yet sufficient distance from Nasserism to see its mixed legacy, to judge whether there was some method, some legitimate achievements, behind its sound and fury. The bases of Nasserism – import substitution, a brand of secular nationalism that was neither collaborationist nor excessively xenophobic, the expansion of educational opportunities – had been mixed. Eventually, those who had been through the whirlwind of Nasserism were destined to take stock of its legacy, to decide whether what was done constituted progress or was merely illusions and theatrics or, more likely, a combination of both. But the time to do so was not yet at hand in the mid-1970s. All that stood out then was the success of the new men and the disaster of the June 1967 defeat. A statement made by a Saudi in 1975 to a visiting American journalist was typical of the mood:

> I was educated in Egypt during the time of Nasser, and when I came back I went into the army, because I thought it was the instrument of progress. But then I saw what was happening in Egypt and in Syria and Iraq. I realized that we were left alone to fight the battle of liberty and free enterprise in the Arab world . . . Now ideology has been stabilized. We have proven to the world that we were right. The proof is in the reception of this country's leadership in an Arab world. Saudi Arabia has become an economic and political model.[22]

In other words, it was not so much the achievements of conservative fundamentalism that won out; the outcome was determined by the failure and exhaustion of the adversaries.

For more than a generation, radicals in Egypt and the Fertile Crescent had been saying that the past must be shed if the Arab Islamic order was to stand up to the outside world. Secular radical nationalism had insisted on its capacity to secure national glory and prestige. But the record told a different story:

> Nowhere has this type of nationalism resulted in an escape from economic dependence and underdevelopment. The only achievements of the great Arab nation in the field of power politics and national prestige have been the work of the oil potentates – the most fundamentalist and conservative of Muslims – in selling their oil with the haggling of skilled businessmen and technocrats (but whose *keffias*,

agals, and *abayas* enable them to be associated with bedouin tradition). As for the ideal of the united Arab nation,
it has grown ever harder in the face of the evident development of regional nationalisms (Egyptian, Algerian, Moroccan, and so on) to maintain that its realization is hampered
only by the "plots" of Israel and "imperialism."[23]

Thus the movement from the era of nationalism and ideology to
the era of commissions and the middlemen. In the former, the
Arabs had subsisted on Nasser's grandeur; some (unfortunately
for them) were taken in by the metaphysics of Michel Aflaq, the
theorist of the Ba'th Party, and his abstractions about Arab unity,
love, and the primacy of the nation. A decade later, they were
being treated to the theatrics of the middlemen, to the great
achievements of Adnan Khashoggi; they were told about the "regional packages" — large deals involving Saudi capital, Egyptian
labor, and Sudanese land that would achieve, without political
struggles and disagreements, the unity that had eluded the pan-
Arabists. In the world view of the middlemen and of the technocrats, if ideology were stabilized and passions expunged, the new
order would prosper and men would telescope history, buy technological progress off the rack, and leap into the industrial world
without disrupting the social mores. There was in this an obvious
desire to sublimate politics, to run away from conflicts. In Albert
Hirschman's imagery, there was a desire to substitute the logic of
"interest" — money making, pragmatic politics, the seemingly benign endeavors of wealth seeking and consumption — for the ca-
priciousness of "passions."[24] It was reasoned that the Arab world
had suffered enough from total schemes and romantic visions, that
there was plenty of wealth to go around, that the area could do
with a bit of normalcy. On the face of it, this was a simple and understandable desire. It seemed benign and safe enough, a Middle
Eastern variation upon Europe's story after World War II. Exhausted and ruined by its passions, tired from attempts at domination, Europe would see in economic recovery and the benign pursuit of economic growth a way of extricating itself from historical
grievances and conflicts. But success and normalcy produce their
own troubles. In an era of intense competition, fatigue points the
way out and people are ready to compromise; in a benign world,
there are always those who stand for principles, who wish to inject
into what they see as a compromised world their own higher ideals
and own lofty motivations.

Just as fatigue places a high premium on normalcy, crass success is vulnerable to the contempt and passion of those who believe that they have higher public projects in mind, things more noble, more historically justifiable than personal success and material aggrandizement. Two such public projects exploded the benign order: the Palestinian quest and the fight of Maronite Lebanon for its version of order and civilization. Both projects revealed that the supposedly rational, restrained order was in an inhospitable habitat. There was something ominous and odd about the mixture of outward pragmatism and rationality and the various political and cultural troubles of the Arab order. The massive technology purchases, the acquisition of new skills, the determination born out of success to engage the outside world without the old resentments and inadequacies, and then the political and cultural troubles undermined the new rationality. The troubles of Lebanon offered a pointed commentary on the outward rationality. By the logic of interest, the Lebanese stood to reap substantial benefits from the new order. Traditionally brokers and middlemen, there was plenty for them to do in the post-October 1973 order. But passions won out and the traditional capacity for bargaining broke down. For the young who manned the barricades on both sides, all considerations of finance were degraded. As the Christians' apocalyptic language put it, their fight was for a civilization in retreat: It was a fight not only for Lebanon but for the West as a whole. The West was lost unless Lebanon (their version of Lebanon, of course) was saved. That the West was unable to see it as such was the result of cowardice and greed. Blackmailed by Arab oil, the West had relinquished its moral duty, betrayed itself. In the words of Amin Gemayyel, the son of the Phalangist leader Pierre Gemayyel, "Lebanon's war was the war of a failed civilization [Islam, the Arab world] that wanted to destroy a successful cultural experiment . . . for the Lebanese the scale of destruction does not matter; what matters is the quality of reconstruction."[25] In other words, if Lebanon needs to be destroyed to be re-created, then men must have the nerves for a task of this kind. As for the Western world, says Amin Gemayyel's brother, Bashir Gemayyel: "Its great sin is to leave a small population, that is the Lebanese population, fighting alone for liberty, democracy, for the dignity of man against peoples and groups that deny these values and try to destroy it and to eradicate this country that still adheres to such values."[26] How is the seemingly banal pursuit of economic interests to accommodate such views and historic fears? In this kind of rule-or-die mentality, all calculations of interests are naive or treasonous. That interest alone governs the world was once rebutted

in a different context and at a different time by a man who maintained that "passion, humor, caprice, zeal, faction, and a thousand
other springs, which are counter to self-interest, have as considerable a part in the movement of this machine."[27] Lebanon supplied a
confirmation of that view: Individuals are not always neutral umpires or middlemen. Their moral calculus is complex. They do not
merely note and philosophically accept large historical and cultural shifts; they become frightened or assertive; they fight for
what they know, and they do so all the more ferociously against
what they perceive to be banal or smug orders to sweep things
under the rug.

Lebanon's traditional role was thought of in apolitical terms: It
was assumed that so long as the pan-Arabists accepted Lebanon's
unique identity and situation, Lebanon could find its place in the
Arab family as a link between the Arabs and the West; as a place
for those who played and lost the game of politics and who then
needed somewhere to go to write their memoirs or plot their return to power; as a playground for Saudis and Kuwaitis who wished
to flee from the climate and puritanism of their own countries; as a
banking haven for Syrians who wanted to flee from the politics and
intrigues of the military and economic irresponsibility of would-be
socialists.

In the view of the "Lebanonists," however, the country had a
special mission: to interpret the Arab world to the West, to act as
an agent for Western civilization. So long as Arabism was not
pushed beyond tolerable limits, Lebanon could have it both ways:
live off the Arab world yet think of itself as part of the Occident.
The so-called National Pact worked out in 1943 was a compromise:
The Christians would accept nominal membership in the Arab
world and the Muslims would give up the notion of Arab unity.
The two leaders who concluded the agreement, the Maronite
President Bishara al-Khuri and his Muslim Sunni Prime Minister
Riad al-Sulh, were both reasonable men who made the best of the
material at hand. The philosopher behind the idea was a Catholic
banker and writer, Michel Chiha, who believed that Lebanon
could maintain a Mediterranean civilization if ideology, fanaticism,
and politics were kept at bay. The Christian elite at the time understood Lebanese economic dependence upon the Arab world and
sought to reconcile this with the cultural affinity with the West. It
believed that it could juggle both worlds: Arabism was far away;
one could pay homage to it and still go about one's business of trad-
ing, publishing, smuggling, or banking.

The alliance between the Maronite militias and the state of Israel that had become public in 1976 was the final nail in the coffin of Michel Chiha's and Bishara al-Khuri's Lebanon. The passing of power in the Christian community from men like these to the Phalangists — who were once thought of by the Christian community as rednecks and lower-middle-class ruffians — symbolizes the triumph of passion in Christian Lebanon over the reasonable logic of interest.

During the struggle for Palestine, the Lebanese Christian bourgeoisie had seen the Israelis as a threat: Both wanted to appeal to the West, both thought of themselves as enclave societies in a culturally alien world, and the Lebanese business community feared that a dynamic Israel would outstrip it economically and be more successful in its appeal to the West. After the establishment of Israel, the Lebanese argued for a division of labor in the Arab world. Other Arab states could pursue a military struggle if they wished, but the Lebanese would appeal to Western opinion and try to awaken the West to the plight of the Palestinians and to the justice of the Arab case.

This worked while the Arab–Israeli conflict was removed from Lebanon's soil — a situation that changed after 1970 when the Palestinians, expelled from Jordan, made their political home in Lebanon. It was then that the glib, superficial Arabism of Lebanon met a test it was destined to fail. The leaders in the Christian community who had known the Arab system and made their peace with it lost to those to whom Arabism and Islam were synonymous and who believed in their own cultural supremacy and in the backwardness of the Arabs. The Maronites, convinced that they were being abandoned by the West (they too heard of the so-called decline of the West), resentful of the post-October 1973 wealth and prominence of the Muslim Arab states, losing control over a country that had become too Palestinianized and radicalized for their taste, and aware that the demographic facts were shattering the myth of Christian majority, did what was previously unthinkable. After a brief reliance on a Syrian connection, they opted for a full break with the Arab system — an alliance with Israel and a full commitment to partition.

Through it all, the advocates of partition would be helped by the obvious culpability of the Arab states that had exported the "sacred Arab cause" — the Palestinian issue — onto Lebanese soil. In other words, the least Arab of countries and the weakest militarily was to bear the brunt of full Israeli retaliation and to accept a parallel and competing system of authority. The Palestinian slogan of nonintervention in the internal affairs of Arab countries was harder to practice than to preach. With Israel willing and able to retaliate for raids into her territory, the Lebanese formula unravelled. The gift of an enlarged Lebanon bequeathed by the French turned into a nightmare, and the Maronite militias took up arms first to defeat the Palestinian-leftist-Muslim alliance and then, a little later, to try to carve out their own state, bidding farewell to the idea of Arab brotherhood. They were now willing to state what had been their conviction for quite some time: that they thought of themselves as a different breed; that they were set apart from the Arab world, in which they were geographically included but culturally separate. Arabism, said a spokesman for the Guardians of the Cedars (one of the Maronite militias) in a tone that reflects the deep-seated fears of a mountainous people, is a backward movement that has nothing to offer Lebanon or the world. "They" (meaning the others, the Muslims, the Arabs, the savages) "would push us into the ocean . . . If they push us we'll take refuge in the mountains and fight to the last man."[28]

The other strand of Lebanese thinking, the case for moderation, was still alive, but the world had grown too grim for it. The son of Bishara al-Khuri reiterated the old case for an apolitical Lebanon all the more urgently when there was so much Arab wealth to share: "In no case should the Christians ignite the antagonism of the Arab hinterlands, where our *interests* are tremendous. The time has passed when the foreign powers protected us. One barrel of oil outweighs all the Christians of the Orient."[29]

But it was no longer Khalil al-Khuri's era or the era of men like him. It was the time of those who thrive on that mixture of fear and "purity" engendered by massive breakdowns and crises. The rise of men like Major Saad Haddad, a renegade officer from the Lebanese army, the chieftain of "Free Lebanon" – a strip of land in southern Lebanon that embodies the desire for purity and escape – was of a piece with the new world around him, a bleaker, more biased world. A reporter came back from "Free Lebanon" with Major Haddad's themes: the betrayal of the West and his and his own men's defense of a decaying, materialist civilization:

I think all of the Christian world knows what is going on. But it is too involved in its own materialist problems. No more human values. Religion, it is only by name now. We have been born a Christian, so we say we are Christian. Even my Pope doesn't help. He is supposed to tell all the Christians of the world to wake up, their brothers in Christianity are in danger of being exterminated and they

have to help. By saying a few words he can change the pic-
ture. I wrote to the Pope and never got an answer. He is
supposed to be our spiritual father on the ground, and each
father is supposed to protect his son, even if he is wrong.
How come we are right and he is not supporting us? The
terrorists are getting volunteers from Iran, Libya, Iraq,
Saudi Arabia, from all the Communist countries, to fight
for them. What prevents the Christians from sending
funds or coming as volunteers to help us? We feel left out
from all the world except by Israel. We are fortunate that
we found Israel on our border to help us. Israel understood
our problem, that we are a minority threatened with exter-
mination, and extended its hand to us. They ask for
nothing, and for whatever they give, I am thankful. I have
no right telling them I need this and this. But I have a right
to ask my brother in Christianity.[30]

The Lebanonists once hid behind the notion of majority rule:
Lebanon was said to be more Christian than Muslim, so the Christians governed. Implicitly and explicitly they felt that the West
would continue to dominate and that those who spoke its language
and shared its religious heritage would be partners. The world
changed. The demographic realities were no longer the same. The
previously inaccessible Muslim Arabs to the east of Lebanon were
now, in their own way, joining the world; besides, the outside
world had come anxiously courting the Arabs of the peninsula.
This was a nightmare and a challenge to Lebanon's raison d'être
and to the mental geography of the Lebanese, secure as they were
in their belief that they played an indispensable role. Now the ideological position had to harden: The claim to power would no
longer rest on demography and majority rule but on the supposed
superiority of the minority civilization. To counter the Muslim demographic edge there was the excellence of the Christian minority. This was openly stated: People would no longer hide behind
arguments borrowed from Western parliamentary systems — they
would simply state that their existential predicament made their
political dominance a necessity for survival. "The problem of Lebanon," we are told by a pamphlet of the Phalanges published in
1977, "is the old problem of minorities in the Middle East; it is the
old Oriental Question. The Muslim majority, first by virtue of it
being a majority and second by virtue of it being a Muslim majority,
is tyrannical whether it wishes it to be so or it did not." Because it
is in the nature of such a majority to dominate, Christian Lebanon

must look for a way of resisting the encroachment of the majority, and the answer lies in "superior man," in militias, in guarantees to Christians.[31] A country that had juggled different worlds was up against the wall, growing more incoherent and frightened, more irrational. To its own troubles were added the ambition and schemes of others — the burden of the Arab — Israeli conflicts, the ambitions of young Libyan officers, the schemes of Iraq, the fears and ambitions of Syria. The Lebanese, who had prided themselves on their modernity, were to treat the world to a ghastly night-mare. "Right" and "left" alike, Christian and Muslim, were dwarfed by forces more powerful than they were.

Lebanon was one problem, the question of Palestine another. Here too there was a matter of principle and passions, one that provided an embarrassing contrast of its own to the smugness of the new era. Nothing so visibly demonstrated the peculiar nature of Arab wealth — its inconvertibility to real power, that frustrat-ing difference between power as resources and power as the ability to affect outcomes — as the incapacity of the dominant order to resolve the Palestinian question. Having exaggerated the achievements of the October War, the leaders themselves fed the unrealistic expectations of the masses as to how quickly things could happen. In the popular mood that prevailed in 1974 and 1975, the recovery of the West Bank and Gaza was just around the corner. After all, the Arab armies had defeated Israel, and Arab oil had cornered America, the power that holds the cards. It was the claim of Arab pragmatism that, once total visions were shed, once the old language and assumptions were transcended, once America was won over, the Palestinian question would be settled in an honorable way: either in the "Jordanian solution" to the West Bank problem — probably the real commitment of the Arab order — or in a Palestinian state, the public commitment stated in the Rabat summit conference of 1974. Meanwhile, the Arabs could find their way into the modern world (into the Western interna-tional system, of course) without old complexes and resentments. They could invest their new wealth and assume their newly ac-quired status in the world system.

Having been repeatedly told that the world after October 1973 was a different world, the guardians of the Arab order — the new men — were hard pressed to reconcile their own optimism about a more moderate world with the persistence of that old historic claim against Israel. The fight with Israel stood out as a large un-finished item from yesterday's world: It seemed to defy the out-ward displays of rationality, the steady insistence that the Arabs were no longer the victims of history. In the short run, the new men's bet was on the possible benefits of the Arab world's "reversal of alliances" (Kissinger's term) away from the USSR and toward the United States. If the world was shaped by America's will, if Israel's policies were a mere echo of American wishes, then the Arab turn from the USSR would be rewarded with a comprehensive settlement that would make it easy for the established Arab order to claim that it led a historic fight to an honorable solution: halfway between the utopia of eliminating Israel from the region and the hell of the post-1967 status quo.

As Kissinger wanted it and phrased it, the Arab elites came to "realize that it is the U.S. and not the USSR that holds the key to what they want."[32] In the post-October 1973 configuration of power, the principal Arab advocates of the American connection justified their power by their ability to deliver the superpower that could deliver Israel. Such was the Saudi claim, which made the deradicalization of Arab domestic and foreign policies part and parcel of a reorientation of U.S. attitudes toward the Middle East. And that too was the position of Sadat, who maintained immediately after the October War that "that man [Kissinger] is the only person who can order that woman [Golda Meir] to get out and be obeyed"[33] and who would claim in April, 1977, that he had successfully "convinced" President Carter of the "necessity of establishing an independent Palestinian state."[34]

Mr. Sadat's dramatic deed — his journey to Jerusalem a few months later — showed his impatience with his own dictum. By then Israel had successfully withstood American pressure, it had mocked the Ford–Kissinger threat to reassess American Middle Eastern policy and dashed the expectations that the Carter Administration could effect a comprehensive settlement. Sadat's deed was to face America with a fait accompli: direct diplomacy between the region's two most formidable military entities. It was not to America's liking, but the Egyptian – Israeli relation had to be underwritten; that was the meaning of the Camp David meeting and then of the Egyptian – Israeli treaty of March, 1979. It was initiated by the two parties and blessed by a cornered America. President Sadat provided his own clarity to the Middle Eastern situation. For him the question was not Palestine but Egypt. The American connection was not inspired by the Palestinian dilemma; it was a politicoeconomic and cultural choice.

The Palestinian question was not felt with equal intensity in the Arab monolith. Frustrated by the incapacity of the superpower to get them off the hook, the Arab states went their separate ways:

The Arab center – the moderate camp of Syria, Saudi Arabia, and Egypt – fragmented. The dominant order rode high in the glow of the October War; it made too many promises and it had to pay for them. Egypt was pushed farther down the road of isolation than its president realized; the Syrians hurried to solidify their position and to claim their place as the "principal confrontation state," to "pacify" Lebanon, and to take on the Palestinians in 1976. This was not exactly what the Saudis had in mind when they set out to deradicalize Arab politics in the aftermath of 1973. Egyptian and Syrian policies taught them that allies – even financially dependent ones – can be unwieldy and troublesome. The turn that Islamic fundamentalism took and the attack on the Grand Mosque in Mecca in November, 1979, showed them that the weapons and ideas one brandishes take on a life of their own and are often subject to hostile interpretations, that the forces people unleash and pay homage to can be turned against them and that one can die at the gallows one sets up for others.

THE QUESTION OF AUTHENTICITY AND COLLABORATION

Would-be modernizers are toppled by the changes they seek; would-be reformers (witness post-Maoist China) push for a moderate critique of a particular order, but they throw open the floodgates of criticism and are outflanked by young dissidents who carry the critique of authoritarianism to its logical conclusions. We are free to choose the symbols we wish to fight others with, but the symbols we use make their own demands.

In doing battle with the polished, compromised liberals and atheistic Marxists, the Saudis found it natural to raise the banner of Islam. Their power and wealth, like all power and wealth, required a cover of some kind, a system of legitimization. The Saudis were still fighting yesterday's battle, and under those circumstances their choice seemed safe and sensible. Having made the choice, they had to live with it. It dictated certain things and precluded others. But the choice turned out to be a problematic one. This would be made clear to the Saudis by the Iranian upheaval.

All along, the so-called Saudi era was less stable than was assumed from afar. In the post–pax American view, Saudi Arabia was a regional power – "regional influential" in Zbigniew Brzezinski's facile language – one of those handful of Third World countries chosen for deputizing by an America traumatized by Vietnam and too weary to go it alone. From the perspective of poor Muslim states, Saudi Arabia was another foreign aid donor in a world of scarcity and constraints. But the same kinds of troubles identified earlier in our discussion of the Third World challenge to the West foreshadow the troubles of the Saudi-organized Arab order that emerged out of the October War. There were weaknesses that victories on the world stage could not correct.

For all its wealth, Saudi Arabia was still an underpopulated, weak country in a region seething with unrest. In its post—October 1973 exuberance, Saudi Arabia could entertain all sorts of possibilities — it even became fairly convinced that it must combat Euro-communism and try to do something about the left in France and Italy.[35] But all the principal weapons in the Saudis' arsenal turned out, upon investigation, to be double edged. Acquiring arms risked exposing the Saudis to external attack and spawning a military apparatus that has ended the reigns and taken the lives of other dynasts. Industrialization meant the introduction of foreign workers who would "pollute" the moral universe of this once insular kingdom. Aid was a bottomless pit. Gratitude is an elusive thing; most aid recipients are hopelessly uncontrollable. You can't give enough to keep them afloat or to guarantee that they will do what you want them to do. The American connection too was a mixed thing. The great ally was busy on too many fronts, and besides, the Saudis knew their own history: in their defeat of the Hashemites a century before, they emphasized the foreign collaboration — the British connection — of the Hashemites and stressed their own fidelity to tradition, their own independence. That is why the Saudis seemed to alternate between a Kissingerian kind of gloom about the decline of American power and a reluctance to associate themselves with the United States whenever the United States sought to project its power in the region, to set up military bases or the like.

There was another weakness. Saudi Arabia was not a particularly articulate society, and in a political culture like the Arab world, that operated to its detriment. Saudi Arabia produced few if any books and had very little cultural allure. In the battle of ideas, the Saudis were no match for the traditionally eloquent Egyptians or for the intelligentsia based in Beirut. When Saudi Arabia produced books, they tended to be editions of the works of Sayyed Qutb, the prolific activist of the Muslim Brotherhood. But Sayyed Qutb was an Egyptian, and besides, his brand of social discourse preached the virtues of austerity and had a radical socioeconomic thrust, an embarrassing contrast to the luxury and corruption engendered by the new wealth.

All these were limits to the power of those in Saudi Arabia who pondered a restorationist course for the region. But there was another dilemma, which had to do with the claims of authenticity and the realities of dependence. Islam and the American connection were a tough juggling act. Tradition mongering was the Saudis' choice, but once restored to, it made its own claims. The combination of foreign collaboration and conservative religion is a trauma in a region where that combination has been attempted and exposed over and over again. The special relationship between Saudi Arabia and the United States could be defended, perhaps even proudly displayed, so long as the power from afar promised or was said to have promised a comprehensive Middle Eastern settlement. If the same superpower could deliver the technology of war, a settlement on Jerusalem and the West Bank, and a tantalizing array of gadgets and development projects, then surely the American connection made sense. The Russian connection of yesterday's radicals came with atheistic communism; it defiled and challenged the ways of religion. Presumably the American connection came culture free and could be safely contained in the realms of technology transfers, arms sales, and diplomatic deals. Of course it could not, but the separation between power and culture was made for the United States and denied to the Soviet Union.

This could work so long as the American presence was reasonably discreet and modest and so long as diplomacy delivered tangible gains. But the American push into the region was of a far greater magnitude than had been hitherto known, and the frustrations of diplomacy were infinitely greater than expected. The beneficiaries of the post–October 1973 order had a difficult time squaring their own claims of a new world with the pervasive American presence that the new wealth had invited. It was "strange," writes John C. Campbell in a perceptive essay, that "the moment of crisis [the October War] for the United States, which revealed this vulnerability to the new economic power of OPEC, also left it in a stronger position than ever before, as it gained new influence in the Arab world without losing its special relationship with Israel, and as it stepped forward as the principal partner in the security and economic development of the oil producing states of the Gulf."[36] And for a while the post–October 1973 American structure in the Middle East looked awesome indeed. Based on an alliance with the regimes in Riyadh, Teheran, Cairo, and Jerusalem and the acquiescence of the one in Damascus, it suggested the possibility of taming the region's conflicts, containing the Soviet Union, and keeping "castrated" Europe dependent on the United States.

There were tangible American interests at stake, but there was also the challenge of a new frontier. The Middle East was to be what Southeast Asia turned out, after the outpouring of so much blood and money, not to be: a place where America makes a differ‐ ence, where resources are committed for good reasons. At a time when technology was under fire in the West, a time of debates about limits to growth, the American model was being vindicated in the Middle East. There was an old civilization turning on a large scale to the technology and wares of the United States. The ma‐ terial incentive to recycle petrodollars, to restructure the interna‐ tional system — as the jargon then had it — and to bring the Mid‐ dle East into it, was propelled, as all such endeavors are, by a cultural drive. Technology, it was believed, could perhaps tame the romanticism of the area, make the Arabs more like others, bring them into the world. This required massive American pres‐ ence, at a time when the ruling elites in the Arab lands and in Iran had claimed that they had entered a new era and secured a new place in the sun. Thus began what a wise old Saudi jurist described as the "secular pilgrimage" to the peninsula. And the outside world came in bearing its cultural messages and its wares, raising questions of identity, generating an even greater need to conceal, to play up fidelity to tradition. The drama required a brilliant and restrained effort at cultural and technological traffic control, but such an effort, even if it were possible, was aborted by the magni‐ tude of the wealth and the dreams that were entertained by people who had historically lived on the margins of things and by the huge commissions that were there to be made. The Western world had lost the battle of oil pricing; it had to recoup its losses. An erosion of the power of the dominant organizer of the world economy made it possible for the hitherto "insignificant"[37] to raise oil prices, to claim a new place for themselves. The so‐called winners of October 1973 could now have the world, or so they believed. The serious questions about their willingness and ability to handle that world, about their capacity to withstand its assaults and temptations were not even raised, let alone answered. Here and there, there must have been some doubts, some fears, but they proved no match for the new ambitions and possibilities. Hard as the regimes would try to wrap themselves in the garb of authen‐ ticity, people were witnessing the surrender of their own elites to models and temptations from afar. For a while the contradiction could be wished away by sermons about the supremacy of Islam or the supremacy of Persian kingship over American and Western in‐ stitutions. But this was a difficult dilemma: the dilemma of any so‐

ciety trying to borrow alien things without falling apart. The se-
ductive machines that produce power for others come with
foreign technicians who must work them, and the latter become
living reminders of dependency and weakness.

Beyond the issue of a diplomatic settlement, Israel's presumed
susceptibility to American influence helped those who opted for an
American connection – Sadat, Saudi Arabia, the more cautious
regime in Syria – justify and legitimate their broader politicoeconomic identification with the United States. Deep down, there
was a psychological vulnerability to America and things American.
With or without America's diplomatic power with Israel, the critical and dominant interests in Saudi Arabia and the Gulf states, in
Egypt, and to a lesser extent in Syria, were overwhelmingly at-
tracted to the United States. They were convinced that an Amer-
ican-organized regional system was their best choice. It is commonplace that this was the case in Egypt and Saudi Arabia. But
Syria too was in this group, less hostile than its rhetoric would
suggest. In this regard the memoirs of both Kissinger and Nixon
are instructive. In Kissinger's memoirs – in which a Manichean
distinction is maintained between "radicals" and "moderates" –
President Asad is given positive marks. After praising Sadat as a
great statesman (forgotten are the days when he considered him a
clown), Kissinger writes of Asad: "Another less significant result
of the autumn of crises [1970] was the accession of Hafez Asad to
power in Syria in November of 1970. Less visionary than Sadat, he
nevertheless gave Syria unprecedented stability and, against the
background of the turbulent history of his people, emerged as a
leader of courage and relative moderation."[38] Nixon, desperately
battling to save his political life in 1974, was still lucid and insightful enough to note the Syrian attitude during his Middle Eastern
trip, and, as the following passage makes clear, to foresee the troubles of the expectations pinned on American power:

> In the Syrian capital of Damascus, the oldest continuously
> inhabited city in the world, American flags were flying for
> the first time in seven years. Everywhere we went large and
> friendly crowds turned out to welcome us, despite the fact
> that our movements and itineraries were given no publicity
> by the Syrian authorities. I viewed this as a measure of the
> people's strong desire for friendship with America, for an
> alternative to the Soviets, and for peace. I noted in my
> diary, "These people want to be friendly with the U.S. and
> it runs right down to the rank and file and it goes to the

fact that they know the Russians. The Americans, of course, may be in that category soon if we are unable to produce on the peace initiatives that we have begun."[39]

What America's (ascribed) diplomatic prowess did was enable those in the Arab world who were psychologically, culturally, and politically inclined toward the United States to conceal (partly from themselves, partly from others) the deeper motivations of their post – October 1973 embrace of the United States to claim that the American connection was a price that had to be paid for a solution of the Palestinian question. If the road to Palestine went through Washington, then America's friends could be forgiven their enthusiasm for things American. This was one way of dealing with what the Egyptian scholar Lewis Awad has described as the "schizophrenia" of the Arab elite's love for America – "Israel's protector" – and their rejection of Israel.[40] But what if the hopes about America's omnipotence were largely the product of wishful thinking on the part of the Arab advocates of the American connection? Then the fundamental ambivalence about the American presence would have to be faced.

The Arab world had long ceased to be culturally autonomous. No political-cultural movement had given it the distance from the outside world that political orders need if they are not to break down and lose their autonomy. The aloofness from the world system given China by a relatively self-contained order and then by the Chinese revolutionaries from 1949 until the early 1970s had no equivalent in Arab history. India's capacity to somehow remain itself while outsiders came and went differed from the situation of the Middle East – an area that had been situated in the path of giants, that had been courted by outsiders, and whose internal defenses faltered in the face of outside temptations.

The Arab world had long seen itself in Western mirrors, judged itself by Western standards. It did so while systematically denying this. America's eruption on the Middle Eastern scene after World War II was initially approved, for, after all, this was a new power: Here was one way one could have the West without the colonialism, the arrogance, the historical baggage associated with the European powers. Historian Bernard Lewis's statement that Arabs refuse to recognize "America as something generically different from Europe, and untainted with the European past"[41] needs to be qualified. Such may have become the outcome in the 1960s and 1970s, for by then the new power had clashed with a growing nationalism and was seen by the end of the 1970s as a rival to the work of Islam. But this was not the case at the end of World War II and in the early 1950s. This is vividly recalled by Mohamed Heikal in a discussion of early phases of the encounter between the United States and the new regime of the Free Officers: "The whole pic-ture of the United States at that time was a glamorous one. Britain and France were fading, hated empires. The Soviet Union was five thousand miles away and the ideology of communism was anathema to the Moslem religion. But America had emerged from World War II richer, more powerful and more appealing than ever . . . Refrigerators, television and all the instruments of the new life seemed to be coming from America. So the United States wore an aura of success and glamour, shining out above the tar-nished failure of the old imperialists, and people were receptive to the idea of the Americans playing a major role in the Middle East."[42]

History, however, took a different turn, and Nasserism clashed with America's designs: Political differences provided a cultural buffer of sorts, kept the United States at bay. The bitterness of the 1967 defeat pushed the Arab world still further from the United States – further than the Arab elite may have wanted. This would be borne out by the turn of events after October, 1973. The success of October enabled the Arab elite to indulge their tastes in alliances, in technology, in models of development – and the American advantage was there for all to see. Americanization and anti-Americanism are two sides of the same coin. The political anti-Americanism displayed in the Arab states and in Iran as the 1970s came to an end was in great measure an expression of the region's rage at itself; it was a display of agony over cultural sur-render. The American push into the region had succeeded all too well. The secular modernized elites, the more cosmopolitan wing of the middle classes and a substantial number of young men and women, had dismantled the defenses of that culture. Its bounda-ries had become dangerously and uncomfortably permeable. Mus-lim fundamentalism – or reassertion, call it what you will – was then summoned, as Joseph Levenson's sensitive analysis of China reminds us, as a psychological device, a self-defense, and a way of bridging the paralyzing split between the Westernized culture of the elite and the popular culture of the masses. The memoirs of the Russian populist Alexander Herzen, in describing the cultural du-alism of the Europe of his time, depict the Arab—Muslim order today as well:

> In the fundamental fact of its everyday life [Western Eu-rope] that its culture is two-fold, lies the organic obstacle

to consistent development. To live in two civilizations, on two levels, in two worlds, at two stages of development, to live not as a whole organism but as one part, while using the other for food and fuel, and to be always talking about liberty and equality is becoming more and more difficult.[43]

To live in two worlds, always talking about self and authenticity (the Arab substitutes for Europe's "liberty and equality"), is becoming more and more difficult. The two worlds in the Arab world were there prior to the October War, as they are in every society. What the new wealth did was encourage and enable the more modern sector in the Arab world to forget the ground on which it stood; it would borrow the language and the trappings of the old world but dispense with its sensibilities and webs of meaning. Fundamentalism symbolized the revolt of the civilization they left behind; it was a desire to close the glaring gap between the claims of authenticity and the realities of everyday life.

In societies of acute cultural dualism, the relatively modernized sectors lay claim to modernity and feel embarrassed about their more backward brethern.[44] Meanwhile, the claim of the more traditional culture is that of orthodoxy and authenticity. Its predominant attitude is hatred toward those who have ceased to be themselves, who gamble, whose women mix freely with men, who feel more comfortable with aliens than they do with their own people. Now the balance of power between these two is the real life-and-death political question. When state power is in the hands of the modernized group, as has traditionally been the case in the modern Middle Eastern state system, war is waged against tradition, belief is steadily undermined, and the so-called backward people internalize the embarrassment about their traditions felt by those who continually trumpet their own modernity and capacity to take on the outside world. But what if the claims of the modern sector become increasingly hollow, their modern management skills are visibly defective and inept, and their dialogue with the outside world turns into an abandonment of national culture? This is where traditions reassert themselves and where the comparative advantage of Islam lies: to be able to assert itself and its uniqueness at a time when technology is seemingly blurring the distinctions between cultures, when models of development tantalize people with promises that in the end they fail to deliver.

We have been witnessing the simultaneous advance of the civilization that technology promised and the determined resistance to it. This has left those engaged and those watching wondering which of the two is more real, more authentic. Wherein lies the truth: Is the process of homogenization winning out over cultural idiosyncrasies and differences, or is the world being suddenly claimed by the past because faith in a successful civilizational model is breaking down and once-defensive cultural outlooks are making a comeback? The easy answer would be to assert one line of reasoning, one reading of history. According to the modern reading, a rational order marches on — as it has since the rise of the European world system — obliterating differences, taming the instinctive and the idiosyncratic in favor of greater predictability and uniformity. A variant of this reading was central to the modernization-of-societies world view that dominated social science and the claims of non-Western rulers a decade ago. According to the theories prevalent then, modernization would act as a universal solvent: The forces of uniformity would prevail, hostile and alien worlds would be understood — in familiar categories, terms, and ways. This, one should note, is common to both liberal and Marxist views of change.

The other reading of history would be to see cultures as far more obstinate than they are depicted by the first view. According to this interpretation, cultures ignore universal messages. They assert themselves by showing people what happens if they cease being themselves in order to enjoin them to remain loyal to who and what they are. Today this interpretation draws power from the evident troubles of Western industrial civilization. The revolt against the West is now armed with the self-doubts of the West. The dominant model, which combined material power, rationality, and freedom of expression, not only is losing some of its grip on non-Westerners but also is challenged at home: by some because it is too squeamish, by others because it is said to have failed to live within ecological bounds, because it has generated profound psychological troubles.

To say that either reading of history wins out is to underestimate humanity's capacity for what Clifford Geertz calls "moral double-bookkeeping."[45] People try to juggle the past and the present: there is around us as much intoxication with machines and gadgets as there is cultural archaeology — people busy trying to revalidate once-discredited traditions and revive once-forgotten symbols. There is both a submission to a dominant culture and a revolt against it. Sometimes the same people do both: They embrace the dominant model for fear of being left behind and denounce it to affirm their uniqueness at the moment that they feel swept by the current.

Fundamentalism and particularism are, then, not riddles at all:

They are a response to the triumph and dynamism of that ascendant civilizational model that began in Europe and of which the United States is today the standard-bearer. The process is illuminated by Immanuel Wallerstein, whose discussion throws light upon the fundamentalism of Muslims, the anguish of that so-called arc of crisis:

> When Western civilization sought to transform itself into civilization pure and simple . . . it was sure that not only God and history were on its side but that all rational men (by which was meant the elites throughout the system, including its periphery) would be on its side as well, at least eventually. Instead what has happened is that everywhere, and more and more, nationalist particularism has been asserting itself. Indeed, if there is any linear equation at all, it is the collaboration of the expansion of capital, the uneven development of the world system, and the claims to differentiation by groups even more integrated into the system — in a dialectical vortex of centripetal and centrifugal forces.[46]

At one point the particularism was expressed in secular nationalist terms. Then fundamentalism took over where pan-Arabism and secular nationalism had failed. Fundamentalism may be too incoherent to govern, but it can topple the world of the elites, shatter their illusions, demonstrate that they have surrendered to the ways of the aliens. Khomeini's appeal no matter how transient — to mass opinion throughout the Arab world, across the deep divide between the Sunni Islam of the majority of Arabs and Iran's Shi'a Islam, across the historical split between Arabs and Persians, underscored the vulnerability of the Arab order. Reduced to its essence, Khomeini's ideology was pure wrath, directed less against dictatorship than against cultural surrender. That is why the expectation of a democratic path in the ayatollah's Islamic republic was an act of reading into Iran Western liberal sensibilities and categories. The new wealth in the region had ruptured its normative order, and greater numbers of men and women were taking to the ways of the outside world.

As the gifted observer Ali Mazrui, has stated, the "barrel of oil" and the "crescent of Islam" were linked and October 1973 represented a resurrection of Islam.[47] But at home, in the Arab states and in Iran, it was clear that the fabric of the civilization was under stress. Extreme Islamic piety and rampant corruption were an unlikely combination; so was the claim to self and authenticity combined with widespread cultural seduction. Having seen the wrath of fundamentalism play itself out in Iran, those people who had only the day before engaged in tradition mongering pulled back. In their own scheme, flouting tradition worked so long as the adversaries were Michel Aflaq and George Habash (both Christians, after all) or the openly secular regime of Abdul Nasser. The new fundamentalism was a more dangerous adversary; it easily pointed out the transgressions of those who had professed their adherence to Islam. The rupture between the traditional ways of the Islamic world and the world of the elite had resulted in acute cultural dualism. The liberal, capitalist West may not openly demand the ideological conversion that Marxism demands, but technology, cultural wares, long and frequent stays in London, Paris, and New York, and the appealing pop culture disseminated by the United States had done their deed. Home was no longer home, so to speak. It is true that Ibn Khaldun had expounded on the virtues of the bedouins: they were "closer to being good than sedentary people," he said, but he had also postulated a condition that the bedouin had to possess: self-sufficiency. Once self-sufficiency is lost, all is lost, and the "Bedouin submits himself to the yoke of the city."[48] Traditions, too, demand their kind of discipline and that was clearly lacking in the new order.

Could it be that these expounders of the virtues of the *turath* were so vulnerable on their own terrain because they were not really traditional at all? Could it be that tradition mongering was carried on so loudly because people had deep down broken with tradition and because tradition had ceased to hold them and that they were left "holding it" (Clifford Geertz's important distinction) without real belief and conviction? Knowing that other ways and other valleys tempt them, people try to tell themselves that they are still at home with their own world. Almost every great upheaval that brings a world close to ruin is immediately preceded by a wave of cultural reassertion, by insistent traditionalism. This is not so much opportunism and hypocrisy – although it includes a dash of it – as much as it is a felt desire to reassure oneself that the ground is solid, that the world is intact.

The people who so devoutly professed their adherence to the *turath* were vulnerable because their world was far more deeply penetrated by Western culture than they wished to admit to themselves or to others. We can see the dilemmas of the standard-bearers of the Saudi era in an essay by Arnold Hottinger:

> The members of the Saudi upper crust who are today earning vast sums are not even in a position to form a unified

group to help exert a stabilizing influence on their country. They regard the kingdom primarily as a kind of money factory. The "homeland" to which they intend to retire sooner or later is more likely to be Texas or California – places where they are already investing their fortunes, have already built luxurious homes and settled the members of their families. It is there that they look toward future stability, not in Saudi Arabia. Many of these people have studied in Texas or California, their youthful memories are there, and it is there that they plan to flee sooner or later from their desert capitals, which their vast but inappropriate projects have turned into places where money is made and spent but where they consider no genuine style of life is possible any longer.[49]

The vast infusion of wealth enabled men (and some women as well) to exit from their austere societies. The great capitals of the West became close and accessible. It was in London and Paris that the freest Arab press was based and it was to these places that men and women in search of cultural freedom journeyed. The phenomenal flight of capital from the Middle East to the West was but the material expression of a wave of cultural escape plaguing the Arab world in particular and beyond it the Third World as a whole. "All over the world," writes V.S. Naipaul in his haunting novel, *A Bend in the River*, "money is in flight. People have scraped the world clean, as clean as an African scrapes his yard, and now they want to run from the dreadful places where they've made their money and find some nice safe country . . . They are frightened of the fire."[50] In no other great story of civilization have the possibilities of exit been so easily available. One could scarcely imagine a viable Japanese recovery in the nineteenth century if the dominant elite of Japan had had the choice of escape that is available to the Arab elite. The Japanese revolution from above worked, because the samurai who accomplished it made a stand for their own world and posed as effective bearers of national culture. The samurai "were men who had been brought up to believe in discipline and firm government, to cultivate martial virtues, to set duties above rights."[51]

None of this could be said of the guardians of order in the Arab states or in the shah's Iran. And that is why the order in Iran crumbled before the ayatollah's austere example and why the conservative regional order built around Saudi Arabia and Iran had such weak foundations in the Arab world. The danger of emptying that important political space, national culture, is that others –

mullahs, radicals, millenarians — will rush to fill it. Where there is a millenarian tendency, as there is in Islam, the failure of practical politics always spawns dreams of resurrection. "Moslems," writes Manfred Halpern, "have been perennially ready for the Mahdi, the messenger of God, who could lead the community in a religio-political leap into immediate fulfillment of all spiritual and material needs."[52] The failure of the dominant order to keep the outside world at bay without falling into the extremes of surrender and xenophobia encourages the latent desire for escape and for totalism.

Thus the resurgence of Islam is a response to the blockage of ideas and the failure of state elites. Nadav Safran's recapitulation of Egyptian political and intellectual history provides an illuminating paradigm that can help explain the drift toward Islamic fundamentalism today. In tracing Egypt's political evolution from the early nineteenth to the mid-twentieth century, Safran identifies liberal and reactionary phases. The strength of the Muslim Brotherhood, which came close to capturing political power, was a response to the failure of liberal nationalism. In the dismal political atmosphere of the 1930s and 1940s, a "romantic, vague, inconsistent, and aggressive" Islamic ideology filled the ideological and political vacuum. During this period, some of the secular nationalists themselves retreated into the fundamentalist fold. Millenarianism spread when the liberal elite failed to live by their own code and when the dominant order seemed blatantly inequitable and compromised.[53]

Recently the noted Egyptian scholar Lewis Awad has echoed Safran's conclusions. He observed that from 1800 onward, the dominant order in Egypt was on the side of progress during phases of achievement and retreated into fundamentalism and mythology during periods of crisis. Thus the order favored change during the times of Muhammad Ali (1805–1842), Ismael (1863–1879), bourgeois nationalism (1919–1936), and Abdul Nasser (1952–1967). Millenarianism prevailed whenever the political order failed. It did so during the reign of Abbas I (1848–1854), from 1882 to the bourgeois revolution of 1919, from 1936 to 1952, and, finally, after the Six Day War.[54]

The analyses of both Safran and Awad deal with Egypt, but their theme goes beyond the Egyptian case. The voice of fundamentalism is so insistent today because moderate revolutions from above have failed and because the world outside has been encroaching on the region. That the world outside is invited in by the region's own elite offers no consolation; it only increases the self-doubts and thus the need for some form of rebellion, for an affirmation of self.

The encroachment of the outside world – really its invitation and purchase – posed for the Arabs the prospect of greater *levantinization* – the process of being an intermediate civilization, being, as a thoughtful young Saudi scholar describes it, "every-man and no-man" at the same time.[55] The levant as an idea, as a system, and as a way of life was once restricted to pockets of the Arab world, to a few cities, to small groups of intellectuals and traders. The urge to import and to mimic is now more widely spread. A conscious kind of Islamization provided protection against the prospects and the costs of being a levantine. One need not be unduly committed to the particularism of civilizations to note the costs and to see the scars of levantine identity; these were perceptively illuminated by Albert Hourani:

> To be a Levantine is to live in two worlds or more at once, without belonging to either; to be able to go through the external forms which indicate the possession of a certain nationality, religion or culture, without actually possessing it. It is no longer to have a standard of values of one's own, not to be able to create but only able to imitate; and so not even to imitate correctly since that also needs a certain originality. It is to belong to no community and to possess nothing of one's own. It reveals itself in lostness, pretentiousness, cynicism and despair.[56]

The determined traditionalization of culture was a response to the displayed forms and mimicry. It was inspired, as all revitalization movements are, by fear that assimilation into alien ways has gone far enough and the usual nostalgia that lives in every vanquished civilization with a long memory for a vanished whole world.

THE RULERS' ISLAM, ISLAM OF THE RULED

Phrases like "the resurgence of Islam" are so powerfully evocative that they make us lose sight of the real struggles that men and societies are engaged in. We think of great crusades, of a powerful desert wind devastating the achievements of progress, of societies being dragged back into the middle ages. But things may not be what they seem. People summon the spirits of the past to help them achieve very precise goals. There is a penetrating passage in Marx that helps explain why we hear from the past precisely at a time of such profound crisis in the Muslim order:

> Men make their own history, but they do not make it just as they please; they do not make it under circumstances chosen by themselves, but under circumstances directly found, given and transmitted from the past. The tradition of all the dead generations weighs like a nightmare on the brain of the living. And just when they seem engaged in revolutionising themselves and things, in creating something entirely new, precisely in such epochs of revolutionary crisis they anxiously conjure up the spirits of the past to their service and borrow from them names, battle slogans and costumes in order to present the new scene of world history in this time-honoured disguise and this borrowed language. Thus Luther donned the mask of the Apostle Paul, the Revolution of 1789 to 1814 draped itself alternately as the Roman Republic and the Roman Empire, and the Revolution of 1848 knew nothing better to do than to parody, in turn, 1789 and the revolutionary tradition of 1793 to 1795. In like manner the beginner who has learnt a new language always translates it back into his mother tongue, but he has assimilated the spirit of the new language and can produce freely in it only when he moves in it without remembering the old and forgets in it his ancestral tongue.[57]

In some cases the spirits are summoned simply because people are trying to find something with which to combat remote, smug, or oppressive state elites. The balance between state and society has been fundamentally disrupted in the Arab–Muslim order. The claims of the state have increased, and so have the resources at its disposal. In previous times, men coexisted with political authority – they made their peace with it so long as it left them alone. Today the state elites wish to turn the world upside down, and the popular culture finds no more effective weapon of resistance than Islam. In Syria and Iraq, narrowly based state elites (the Alawis in the former, the Sunnis in the latter) monopolize power, brandish the symbols of national security, and hoard resources for themselves. Devastating, as they do, other channels of opposition, they leave men with that one thing that the elites cannot monopolize: religious devotion doubling as piety and as a political instrument.

The opponents of the Syrian regime have, as it were, discovered religion, for the men in power and their clan (the Alawis account for ten percent of Syria's population) are of a different breed. To the normal gulf between ruler and ruled have been added historic sectarian differences and suspicions. The tendency of power to seek shelter, to exercise itself in the dark, in small groups, led the Syrian regime into ever-deeper trouble. The insecurity of the man at the helm — itself a rational response to the uncertainty of governing in Syria — led him into greater dependence upon fellow Alawis, a dependence symbolized in his reliance on his brother, Colonel Rifaat al-Asad. Political power presented a traditionally rural, deprived minority with the chance to have its day in power and to hoard wealth. Capricious dictatorship is not a new theme in Syrian history, but this one took on the quality of a grave moral violation, because its perpetrators were of a different breed and because there were so many beneficiaries, so many brothers and cousins anxious to ride the coattails of the group in power.

In the cycle of terror and counterterror between the security apparatus of the regime and the fringe Muslim Brotherhood waged with particular intensity in 1979, the tactics and passions of the true believers in the Brotherhood may have been somewhat extreme, but they served as a vehicle for the resentments of the Sunni majority. The terror displayed the abyss between society and the state. The massacre of more than sixty Alawi cadets in June, 1979, by the duty officer at the Aleppo artillery academy revealed the depth of the hatred. The cadets were no longer the symbol of national security in a sacred fight with Israel but the beneficiaries of a regime of privilege and corruption. The Brotherhood eluded the regime's determination to crush it because it fed off the sympathies of the majority of the population: Its finances came from traditional Sunni merchants; its sympathizers were more than the handful of "extremists" they were said to be in official rhetoric.

We can see the Brotherhood's concerns in an underground publication in October, 1979: President Hafez Asad is a "fox" (in the public imagery the Alawis are devious and conspiratorial), his community a pack of "wolves" known for a history of treachery and collaboration. There are also standard bourgeois themes and moral appeals: the violation of property rights, the sanctity of homes, the honor of women. "It is decency alone," said the Brotherhood, "that prevents us from mentioning those enslaved of our sisters and daughters." Political power had broken all limits, had laid its hands on the wealth and honor, the *'ird,* of others, said the

Brotherhood to the ruler, "so we rebelled for our dignity, for we are Muslims, oh enemy of Islam, . . for the Muslim does not fear and does not grovel . . . we rebelled for our country that you sold cheaply, for our blood that you spilled so callously, for our brothers whom you eliminated in the dungeons of Unity, Freedom and Socialism"[58] [the slogans of the Ba'th party].

A manifesto of the Brotherhood, made public in September, 1979, asks the ruler some questions about "national unity" in Syria:

> How could national unity be realized when the overwhelm-ing majority is enslaved by the minority?

> How could national unity be realized when Rifaat al Asad and his gangsters dominate the army and the regime and monopolize the nation's wealth?

> How could national unity be realized when al sulta [the ruling authority] persists in the corruption of moral prin-ciples, in the subversion of morality and education so as to destroy the spirit of resistance and struggle in future gen-erations? Could national unity be realized by sacrificing the Golan [Heights] and promoting the traitor into a president of the republic?

> If this is what is meant by national unity we refuse it and we call upon all others to refuse and combat it.[59]

Thus Sunni Islam thrives in Syria as a mode of protest against those who have used the power of the state to restratify class rela-tions, to accumulate fortunes unimaginable to those who have to work for a living, to obtain sexual liberties and prerogatives that tantalize and outrage those without them.

A Syrian scholar has analyzed the intersection of religious devo-tion and opposition in a thoughtful unpublished essay. Of the Mus-lim Brotherhood's tactics and of the functions of the mosque, he observes,

> in its strategy to displace the regime, the MBM [the Broth-erhood] has been using the same tactics which were applied by the Muslim guards in Iran to bring down the Shah. The chanting of hymns at dawn and the teaching of religion on the minaret's loudspeakers throughout the day represent an impressive campaign of mass political socialization. For the first time in Islamic history women are invited to the mosques in special sessions to receive Islamic education.

The government has imposed restrictions on the means and times when religious instruction can be given, but it has failed to stop its momentum. Men and women, especially young people, flock to the mosques in increasing numbers in order to pray or to receive Islamic education.

The MBM considers the Alawis to be seceders from Islam, and since it is decreed in the Quran, the Muslim Holy Book, that the blood of seceders shall be upon them, any Muslim who sacrifices his life in carrying out God's order will be a martyr whose place after death is in Heaven.[60]

Likewise Shi'a Islam thrives in Iraq (witness the expulsion of Khomeini once the struggle between Khomeini and the Shah was on), because the one continuity between Iraq under the Hashemites and today's more radical Iraq remains the unequal access to state power that enables the Sunni minority to rule either as a partner of foreign interests, as was the case with the Hashemites, or in the name of revolution, as the military now claims. The forms change, but the world remains the same. In Egypt fundamentalism persists because the political order of the Free Officers has yet to allow the citizenry to enter the political arena. No sooner had the Iranian revolutionaries brought down the Pahlavi dynasty than President Sadat warned against the rise of ayatollahs in Egypt: those who wanted to engage in politics, he insisted, should go to the parliament, those who wanted to engage in religious matters should go to the mosque. There would be no mixing of religious and secular matters in Egypt. Putting aside his statement's doctrinal vulnerability, for classical Islam does not easily accept the separation of politics and religion, Sadat overlooked the emasculation of parliament in his own political system, which has made parliament such a poor rival to the mixture of politics and religion. Were Sadat to offer a viable parliamentary option, there would be a more balanced duel between orderly politics and millenarianism. His failure to do so, part of the broader failure to solve the question of political participation in Arab society, leaves the fundamentalists with ample room for maneuver. Politics has been driven into the mosque and the symbols of opposition have become avowedly religious, because the ruling elites remain bent on monopolizing political power. A young Tunisian — in a relatively modernized, relatively democratic country — put it this way: "There is no other way to hold a meeting except in connection with the mosque, no way to speak out."[61]

For the Arab world, the drama of Iran was the spectacle of men and women in the street making and remaking their own history. Win or lose, they were out there demanding to be counted and heard. All the Arab elite's attempts to say that Iran's troubles were peculiar to that society and to point out the detailed (and legitimate) differences between their own countries and Iran were beside the point. The Arab elite knew, as the guardians of the French ancien régime in 1789 knew that revolutionary ideas spread and that the revolution next door might be a crystal ball in which they could see their own future. Both panacea and plague, the Iranian revolution had to be dealt with psychologically and politically by the neighboring Arab order for reasons long ago spelled out in Burke's masterful statement on the French revolution:

> Formerly, your affairs were your own concern only. We felt for them as men because we were not citizens of France. But when we see the model held up to ourselves, we must feel as Englishmen, and feeling we must provide as Englishmen: Your affairs, in spite of us, are made a part of our interest, so far at least as to keep at a distance your panacea, or your plague. If it be a panacea, we do not want it. We know the consequences of unnecessary physic. If it be a plague, it is such a plague that the precautions of the most severe quarantine ought to be established against it.[62]

The half-hearted attempts at democratization reported, in the aftermath of the Iranian revolution, in Kuwait, Saudi Arabia, and Iraq were part of a frantic attempt to quarantine the Iranian upheaval, to deny the relevance of Iran to the Arab situation. But these measures could only be cosmetic, for at stake was nothing less than the culture's style of authority. The institutions and the habits of mind needed to allow the citizenry to become more than sheer spectators were nowhere to be seen in the Arab–Muslim order. On that score regimes on both the right and the left were equally assailable. Whether they repressed in the name of revolution, in the name of order, or in the name of national security, the results were the same. Nor did the so-called bargain – the denial of political rights in order to obtain some concrete gains – seem to make sense. In the ideology of the hard state, the eggs have to be broken on the deferred promise of the omelet. According to the dogma, men and women get something in return – powerful modern armies that protect them, social welfare, or some other gain. But in the Arab world, Caesar had taken without reciprocating. The brittle states on top had little by way of military victories and socioeconomic achievements to show. To be sure, they had produced a shift in the distribution of world wealth in October, 1973. But this only highlighted the crisis of political authority and gave the struggle over authority a particularly grim dimension.

The crisis of democracy and of authority was no longer the question of political rights granted or denied or of politicians ranting about nationalism or engaged in metaphysical speculations about Arab unity. Access to power now meant phenomenal fortunes — fortunes unimaginable to those located outside the state. The sword had always commanded its share of wealth in the Arab —Muslim world as it has and does elsewhere. Control of the means of destruction had always paid off. Some in the public sector had done reasonably well for themselves under the semisocialist orders of Nasser and the Ba'th. But now the stakes were of far greater magnitude. The returns on other economic endeavors seemed insignificant when compared with the staggering fortunes made by the ruling stratum and by the middlemen who provided the state with weapons and large technological projects. It was difficult to tell where public authority ended and personal plunder began. Even in a world where political power is expected to help itself to wealth, there were limits to public patience. Into the tidy, benign world of the middlemen crept a new force: *hiqd,* resentment, hatred of corruption, a feeling of relative deprivation.

Liberalism, Marxism, and other ideologies are constructs, labels, but resentment is all too human and real. At their best, ideologies still fail to capture reality, to stir emotions. But resentment can be a hurricane. Iran's rebellion and the anguish of the Arab world were fed by resentment, a feeling that the winners had taken too much, that their wealth was all the more difficult to live with because it enabled them to violate established pieties, to do things that ordinary people could not do or get away with. Religious faith and a sense of relative deprivation combined against the new economy of speculation, against the way the windfall society distributed its gains and what those who got the lion's share did with those gains. Woe to him who incurs the wrath of the petty bourgeoisie, writes the Lebanese leader Kamal Junblatt in his political will.[63] The traditional middle class — the artisans, the bazaar merchants, the clerks, those with traditional educations, those living on fixed incomes — summoned God and national culture on their side in a battle that involved the always inseparable domains of interests and values.

The fight over culture and values is never carried out over intangibles and sacred things but rather over power and who will wield it and resources and who will command them. The power to define culture, the permissible, the good is political and economic power. The wrath of the traditionalists, of the middle classes was directed against a powerful new (though classical) triangle that moved the post-1973 outcome: (1) foreign entrepreneurs, with their resources and skills — their access to world markets that dwarfed national capitalism; (2) the local middleman who cuts the red tape at home and moves with remarkable ease abroad; (3) the ruling authority that grants contracts, that buys massive technology, that now more than ever could raise men to new heights of power and foster the growth of new classes if it wished — that could make the lifesavings of a local merchant or of generations of bazaaris trivial in comparison. Nativism became, as it has classically been and will remain, the rallying cry of those who lost out in the boom.

The appeal to national culture was part of the reclamation of the national economy. If foreigners were getting their way with the help of middlemen, it must be because of the fawning devotion of the ruling stratum to things alien; as for the success of middlemen, it must be the product not only of access to court but also of a willingness and capacity to move in the foreigner's universe: to discourse in a foreign language, to move easily in the foreigner's hotels and boardrooms, to allow one's unveiled wife to mix with infidels. Politics and culture intersect, and the only way to break the hold of that triangle on vast national wealth is to break it where it counts: challenge the ruling authority, reclaim the political system in order to perform the twin functions of cultural purification and economic autonomy.[64] Those who lead such a revolt are never those anonymous masses ritually spoken of in radical polemics. They are comparatively better off, they have resources, they are articulate. Of them could be said what Crane Brinton wrote about "revolutionists" in general: they are not "in general afflicted with anything the psychiatrist could be called in about. They were certainly not rifraff, scoundrels, scum of the earth. They were above all *not* worms turning."[65] The temptation to reduce large rebellions and upheavals into theories of psychological unsettledness misses the drama that moves people to take on the power of seemingly awesome military and administrative machines — machines that have very few qualms about liberal rights, that are capable of responding with great zeal and ruthlessness to protect what they have.

That the order seemed to come apart at the seams during a period of relative success and affluence is no riddle at all. As de Tocqueville said, social orders are more likely to be challenged when things are going rather well and when people sense the possibility of improvement than during periods of decline. The post—October 1973 order was unprepared for the contradictions it had brought about. This was a world with a different agenda, all the more so because the dominant order was trying to tone down what had been the legitimating principle in the preceding era: the Arab—Israeli conflict.

The dream of sublimating politics into finance and wealth was short-lived, as was inevitable. Wealth creates dissatisfaction on the part of those who take it for granted, resentment on the part of those who feel that others have more than they do. The simple notion of man as worshipper, man as consumer offered to the region in the aftermath of October 1973 was far more dangerous than was thought: It raised the usual questions of equity and justice and (because wealth had come from the outside and was being spent to acquire stakes in a more glamorous world) of authenticity. In the new situation, a populist strand of Islam offered people a way of attacking inequity without being branded with the stigma of communism or atheism. Against the world of the elite came this way of dissenting while holding onto one's tradition and heritage. Was the smashing of casinos, nightclubs, and gambling spots that cater to the Arab rich and to the wealthy Egyptians during Egypt's food riots of January 1977 an act of Islamic piety or an expression of rage against those who could afford the things denied to the majority?

In a world where the overwhelming majority of people is subjected to severe moral prohibitions and to the grinding demands of material survival, the capacity of the few to get their way generates dangerous strains: Are the inherited values and the established pieties still worthwhile or is the class that violates them in error? Even in a patient society like Egypt things reached the boiling point in January, 1977, and the demonstrators (overwhelmingly young) drew the line for the regime. The official explanation, communist agitation, underlined the gap between the old explanations and the new realities, the flights of the guardians of order into old dogmas and reflexes. More realistic analyses found their way into the official press after the riots were suppressed in a stream of blood and the loss of seventy-nine lives. Egyptian society, observed Lutfi Abdul Azim, a respected editor of *Al Ahram al Iqtisadi,* is full of time bombs: The majority of Egyptians have come to feel like "undesirables" in the new "consumer society." There is a dangerous economic split between the poor majority and the fortunate few. The demonstrators who burned and looted were only one side of the story; the more meaningful one was the "silent majority" that stood by and watched. Why should the average person care, Azim asked, when he hears tales about belly dancers on Pyramid Road earning in one night what would take him several years of toil?[66]

In the rhetoric of the dominant order, the *turath,* the tradition, had been burdened with defending inequality and with fending off egalitarian claims and Marxist groups. President Sadat had consistently used Islam and "authenticity" to battle secular radicals. His prime minister, Abdul Aziz Hijazi, when queried in 1974 about the legitimacy of the new wealth, replied with a verse from the Quran: "Some of you We [God] have placed over others in rank."[67] In 1975 the grand shaykh of al-Azhar Abdul Halim Mahmoud joined the political debate on matters of equity by rendering the judgment in favor of the regime usually rendered by shackled religious institutions: Islam was for private property, discussions of equity are heresy, he who dies without his private property is a martyr. The *fatwas* (learned religious opinions) of the shaykh of al-Azhar on property rights and on Marxism, put together in an extremely shallow book,[68] were an important part of the regime's defense of its economic policies. When his conservative views were contested by others — including some who provided "irreverent" details of the wealth and investments of some of al-Azhar's leading personalities — the regime was quick to note that the shaykh was the "living symbol" of all Muslims and that attacks against him go beyond permissible bounds.[69]

The point of this is that Islam is many things. Those in power who rail against radical Muslim fundamentalists forget that they too mix religion and politics. The quoting of scripture back and forth between those who rule and those who challenge was of course not a matter of piety. Scripture was part of a grubby political process entailing the distribution of wealth and power, the desire of some people to accumulate wealth, and the frustration of others who suspect that the game is rigged. In more secular societies, the scripture is different — it may consist of the myth of private enterprise, the essential oneness of capitalism and freedom or public control of the means of production, the socialist imperative. In political cultures in which the\debate (including the part of the ruling elite) takes on blatantly moral and religious coloring, those on the fringes of power come to phrase their demands and grievances in time-honored categories and precepts that are easily understood and disseminated. The foreign, learned tracts of Marxism are inaccessible and dull and made duller still by those in the

Arab world who translate them literally and rigidly, who ritually parrot their verbiage in small circles of alienated, ineffective intellectuals. In contrast, the popular sermons of Shaykh Abdel Hamid Kishk — a spellbinding Cairene orator whose commentaries cover the entire gamut of social and political issues, such as official corruption, the oil money that should go to liberating al-Aqsa Mosque in Jerusalem but instead goes to European vacations and investments, wild rents, and furnished apartments in Cairo where the wealthy violate public morality — are couched in a familiar and moving idiom.

Our urge to reduce the world to a battle between liberalism and liberalism's stepchild, Western Marxism, has led us to believe that the world has become more and more uniform. But the entry of broad segments of the population into the political process has shattered these assumptions. For when hitherto marginal and dispossessed people came into the political arena, they brought with them their language, their folk ways, and their old memories as well as their new grievances. The facade put up by the more cosmopolitan rulers and the intellectuals cracked. Faced with the local idiom and sensibilities, all ideological constructions seemed thin and contrived. The popular culture was less changed than the modernists had told themselves and others. The Islamic world is no more Islamic today than it was a decade or a quarter century ago. It only seems more so, because mobilization has succeeded in bringing into the political arena classes and individuals traditionally cowed by political authority and convinced that power is the realm of people other than themselves. The invincible leaders of yesterday, so sure that they had the answers, are no longer sure today. Fewer and fewer people in the Muslim world today are convinced that Mustapha Kemal Ataturk, the prime secularizer who served as an example for the shah in Iran and for Abdul Nasser in Egypt, was the genius he was once perceived to be. The Turkish state that led the movement to secularism is now in shambles, its politics a theater for rightist and leftist violence, its parties a pale reflection of one another, its economy a captive of the International Monetary Fund. The cultural price paid by Turkey for this change was immense; the benefits are not easy to see.

Inflation and other complicated economic matters may seem to be beyond the reach of the local mujtahid and of the average member of the urban petty bourgeoisie, but the sophisticated technocrats and economists who man the bureaucracy do not show that much more skills and talent. If we were to take the modernists at face value, the duel between the state and its fundamentalist challengers fight between reason and faith, sustained modern inquiry and dogma. But such is not the case. The tracts of the Muslim Brotherhood on economic matters may strike a skeptical reader as hopelessly out of date, imprecise, and naive. But so do governmental pronouncements. In a detailed study of the economic liberalization in Egypt we found, for example, that the writings of the Muslim Brotherhood were hopelessly theological and simplistic and their views on the "Muslim economy" they would want to build not particularly illuminating.[70] The open-door economy, they insisted, was doomed, for it was an "un-Islamic" economy. One did not have to borrow alien models; Islam had a "total economic system." True prosperity required self-reliance and persistence: The only hope for Egypt was through increased production, and the root cause of nonproductivity was deviation from Islam. Islam alone was capable of increasing productivity, for "it turns labor and work from a routine task to an act of worship."[71] But we found the arguments of the proponents of the open-door economy – the importers who dismantled the tariff system, the representatives of multinationals who insisted that taxes should be done away with and that legislation protecting workers should be scrapped so as to attract foreign investors – equally shallow and simplistic. At a time of intense economic nationalism the world over, the proponents insisted that government intervention is the root of all evil, that a totally free economy – whatever that means – will provide enough income and employment, that the civilized world will come to Egypt's aid through a Carter plan or a new variation on the Marshall Plan. If the polemics of al Daw'a (the organ of the Muslim Brotherhood) were escapist, so too was the world portrayed in the glossy and glib October magazine, which is the regime's mouthpiece. If al Daw'a runs away from reality and toward some imagined pure, just, Islamic economy, October's vision of life – its tantalizing advertisements, the high life it depicts, its society pages – is equally removed from Egyptian realities. One dogma battles another; one form of escape matches another.

Beyond this lies another, broader matter: the quality of the political imagery, the style of authority debated between the dominant order and its challengers. The polemics of Khomeini and the literature of the Muslim Brotherhood in Egypt and Syria are full of holes. But what of the censored official press in the Arab world? Does it fare any better, does it offer more penetrating and living inquiries? The lamentable quality of the secular discourse, its embarrassing subservience to the powers that be, and its demeaning of the truth in favor of flattery and hypocrisy leave all but the most naive and trusting skeptical about the claims of the state, dubious about what they read, vulnerable to rumors and messianic calls.

Both the dominant order and its challengers ask people to sus-pend disbelief. The men in power do not offer more open, honest, empirical discussions of social problems than their messianic chal-lengers. They offer the citizenry only faith. If faith is all it takes, then inherited religious dogmas have a chance, for they meet the claims of the state on the religious dogmas' own terrain.

From a distance, some of the guardians of order in the Arab and Muslim states appear modern, secular, rational, reformist, what-ever the labels may be. This was the cultivated image of the shah of Iran; this has been the overwhelming impression of a Sadat or of the Tunisian Habib Bourguiba; this is the impression these men wanted to create in that part of the world whose approval they sought and whose trappings they admired. But are these men really modern men: Are they as different at home from their fundamen-talist challengers as it is presumed in the West? Or do these men show a different dimension of themselves at home, a more dictato-rial, more superstitious one, with the result that the political cul-ture suffers the ailments and limitations of tradition yet without the webs of meaning that softened it and made it bearable? We know that the Shi'a imam in Iran or the Supreme Guide of the Muslim Brotherhood claim that their deeds are inspired by divine revelation, that they carry out God's will, and that disobedience to them amounts to waging war against God's design. But the secular rulers, the men who tell us how modern they are, also put forth claims that amount to divine inspiration. "I am not entirely alone," said the shah to an interviewer, " . . . I am accompanied by a force others can not see. My mystical force. And then I get mes-sages. Religious messages . . . I believe in God, in the fact of having been chosen by God to accomplish a mission. My visions were miracles that saved the country. My reign has saved the country . . . "[72] Sadat too has claimed divine inspiration. In his reconstruction of his life's events − all the way from escaping drowning as a child to his "mission" to Jerusalem in November, 1977 − he cultivates a sense of destiny and divine guidance: He is saved from certain death; he survives an era of turmoil and mad-ness (the Nasserist phase) largely through his "faith"; then he sees his way to a "sacred mission" to spread the gospel of love and brotherhood. "This is the story of my life," he writes in the pro-logue to his autobiography, "which is at the same time the story of Egypt since 1918 − for so destiny has decreed."[73] And short of di-vine inspiration, the presidency-for-life of a "modern" man like

Bourguiba is clearly at odds with his claims to being a "new" man: Even when ailing, he remained the supreme source of authority.

The shackling of society at the behest of the exalted leaders had confirmed the traditional style of authority; the modern veneer given that leadership, either through its command of a foreign language or through the steady cultivation of a progressive image was put on more for export than for home consumption. At home the leadership continued to relegate the citizenry to a marginal place. The infallible leader was but an extension into today's world of the infallible imam (as in Shi'a thought), the official governmental line an extension of religious orthodoxy (as in Sunni orthodoxy). The Egyptian scholar Hassan Hanafi has interpreted this phenomenon in an essay that helps rehabilitate the question of political democracy in the Arab world and restore it to its rightful place. In considering the question of political authority and liberty in the Arab world — "our thousand years crisis," as he calls it — Hanafi connects the orthodox religious view of the world as a reflection of God's will with the dominant style of political authority:

> From such a static view of the world issued the idea of the Only Leader (al Za'im al awhad), the Grand Saviour, the Faithful President, the Divinely Inspired One, the Teacher who commands to be obeyed, who expresses the interests of all the people, who embodies all, who borrowed all the characteristics of God in knowledge and ability, who hears and observes everything, who pronounces on every occasion either directly or through the channels of censorship and communication. As a result, there is no longer any difference between Sunni thought which emphasized institutions and Shi'a thought which focuses on the Infallible Imam who will fill the earth with justice as it had been dominated by oppression.[74]

The equating of opposition and religious unbelief and of the dominant order and orthodoxy is an old political stratagem. While it persists, both the rulers and their opponents will tax the *turath* with their claims: the rulers with demands for total obedience, for religious vindication of what has been done in this grubby world; their opponents with a vision of a successful order that makes today's necessities and shortcuts look like treason and more compromise. The struggle becomes all the more difficult, for once religious orthodoxy is called upon to sustain political authority there is a natural urge on the part of those pushed out of the world of power to claim that they too wish to re-create God's world and to purify the religious heritage.

The task of what one Arab analyst calls the "dissociation" of religious and political authority remains: It is a task that Arab—
Muslim societies are yet to face up to candidly.[75] Because the
realm of politics and human affairs is never clear, it is simplistic to
say, as Arab radicals are prone to say, that people have to destroy
their past and do away with historical forms and inhibitions. The
disjunction between what people say and what they do is always
present; change is introduced in spurts. The modest, grubby domain of politics must be distinguished, to the extent possible, from
God's realm, lest the former become unduly messianic and the
latter unduly contaminated. This has more to do with the quality
of what political man does than with the inhibitions and injunc-
tions of classical scripture.

So far the attempt has been avoided not only by the conservative
dominant interests but also by those who claimed to represent the
new politics. Of the latter regimes, the writer just cited observes:
"Instead of confronting *al Salafiyya* [the dominant religious orth-
odoxy] they turned it, whenever in power, into an instrument and
a pillar for their power. Thus the ideology of the Religious Institution and a pillar for their power. Thus the ideology of the Religious
Institution became the ideology of the rulers — even the revolutionary ones among them."[76] The task of distinguishing the two
will leave the dominant order without the crutch of religion, and
that is why the men in power have refrained from such an undertaking. But in the long run it will tone down messianic expectations, it will remove from the push and pull of political life the expectation that some perfect utopia can be resurrected, and
perhaps it will enable societies made up of Christians, Shi'a,
Sunnis, Alawis to arrive at a modicum of national unity. It may be
useful in the short run to unleash Islam against Marxism, but what
will this do to a society with a substantial Coptic minority? Sadat's
war against *al mabadi al mustwarda* (the imported doctrines)
can backfire, as the recurring strife between Muslim fundamentalists and Copts shows. In the absence of a more secular orientation,
the prospects for any measure of unity in Syria between the
Alawis — who are considered seceders from Islam by orthodox
Muslims — and the Sunnis must be poor at best.

Likewise, Saudi Arabia's Wahhabi heritage, a memory from its
simpler, more pristine past, may enable the Saudis to play up their
fidelity to tradition, their role as bearers of Islam's original simplicity, their homeland as site of its initial triumphs. But this too can
backfire. By the vision of original Wahhabism, much of today's
Saudi Arabia — its wealth, the ways of its young men and women,
its friendship with infidel powers — represents a compromised,

hopelessly corrupt society. Furthermore, what does Wahhabi or-thodoxy have to say about those who inhabit the Arab world but belong to other sects (Shi'a, Druze) or to other religions — specifi-cally, Christian Arabs? The Saudi call for a single Islam may be an elegant variation upon the theme of consensus that they push in inter-Arab circles. But whose Islam would prevail? Whose sense of the right and the just? Even political stability — not a particularly exalted goal — will remain elusive so long as the men in power summon ghosts whose fury they underestimate and misjudge.

More than half a century ago, Ali Abdel Raziq, a young Azhar-educated judge, had the daring and insight to publish a book that openly called for the separation of religion and state, that stated that Islam was a spiritual – ethical construct that had nothing to do with political matters. According to Raziq, the mixing of poli-tics and religion was the deed of the caliphs who governed like any other mortals but hid behind religious justifications. In reality, the caliphate had nothing to do with religion: It was a secular, admin-istrative institution of men who usurped power in the way men normally acquire political power. The sooner Muslims understood this the better: Faith would then become strictly faith, politics would be what politics have always been about — the exercise of power, the governing of people and goods.[77] It is sad — at least for a secularist — that the simple case made by Abdel Raziq is yet to be learned, that people remain tied to old chains, doomed to repeat the old themes and to resort to the old lines of escape.

The Islamic state that tantalizes the true believers and frightens those in the West who worry about the receding of civilization is a memory that makes the present order look hopelessly compro-mised. No one knows what an Islamic state would or would not do, would or would not look like. Memory may imagine and resur-rect — on paper, in sermons, in the tracts of the true believers — a world that was once whole and autonomous. But past orders cannot be resurrected. Ideas and systems — liberal, Marxist, Muslim, whatever — become a cover for power, an apology for decay. Behind the labels lurk the struggle for power and the fears and ambitions of men. Reality devours the scheme, and people are left insisting that it was betrayed or disfigured only by greed or in-competence. Or they are left using the forms of a particular civili-zation — its methods of punishment, its sacred words, its outward displays of devotion — as a smokescreen behind which they engage in sordid or banal matters. Then the fight begins anew over the symbols themselves. What was presented as a solution becomes a new battleground.

Where is the true Islam — in Khomeini's view of things or in Sadat's, in Saudi Arabia or in Qaddafi's Libya? Radical-fundamentalist Islam is one form; bourgeois Islam is another; reactionary Islam is yet another. Some read socialism into Islam. They insist that their radical economic policies can be found in this or that scripture, in the record of this or that caliph, in this or that *hadith* (saying of the Prophet), but their adversaries find in the same Islam high regard for private property and inequality. The Muslim Brotherhood condemns the Egyptian treaty with Israel, but al-Azhar, Egypt's and the Muslim world's most distinguished institution of Islamic learning, gives its approval to the treaty as the opinion of Islam. "The ulama of al Azhar," we are told in an official opinion, "believe that the Egyptian — Israeli treaty is in harmony with Islamic law. It was concluded from a position of strength after the battle of the *jihad* and the victory realized by Egypt on the tenth of Ramadan of the Year 1393 [October 6, 1973]." And to show how flexible traditions can be, al-Azhar found a precedent for the Egyptian — Israeli accord in the Prophet's diplomacy and conduct of war and peace and the treaty he concluded in 628 — the Hudabiyah Treaty — with the clan that then controlled Mecca.[78] Once again the question arises: Where is the opinion of Islam — in the tracts of the Muslim Brotherhood or the rulings of al-Azhar? There is no happy conclusion to the drama of politics, no shortcut to justice.

THE WAYS OF THE ANCESTORS, THE WAYS OF THE WORLD

The quoting of scripture can lend courage when courage is needed for difficult undertakings; it can connect people and societies to their origins and remind them of the path they have traversed. For as we were long told by Edmund Burke, a society wrenched away from its past and its roots may be a society without a future. Wholesale indictment of a political order and open warfare against a society's history may be polemically elegant but they can turn into a nightmare: "No one generation could link with the other. Men would become little better than the flies of a summer."[79] But here is to be found a warning: Fidelity to the past and a connection with it must be honestly felt. One cannot simultaneously bulldoze the past (as so many of the wealthy oil states have done) and claim honesty to it. The huge construction projects reveal, if anything, a broken connection with the society's world and history, a desire to

{ 193 }

obliterate and forget, a contempt for the past. In this frenzied world, people have indeed become "summer flies," and some have become vultures. Caught between insistent trumpeting of tradition and heritage on the one hand and open and real violations of the past and the traditional on the other, societies can push the gap between reality and symbols beyond tolerable proportions.

The great Iranian upheaval, in whose shadow discussions of Islam and restoration will go on for some time, will eventually be seen as an internal affair that is bound by political expediency. But the Arab dilemmas explored here will persist, as all dilemmas do. The Iranian revolution burst on the scene with Khomeini claiming that the final victory of Iran's Islamic revolution will be on the day when Islam comes to rule the whole world. That was the promise of the Bolsheviks as well, whose revolution ended only when the world revolution and socialist internationalism won out. But just as the Bolsheviks came to realize that revolutionary happiness cannot be exported and to settle for socialism in one country, Iran's Islamic revolution will have to make its stand at home. There was a great deal of insight in Stalin's criticism of Trotsky that the theory of permanent revolution was a theory of "permanent hopelessness."[80] Revolutions must come to terms with the world if they are not to degenerate into hopelessness and incoherence. The test of Iran's revolution will be the cold one of performance: whether it can close the gap between those Iranians long swept away by secular disaffection and the rest of the populace, whether it can run an economy, restore Iran's agricultural capacity, and so forth. All sorts of doctrinal justifications can, of course, be found for this coming to terms with the world. Like the Bolsheviks, the Iranian revolutionaries can claim, as they began to claim a year or so after their triumph, that the best way to export their revolution is by example: Build a just Islamic society and others will have to emulate it.[81]

During what passed for the liberal age in the Arab–Muslim world, the liberals searched for the West's success and ended up importing its disembodied forms and pretensions, alienated from their habitat, and, when things really mattered, betraying their own principles. In Marxist movements and groups, sterile molds and the usual phrases about the "proletarian revolution" and the "petty bourgeois" failed to capture the predicament of that world; that is why there is no living Marxism in the Arab world. Now the traditionalists insist that they have the proper remedy: Islam, the *turath,* the ways of the ancestors. They say nothing about what they intend to do with young men and women who have seen other

{ 194 }

ways and who do not wish to return to some imagined pure tradition. The discourse of the traditionalists is hopelessly simple in its
assertion that the tradition lives and that there is an Islamic way of
education, of income distribution, of government. It has yet to face
up to the change that has swept the Muslim world.

The people who surrender to the ancestors are, strictly speaking, surrendering to strangers. Between those branded as followers of Western models (either liberal or Marxist) and those insisting on the ways of the ancestors, the fight should be carried out
with mirrors. Both want a world with preconceived models; both
want to spare men and women the agony of choice and of experience. Authenticity can be as much an escape as dependence and
mimicry can be. Joined together, as they often are in the Arab
world, they tell us that a civilization has ceased to work. The point
is thoughtfully made by the Egyptian Ghali Shukri in an attack
against the polemics of authenticity: Despite their seeming opposition, the two views — the one that sees salvation in return to Arab
— Islamic or Phoenician or pharaonic roots and the one that sees it
in escape to European or American civilization — converge. Both
abandon present reality in favor of a deal offered either by the
strangers or the ancestors. In this way they forfeit the opportunity
to learn from both strangers and ancestors. Both created their own
models.[82]

None of the talk about authenticity or ancestors has given the
Arab world the self-confidence to sort out its relationship to the
West or to choose among the ideas, technologies, and development
models tantalizingly held before it and come up with a viable mix.
Side by side with the talk of autonomy and authenticity has been a
paralyzing vulnerability to the wares of the West that manifests itself in the urge to buy the latest inappropriate technology, the
largest kinds of technical projects. An arid technicalism has swept
the region — concrete and steel, prefabs, nuclear power, construction projects, financial deals, talks of financial deals, and so
forth: the West devoid of the social system that gave rise to it, the
West without its ideas, its art, its books, its counterculture.

In the affluent Arab states, as in Iran under the shah, a merger
has taken place between the technology of the Occident — its
harsh side, its salesmen, its brutal empiricism — and the despotism
and tribalism of Near Eastern traditions. There is no place in such
a hybrid for books, for artisans, for folk culture, for ideas — no
honest encounter with the discontents of civilization. Once upon a
time, the Orient — to use that overused artificial distinction between Orient and Occident — prided itself on its spiritualism and

divided the world into a spiritual East and a materialist West. Nowhere is the idea of the materialist West as firmly entrenched as it
is in the Arab world today. The real West is a mix of ideas and
techniques, technologies and social institutions; the other West —
the one bought by Arabs and others — is dry and oppressive and
ultimately a weak cardboard structure. The "Asian Germany"
that the Shah wanted to turn Iran into (as he described it) epitomized the dream and its fate. It was decreed by administrative fiat
that traditions be obliterated, that "embarrassing" popular celebrations be banned and forgotten. The dark side of Iran had to be
expunged and the gadgets and machines had to be displayed as an
alibi for civilization.

No sooner had Iran collapsed than the tired theme was replayed
in Iraq with all the talk about a rising regional power, all the statistics about capabilities and achievements. Consider the following
report about Iraq's quest for modernization, which highlights the
mixture of technology and regressive social structure. The country bent upon entering the nuclear age, we are told in this report,
strictly regulates the usage of privately owned typewriters. Only
friends of the government are given licenses to acquire them.
Typewriters smack of political freedom, of pamphlets and agitation. What is allowed is a wide range of luxury goods from the
West: "perfume from France, clothes from Italy, and toys from
the U.S." All is stocked in government-owned stores and made
available to the new elite:

> Life for this new educated elite can be sweet indeed, pro-
> vided mouths are kept shut and fingers don't pound type-
> writers. In Baghdad, Iraq Stores Co., a downtown depart-
> ment store, looks like Christmas-time as crowds of affluent
> young Iraqis shop for everything from Chanel No. 5 to bas-
> ketballs endorsed by Bob Cousy, the Boston Celtics player
> of the 1950's.

> For the children of this elite there is aisle upon aisle of
> clothes and toys. The store's director explains that a spe-
> cial blue-ribbon committee made up of representatives of
> all the important ministries meets once a week to decide
> which clothes and toys should be imported from the West.
> "The needs of the children come first, he says.[83]

Anything for the children: anything, of course, but typewriters
and political freedom. For them the West is to be bought without
its anguish, its troubles, its creativity, its cultural freedom. We

shall provide the glamor of the world for them, but we shall spare them the path that the West took to get it. We shall not dwell on thought and dissent, but there are plenty of Pierre Cardin fashions — proof that a once-backward world has finally arrived at modernity.

Writing at a time when illusions were easier to entertain, the French scholar Jacques Berque expressed a wish for a marginal civilization to combine advanced technology and its own social structure and come up with something better, not only for itself but also for others:

> Whereas in so many more "advanced" countries the machine dissociates man from nature and imprisons him far from the green shade of the tree of life, in the gloomy landscapes of artificiality, the Arab can, through the machine, recover nature and become natural again. Even the very suddenness of his contemporary history may serve him, after having burdened him; it has not left him time to forget his unifying mission. He has overlept our bourgeois centuries. To the modern world, divided and hard pressed, the beneficiary and victim of analysis, he will be a harbinger of freshness through the completeness of his attitude to life.[84]

The statement was pure sentimentalism when it was written; it is more obviously so now. It was one of those illusions that outsiders come to fix onto a region they adopt — that not only will it find its own way but that it will help others as well. We may of course want to enquire why such illusions are entertained and expressed, but that is another tale. What matters is that they are expressed and then imported by the people to whom they refer. Nature imitates art and such illusions become part of national self-delusions. The "overleaping of bourgeois centuries" foreseen by Berque did not and could not happen. The result was the hybrid of cultural and technological mimicry with regressive social institutions, the lack of fit between people's ideas and habits on one side and their machines on the other.

Less than two decades after Berque made his prognosis, he came face to face with a different reality. This time, in an interview in 1980, he lamented the demise of "the Orient," "the East." Orientalism, he observed, was over, because the East was no longer distinctive. The Muslim world had entered "the game," he said; It now plays it just like the others do. Berque was baffled; his East had failed him and become occidentalized.[85]

But just as his early image of overleaping bourgeois centuries was wrong, Berque's latter assessment is mistaken as well. "Normalization" too — his term — is illusory, another easy way out. The problem has to do with the mixture of hyperauthenticity on the one hand and civilizational vulnerability on the other. Underneath the hyperauthenticity there is a vulnerability to outside models that must be candidly faced. Like all prohibitions and denials, this vulnerability grows more powerful and obsessive the more it is denied and covered up with exaggerated cultural rebellions and exaggerated claims to radicalism.

When the liberal generation in the Arab world pondered the great issues facing them, they did it against the background of total confidence — their own and the West's — in the Western model. Likewise, the Marxists who wrote the trenchant tracts were sure that Marxism blew away historical inadequacies, ethnic biases, and created a new man. Today these illusions are denied to those who engage in political struggles and those who interpret them from a safe distance. We ponder these questions at a time of great uncertainty in the West itself; we also do so at a time when the excesses of what passed for Marxist revolutions — Vietnam, Cambodia — have demonstrated the thin line between the drive for ideological purity and genocide.

The failures of the Arab order have been many, and I have elaborated them (repeatedly and unfairly, it may be said) without a conviction of a finished model that makes things work, of an alchemy that makes people and societies behave justly or rationally.

Caught in the midst of a massive historic crisis, buffeted by powerful outside forces that have made their world pivotal and exposed, the Arabs have fallen back on the symbols and weapons they know best: their religious identity. The skeptic may call this illusion and frustration; those bigoted in favor of Western civilization will dismiss it as a revolt against modernity, a return to the middle ages, as evidence (in the words of the *Wall Street Journal*) of "barbarism." "Civilization," it lamented in an editorial in the aftermath of Iran, is "receding before our eyes" because of "the decline of the Western powers that spread those ideas to begin with."[86]

But history is not the domain of judgement. It is easy to judge but hard to understand the ghosts with which people and societies battle, the wounds and memories that drive them to do what they do. Even if we disagree with people's choice of allegiance, we must understand the reasons for their choice, the odds they fight against, the range of alternatives open to them. The renaissance of civilizations is used as a weapon because so many in the Muslim world and the Third World as a whole feel that they live in a world constructed and maintained by others. They constantly feel judged, scrutinized: Human rights campaigns point out their brutality; successful and sophisticated media put them and their methods of punishment, the way they treat one another, on display. A more energetic Occident plays havoc with their sensibilities, gets more done, even recovers their own history for them. "All that I know of our history and the history of the Indian Ocean," laments Salim, a character in V. S. Naipaul's *A Bend in the River*, "I have got from books written by Europeans. If I say that our Arabs in their time were great adventurers and writers; that our sailors gave the Mediterranean the lateen sail that made the discovery of the Americas possible; that an Indian pilot led Vasco de Gama from East Africa to Calicut; that the very word *cheque* was first used by our Persian Merchants – if I say these things it is because I have got them from European books. They formed no part of our knowledge or pride. Without Europeans, I feel, all our past would have been washed away . . . "[87]

To deal with the predicament of their place in the world, the losers in the world system have alternated between the quest for the Occident's power and success and the desire to retreat to their own universe, to try to find their own values, to rebel and say no to those who judge and penetrate. Entry into that alien, glamorous world has proven as difficult as return; hence the incoherence and breakdown of so many Third World societies.

The renaissance of civilization may be a mode of resistance, but only "up to the point that the detour becomes the journey."[88] The resurrection of Islam puts before Muslims the solution of their own tradition, and if that helps them conquer some of the self-contempt that colonized people feel in the modern world, then it must be seen as a positive development. What people who profess to be Muslims will do with the solution, how they will interpret that tradition, remains to be seen. "The quality of a faith," writes V. S. Naipaul, "is not a constant; it depends on the quality of the men who profess it."[89] Imitating the relative reticence of secular ideologies, great religious orders will have to be more modest in their claims, less ambitious in their search for purity, more willing to tread carefully, for there are far too many mines and far too much skepticism.

A Japanese critic observed that my usage of the terms "fundamentalist" and "fundamentalism" to describe the kind of Muslim sensibility illuminated above was misleading. Why not, he asked, use the terms "nativist" and "nativism"?

> What is a nativist? He is a man who sticks to the perception of the world lost. To him the whole world should be in the Arab world, instead of the Arab world in the whole world. To him the Arab world must be the self-completed world. It is a great pain to every people who had once lived in a self-completed world to admit that their world is nothing other than a small part of the whole world . . .

> The opening of Japan to the outside world was done in 1868. I have never lived in Japan when Japan was the whole world to the Japanese. But still I am sharing this nativist's sorrow. This sorrow was conveyed from father to son, then to grandson.[90]

There is in this statement an invitation to the Arabs to accept that theirs is no longer a self-completed world. To it might be added the consolation that few people, if any, live in "self-completed" worlds any longer, that "we" and "they" alike have been dragged into a world inhabited by others, that we must hear and honor other claims, that our will and our material interests must come up against those of others.

At the root of the nativist view of the world is a utopia — a memory of a world that once was that can be adorned, worked over, and embellished to suit current needs. In the modern world, utopias can serve as correctives, as antidotes to cynicism, as sources of inspiration. But utopias can be pushed too far. Our imagined utopias turn out to be the source of much of our misery: We never quite approximate them, and we feel all the more diminished for failing to replicate the glories of our ancestors or the perfection of our plans.

Notes

ɷɑɾ

Translations of Arabic titles are my own.

Introduction

1 Clifford Geertz, *The Interpretation of Cultures* (New York: Basic Books, 1973), p. 23.

2 Jihad al-Khazin, in *al Sharq al Awsat*, March 7, 1980.

3 See Bernard Lewis's *History: Remembered, Recovered, Invented* (Princeton: Princeton University Press, 1975), pp. 67–69.

4 T. E. Lawrence, *Seven Pillars of Wisdom* (New York: Penguin, 1962), p. 42.

5 Malcolm Kerr, *The Arab Cold War* (New York: Oxford University Press, 1971), p. v.

6 Jubran al Tueni, in *al-Nahar al Arabi wa al Duwli*, January 13, 1980.

7 Michel al-Hayek, "The Seventies of Lebanon, the Eighties of the Arabs," *al Nahar al Arabi wa al Dawli*, January 13, 1980.

8 Bernard Lewis, "The Palestinians and the PLO," *Commentary*, January, 1975, pp. 41–42.

9 Fouad Ajami, "A Malady in the Mideast," *The New York Times*, December 27, 1978, p. 23.

10 Abdallah Laroui, *The Crisis of the Arab Intellectual* (Berkeley: University of California Press, 1976), pp. vii–viii.

11 Dunstan Wai, "Revolution, Rhetoric, and Reality in the Sudan," *Journal of Modern African Studies* 17, 1 (1979): 71.

12 Claude Levi-Strauss, *Tristes Tropiques* (New York: Atheneum, 1974), pp. 401, 403–404.

13 Michel Foucault, *The History of Sexuality*, Vol. 1, *An Introduction* (New York, Vintage, 1978), p. 95–96.

14 Michael Oakeshott, *Experience and Its Modes* (Cambridge: Cambridge University Press, 1966), pp. 107–108.

15 Oriana Fallaci, "An Interview with Col. Muammar el Qaddafi of Libya," *The New York Times Magazine*, December 16, 1979, p. 128.

16 Levi-Strauss, *Tristes Tropiques*, p. 405.

17 Franz Kafka, in *The Great Wall of China* (New York: Schocken Books, 1946), pp. 160–161.

18 Saad Ibrahim, *Itijahat al Rai'al 'Am al-Arabi Nahwa Massalat al Wahda* [The Attitudes of Arab Public Opinion on the Question of Unity] (Beirut, 1980), p. 75. This is the report of a team of Arab social scientists whose effort, carried out in ten Arab states, was to determine attributes toward pan-Arabism, Arab economic integration, and related matters.

NOTES

1. One's World As It Really Is

1 Abdallah Laroui, "The Arab Revolution Between Awareness and Reality," *Mawaqif* 10 (July – August 1970): 138.
2 The Center of Political and Strategic Studies of al-Ahran, *Watha'ig Abdel Nasser* [The Documents of Abdul Nasser], vol. 1 (Cairo, 1973), p. 226.
3 Adonis, "Introduction," in *Mawaqif* 1 (October – November 1968): 4. Adonis is the pen name of the Syrian writer Ali Ahmad Said.
4 Alexis de Tocqueville, *The Old Regime and the French Revolution* (Garden City, N. Y.: Doubleday, 1955), p. 147.
5 In *Sources of Chinese Tradition,* ed. William Theodore de Bary, et al. (Garden City, N.Y.: Doubleday, 1955), pp. 147, 164.
6 Michel Aflaq, *Nuqtat al Bidaya* (Beirut, 1971). This is a collection of Aflaq's post-1967 statements.
7 Halim Barakat, "Alienation and Revolution in Arab Life," *Mawaqif* 5 (July – August 1969): 38 – 39.
8 Zaki Neguib Mahmud, *Tajdid al Fikr al Arabi* [The Renewal of Arab Thought] (Beirut, 1971). See also his essay in *Mawaqif* 1 (October – November 1968): 5 – 14.
9 Marshall Hodgson, *The Venture of Islam,* vol. 2 (Chicago: University of Chicago Press, 1974), pp. 194 – 195.
10 Bassam Tibbi, "On Contemporary Arab Thought: Descriptive Writing and Revolutionary Writing," *Mawaqif* 3 (March – April 1969): 96.
11 Ibid.
12 Adonis, "The Problems of Literature and the Intelligentsia," *Al Adab* 6 (June 1968): 4 – 5.
13 Ibid.
14 Adonis, "Introduction," in *Mawaqif* 2 (January – February 1969): 3 – 4.
15 Sadeq al-Azm, *Al Naqd al Dhati Ba'd al Hazima* [Self-Criticism after the Defeat] Beirut, 1968).
16 Malcolm Kerr, *The Arab Cold War* (London: Oxford University Press, 1971), p. 135.
17 Azm, *Self-Criticism after the Defeat,* p. 58.
18 Ibid., p. 133.
19 Ibid., p. 112.
20 Ibid., pp. 118 – 119.
21 Adonis, "Introduction," *Mawaqif* 4 (May – June 1969): 3 – 4.
22 Abdullah al-Qusaymi, "So that Harun al Rashid Would Not Return," *Mawaqif* 1 (October – November 1968): 24 – 40.
23 Taha Husayn, *Mustaqbal al thaqafa fi misr* [The Future of Education in Egypt] (Cairo, 1938): pp. 18 – 19.
24 Sami al-Jundi, *Arab wa Yahud* [Arabs and Jews] (Beirut, 1968); *Sadiqi Ilyas* [My Friend Ilyas] (Beirut, 1969); *Al Ba'th* [The Ba'th] (Beirut, 1969); *Athadda wa Attahim* [I Challenge and I Accuse] (Beirut, 1969).
25 *Al Watha'iq al Arabiyah,* 1967, pp. 690 – 692.
26 Jundi, *Al Ba'th,* p. 10.
27 Clifford Geertz, "After the Revolution: The Fate of Nationalism in the New States," in *The Interpretation of Cultures* (New York: Basic Books, 1973), p. 235.
28 Jundi, *Al Ba'th,* p. 160.

NOTES

29 Ibid., p. 35.
30 Ibid., pp. 144 – 145.
31 Ibid., p. 157.
32 Ibid., pp. 17 – 18.
33 Jundi, *Arab wa Yahud*, pp. 40 – 47.
34 Ibid., p. 43.
35 Ibid., p. 44.
36 Ibid., p. 55.
37 Albert Camus, *The Rebel* (New York: Vintage Books, 1956), p. 150.
38 Jundi, *Athadda Wa Attahim*, pp. 56 – 57.
39 Jundi, *Arab Wa Yahud*, p. 181.
40 Ibid., p. 180.
41 Jundi, *Sadiqi Ilyas*, p. 86.
42 Nadim Bitar, *Min al Naksa ila al-Thawra* [From Setback to Revolution] (Beirut, 1968); Sadeq al Azm, *Naqd al Fikr al Dini* [Criticism of Religious Thought] (Beirut, 1969).
43 See Elie Kedourie's essay, "Religion and Secular Nationalism in the Arab World," in A. L. Utovich, ed., *The Middle East: Oil, Conflict, and Hope* (Lexington, Mass.: Lexington Books, 1976), pp. 181 – 194.
44 Muhammad Jalal Kishk, *Al Naksa wa al Ghazw al Fikri* [The Setback and Cultural Invasion] (Beirut, 1969); and *Al Ghazw a Fikri* [Cultural Invasion] (Kuwait, 1967). See also *Al Marksiyah wa al Ghazw al Fikri* [Marxism and Cultural Invasion] (Cairo, 1965); *Al Qawmiyah Wa al Ghazw al Fikri* [Nationalism and Cultural Invasion], (Beirut, 1970).
45 Kishk, *Al Marksiyah*, p. 42.
46 Ibid., p. 41.
47 Ibid., p. 88.
48 Kishk, *Al Qawmiyah*, p. 67.
49 Ibid., p. 167.
50 Clifford Geertz, *Islam Observed* (New Haven: Yale University Press, 1968), p. 64.
51 For a perceptive interpretation of the role of Islam in "revolutionary" Algeria, see Ernest Gellner, "The Unknown Apollo of Biskra: The Social Base of Algerian Puritanism," in *Government and Opposition* 9, 3 (Summer 1974): 277 – 310.
52 Kishk, *Al Qawimayah*, p. 233.
53 Daniel Lerner, *The Passing of Traditional Society* (New York: The Free Press, 1958).
54 Islamic fundamentalism, like any other system of beliefs, can lend itself to a variety of interpretations. Imaginative people can read virtually anything they want into a particular tradition. Both the Muslim Brotherhood and King Hassan of Morocco would staunchly defend their adherence to the Quran and the strictures of Islam. Which of the two is more authentically Islamic? The question is the stuff of which bloody struggles are made.
55 Wilfred Cantwell Smith, *Islam in Modern History* (New York: Mentor Books), p. 161.
56 As reproduced in Sa'd Jumah's *Al Mu'amarah Wa Ma'rakat al Masir* [The Conspiracy and the Battle of Destiny] (Beirut, 1968), pp. 239 – 240.
57 Salah al Din al Munajjid, *Amidat al Nakba* [The Pillars of the Disaster] (Beirut, 1967), p. 40.
58 As quoted in *Munajjid*, pp. 61 – 63. For an analysis of the episode and its sig-

nificance, see Bernard Lewis, "The Return of Islam," *Commentary* 61, 1 (January 1976): 47.

59 See Munajjid, *Amidat al Nakba,* pp. 119 – 120; and Bitar, *Min al Naksa,* p. 155.

60 See Muhammad Izzat Nasr Allah, *Al-Radd ala Sadeq al Azm* [An Answer to Sadeq al Azm] (Beirut, 1970), pp. 207 – 209; Sadeq al-Azm, *Naqd al Fikr al Dini,* p. 48.

61 Nasr Allah, *Al-Radd ala Sadeq al Azm,* p. 208.

62 Sa'd Jumah, *Al Mu'amarah,* p. 215.

63 Al-Munajjid, *Amidat al Nakba,* p. 95.

64 Ibid., p. 10.

65 Ibid., p. 136.

66 Ibid., p. 49.

67 Ibid., p. 49.

68 Ibid., p. 47.

69 Ahmad Baha' al-Din, *Thalath Sanawat* [Three Years] (Beirut, 1970), p. 163.

70 E. H. Carr, *The Twenty Years' Crisis, 1919 – 1939* (London: Macmillan, 1946), p. 147.

71 De Tocqueville, p. 146.

72 See the thoughtful analysis of the connection between "situationism" and leadership in Robert C. Tucker's essay, "Personality and Political Leadership," *Political Science Quarterly* 92, 3 (Fall 1977): 383 – 393.

73 Alexander Herzen, *My Past and Thoughts* (New York: Knopf, 1973), p. 333.

2. Egypt As State, As Arab Mirror

1 Jean and Simone Lacouture, *Egypt in Transition* (London, Methuen, 1958), p. 33.

2 Jamal Hamdan, *Shakhsiyat Misr* [Egypt's Personality] (Cairo, 1970), pp. 495 – 499.

3 Muhammad Jalal Kishk, *Kalam Li Misr* (Speaking to Egypt), (Beirut, 1974), pp. 102 – 103.

4 See Nadav Safran, "Engagement in the Middle East," *Foreign Affairs* 53 (October 1974), pp. 45 – 63.

5 Quoted in Edward Said's *Orientalism* (New York: Pantheon, 1978), p. 84.

6 Leo Tolstoy, *War and Peace* (New York: New American Library, 1968), p. 732.

7 Anwar el-Sadat, *In Search of Identity* (New York: Harper and Row, 1978), p. 180.

8 Najib Mahfuz, *Al Maraya* (Cairo, 1972), p. 196.

9 Muhammad Ahwad Mahjub, *Al Dimuqratiyah fi al Mizan* [Democracy in the Balance] (Beirut, 1973), p. 162.

10 Malcolm Kerr, *The Arab Cold War* (London: Oxford University Press, 1971).

11 Ahmad al Shuquiri, *Al Hazima al Kubra,* [The Big Defeat] (Beirut, 1972), p. 208.

12 See Mahjub, *Al-Dimuqratiyah fi al Mizan,* p. 162, and the recollections of President Boumedienne, in Lutfi al-Khuli, *An al Thuwara, fi al Thawra, wa bi al Thawra* [About the Revolution, In the Revolution, With the Revolution], (Beirut, 1975), p. 169.

13 For different accounts of the student rebellion, see Muhammad Jalal Kishk,

NOTES

Madha Yuridu al Talabah al Misryyun? [What Do the Egyptian Students Want?] (Cairo, 1968); Mahmoud Hussein, *Class Conflict in Egypt,* (New York: Monthly Review Press, 1973); and the excellent memoir by Wa'il Uthman, *Asrar al Haraka al Talabiyya* [The Secrets of the Student Movement] (Cairo, 1976).

14 Uthman, *Asrar al Haraka al Talabiyya,* pp. 28 – 29.

15 Ibid., p. 16.

16 The statement is reproduced in Kishk, *Madha Yuridu al Talabah al Misryyun?*, pp. 95 – 98.

17 See *Wathaiq Abdul Nasser* [The Documents of Abdul Nasser], (Cairo, 1973); vol. I, for the proceedings of the Arab Socialist Union of September 14 – 18, 1968. The proceedings were dominated by a lively exchange of opinions and reflections by students, workers, and others. For the statement cited, see p. 542.

18 See Ibrahim Issawi and Muhammad Nassar, "An Attempt to Estimate the Economic Losses Inflicted on Egypt by the Arab – Israeli Wars Since 1967," Third Conference of Egyptian Economists, Cairo, March 1978 (in Arabic).

19 Avi Shlaim and Raymond Tanter, "Decision Process, Choice, and Consequences: Israel's Deep Penetration Bombing in Egypt, 1970," *World Politics* 30 (July 1978), pp. 498 – 499.

20 Arnold Hottinger, "The Depth of Arab Radicalism," *Foreign Affairs* 51 (April 1973), p. 504.

21 See Tawfiq al Hakim, *Wathaiq fi Tariq Awdat al Wa'i* [Documents on the Road to Awareness] (Cairo and Beirut, 1975), p. 47.

22 For the view of Mustapha Amin, and others who share his perspective, see *Madha Ba'd Harb Uktubir?* [What After the October War?] (Cairo, 1974) pp. 23 – 24.

23 See John Waterbury's "The Opening: Part III: De-Nasserization," *American Universities Field Staff* 4, (1975), p. 1; Tawfiq al Hakim, *Awdat al Wai,* [The Return of Awareness] (Beirut, 1974).

24 Tawfiq al-Hakim, *Awdat al Ruh* [The Return of the Spirit] (Cairo, 1933).

25 Najib Mahfuz, *al Karnak* (Cairo, 1974), p. 57. This novel, it should be noted, was written in 1971.

26 See Fuad Mattar's dialogue with Mohamed Heikal, *Bisarah An Abdul Nasser* [Frankly Speaking about Abdul Nasser] (Beirut, 1975).

27 Muhammad Anwar el-Sadat, *Waraqat Uktubir* [The October Paper] (Cairo, 1974).

28 Sayyed Marei, *Awraq Siyyasiah* [Political Papers], Vol. 3 (Cairo, 1978), pp. 738 – 756. Marei's memoirs provide an extremely useful perspective and an abundance of information on contemporary Egyptian politics. Marei was an ancien régime politician who did well during the revolutionary years and then went on to become one of Sadat's closest advisors.

29 The quote is from a personal discussion with Tahseen Basheer in Cairo in December, 1978.

30 Kamal Junblatt, *Pour le Liban* (Paris: Stock, 1978), p. 171.

31 *Al Akhbar,* December 5, 1978, p. 5.

32 Center for Political and Strategic Studies, *Muatamar Kamp David* [The Camp David Conference] (Cairo, 1979), p. 136.

33 Taha Husayn, *Mustaqbal al Thaqfa fi Misr* [The Future of Education in Egypt] (Cairo, 1944), p. 389.

34 *Al Ahram,* October 11, 1979.

35 Anwar el-Sadat, *In Search of Identity* (New York: Harper & Row, 1978), p. 137.

36 Abdulla Laroui, *The Crisis of the Arab Intellectual* (Berkeley: University of California Press, 1976), pp. 31 – 32.

37 See the interview with Boutros Boutros Ghali conducted by Jean-Pierre Péroncel-Hugoz, "Quelle Diplomatie Pour d'Egypte En Paix," *Politique Internationale 5*, (Autumn 1979): 11.

38 Lecture delivered at the Johns Hopkins School of Advanced International Studies, Washington, D.C., April 9, 1980.

39 Edward Sheehan, "Step by Step in the Middle East," *Foreign Policy, 22* (Spring 1976): 18.

40 Quoted in John Marlow, *Spoiling the Egyptians* (London: Andre Deutsch, 1974), p. 105.

41 Nadav Safran, *Egypt in Search of Political Community* (Cambridge, Mass.: Harvard University Press, 1961), p. 34.

42 David Landes, *Bankers and Pashas* (London: Heinemann, 1958), p. 209.

43 Husayn, *Mustaqbal al Thaqafa fi Misr*, pp. 18 – 19.

44 Sheehan, "Step by Step in the Middle East," p. 7.

45 On this topic see one of Sadat's most revealing interviews, in *Al Ahram*, December 26, 1978.

46 Blanchard Jerrold, *Egypt under Ismail Pacha* (London: Samuel Tinsley & Co., 1879), pp. vi – vii.

47 Ibid., p. vii.

48 *Flaubert in Egypt*, ed. and trans. Francis Steegmuller (Chicago: Academy Chicago Limited, 1979), pp. 42, 29.

49 Leonard Binder, *The Ideological Revolution in the Middle East* (New York, John Wiley, 1964), pp. 198 – 229.

50 The views of Hakim and Fawzi and their critics are brought together in an extremely useful work edited by the Egyptian scholar Saad Ibrahim, *Urubat Misr* [Egypt's Arabism] (Cairo, 1978).

51 *Urubat Misr*, p. 109.

52 Ibid., p. 112.

53 Ibid., p. 114.

54 Nadav Safran, *Egypt in Search of Political Community*, p. 140.

55 Sayyed Qutb's answer to Taha Husayn carries the same title as Husayn's work, *Mustaqbal al Thaqafa fi Misr*. Jedda, 1969 edition.

56 Fundamentalist views are expressed in the Muslim Brotherhood's monthly magazine *Al-Daw'a;* the critique of Camp David was in the November, 1978, issue.

57 The story of the Muslim Brotherhood and its Supreme Guide Hassan al-Banna has been masterfully told, with new evidence, by Rifa'at al-Said in *Hassan al Banna* (Cairo, 1977).

58 Crane Brinton, *The Anatomy of Revolution* (New York: Vintage, 1965), p. 47.

59 Mohamed Heikal, *The Sphinx and the Commissar* (New York: Harper & Row, 1978), p. 50.

60 Ghali Shukri, *Mudhakkirat Thaqafa Tahtadir* [Memoirs of a Dying Culture] (Beirut, 1970), pp. 369 – 371.

61 Mohamed Heikal, *Hadith al Mubadara*, (Beirut, 1978), pp. 56 – 57.

62 See Ibrahim, *Urubat Misr*, pp. 127 – 128.

63 Khairi Aziz, in Ibrahim, *Urubat Misr*, p. 72.

64 Ahmad Baha'a al-Din, in Ibrahim, *Urubat Misr*, pp. 139 – 140, 144 – 146.

NOTES

65 The letter has been reproduced in al Taqqadum (an irregular pamphlet of the leftist group the Progressive Assembly of National Unionists), October 11, 1978, pp. 5 – 9.
66 Mohamed Heikal, "Egyptian Foreign Policy," Foreign Affairs 56 (Summer 1978):726.
67 Ahmad Baha'a al-Din, Iqtirah Dawlat Filastin [Suggestion of A Palestinian State] (Beirut, 1968), p. 53.
68 Walid Khalidi, "A Sovereign Palestinian State," Foreign Affairs 56 (Summer 1978): 695 – 713.
69 Tawfic Farah, "Group Affiliation of University Students in the Arab Middle East (Kuwait)," Reports and Research Studies, Department of Political Science, Kuwait University, 1977. I am deeply grateful to Professor Farah for sharing with me his findings and for a helpful discussion of the issues discussed here.
70 Khalidi, "A Sovereign Palestinian State," p. 695.
71 Bernard Lewis, The Middle East and the West (New York: Harper & Row, 1964), p. 94.
72 U.S. Senate, Committee on Foreign Relations, International Debt, the Banks, and U.S. Foreign Policy, 1977, p. 36.
73 Al Sharq al Awsat, March 13, 1980.
74 Abdallah Laroui, The Crisis of the Arab Intellectual, pp. 177.
75 See Michel Crozier, The Stalled Society (New York: Viking Press, 1973), Stanley Hoffmann, Decline or Renewal: France Since the 1930's (New York: Viking, 1974).
76 The escape from politics into piety best illustrated by Sadat's revealing "law of shame," proposed to parliament and in 1980. Instead of political arguments and the terror of the state, the "law of shame" — an ambiguous doctrine that would seek to shame those who dishonor the "Egyptian family," who disagree with the president, who say things that should not be said about the economy and about peace treaties — would rely on the society's oldest and in many ways most stifling chains: the fear of 'ar (shame), the disapproval of the community, moral prohibition.
77 Albert Hirschman, Exit, Voice and Loyalty (Cambridge, Mass.: Harvard University Press, 1970).
78 The survey and the larger problem of emigration is tackled in Adel Husayn's essay, "Wealth as an Obstacle to Unity," Al Mustaqbal al Arabi, 5 (1979): 28.
79 E. W. Lane, Manners and Customs of Modern Egyptians (London: Ward Lock & Co., 1890), p. 272.
80 Jean and Simone Lacouture, Egypt in Transition, pp. 29 – 30.
81 Lewis Awad, The Seven Masks of Nasserism (Beirut, 1976), p. 177.
82 Ibid., pp. 154 – 155.
83 See Jonathan F. Pedersen, "Fighting for Security: Egyptian – American Responses to Middle Eastern Change," senior thesis, Woodrow Wilson School of Public and International Affairs, Princeton University, 1980, p. 24.
84 Ibid., p. 44.

3. Fractured Tradition

1 Joseph Levenson, Confucian China and Its Modern Fate (Berkeley: University of California Press, 1968), p. 124.

NOTES

2 Hanna Batatu, *The Old Social Classes and the Revolutionary Movements of Iraq* (Princeton, N.J.: Princeton University Press, 1978), p. 1035.

3 Levenson, *Confucian China and Its Modern Fate,* pp. xxix – xxx.

4 Hannah Arendt, *Between Past and Future* (New York: Viking, 1968), p. 26.

5 Albert Hourani, *Arabic Thought in the Liberal Age* (London: Oxford University Press, 1970), p. 344.

6 See Al *Mawaqif* 6 (November – December 1969):5 – 76.

7 Jean-Pierre le Dantec, as quoted in Albert Bressond and Thierry de Montbrial, "The Ups and Downs of Mutual Relevance," *Daedalus* 108 (Spring 1979):112.

8 See the thorough and self-critical work put together by the publicists of the PLO Research Center in Beirut, *Al-Muqawamah al Filastiniyah wa Nizam al Urduni* [The Palestinian Resistance and the Jordanian Regime] (Beirut, 1971).

9 Ibid., p. 123. My translation.

10 Ibid., pp. 325 – 336, 337 – 360.

11 *Arab Report and Record* 12 (1976): 398 – 399.

12 Arnold Hottinger, "The Depth of Arab Radicalism," *Foreign Affairs* 51 (April 1973):504.

13 Sadeq al-Azm, *Dirasah Naqadayah Li-Fikr al Muqawamah al-Filastiniyah,* [A Critical Study in the Thought of the Palestinian Resistance] (Beirut, 1973).

14 Husam al-Khatib, *Fi al-Tajnibah al Thwariya al Filastiniyah* (Damascus, 1972), p. 17.

15 Al-Azm, *Dirasah Naqadayah Li-Fikr al Muqawamah,* pp. 122 – 123.

16 Hussein Munis, "The Return of the Arab to his Place in History," in Mustapha Amin and others, *Wa Madha ba'da Harb Uktubir?* [What After the October War?] (Cairo, 1974), pp. 69 – 70.

17 Edmund Burke, *Reflections on the Revolution in France* (1790; New York: Liberal Arts Press, 1955), p. 181.

18 Edward Sheehan, "Step by Step in the Middle East," *Foreign Policy* (Spring 1976):47.

19 For the text of the interview see Oriana Fallaci's collection, *An Interview with History* (New York: Liveright, 1976), pp. 262 – 287.

20 Mohamed Heikal, *The Sphinx and the Commissar* (New York: Harper & Row, 1978), pp. 261 – 262.

21 Fehmy Saddy, "Attitudes of Arab Traditionalists and Modernists toward U.S. Foreign Policy in the Middle East," paper delivered at the Twentieth Annual Convention of the International Studies Association, Toronto, Canada, March 21 – 24, 1979, p. 2.

22 Joseph Kraft, "A Letter from Saudi Arabia," *The New Yorker,* October 20, 1975, p. 111; see also Salim Daher's essay, "United States – Saudi Relations Since 1973," Department of Government, Harvard University, January, 1978.

23 Maxime Rodinson, "Islam Resurgent," *Gazelle Review* 6 (1979):6.

24 Albert Hirschman, *The Passions and the Interests* Princeton: Princeton University Press, 1977).

25 In *Al-Amal al-Shahri* (Beirut), 2 (April 1977):71.

26 In *An Nahar al Arabi wa al Dawli,* May 14, 1977, p. 5.

27 Anthony Ashley Shaftesbury, quoted in Hirschman, *The Passions and the Interests,* p. 46.

28 See Eric Rouleau's sensitive report, "Civil War in Lebanon," *SWASIA: North Africa* 2, 41, October 17, 1975, p. 7.

NOTES

29 Ibid., p. 8. My emphasis.
30 Ray Errol Fox, "South Lebanon's 'Chief,'" *The New York Times*, May 19, 1980, p. A-21.
31 See *Al-Manar*, November 26, 1979, p. 8.
32 Henry A. Kissinger, *White House Years*, (Boston: Little, Brown, 1979), pp. 1276 – 1300.
33 See Mohamed Heikal's account in "Egyptian Foreign Policy," *Foreign Affairs* 56 (July 1978):714 – 727.
34 *Al Ahram*, April 6, 1977, p. 6.
35 See *al Ahram*, December 30, 1977, p. 4 for Saudi worries about Euro-communism; see also Daher, "United States – Saudi Relations Since 1973."
36 John C. Campbell, "The Middle East: Burdens of Empire," *Foreign Affairs*, 57 (1978):613 – 632.
37 "Insignificant nations" was the term used by Irving Kristol in the aftermath of October 1973 to bemoan the way the "significant" nations allowed their power and control to slip. "Where Have All the Gunboats Gone?," *The Wall Street Journal*, December 13, 1973, as quoted in Noam Chomsky, *Peace in the Middle East* (New York: Vintage, 1974), p. 6.
38 Henry A. Kissinger, *White House Years*, p. 1277.
39 Richard M. Nixon, *The Memoirs of Richard Nixon*, vol. 2, (New York: Warner Books, 1978), p. 592.
40 Lewis Awad, *Li Misr wa al Hurriyah*, [For Egypt and Liberty] (Cairo, 1977), pp. 118 – 119.
41 Bernard Lewis, *The Middle East and the West* (New York: Harper & Row, 1964), p. 129.
42 Mohamed Heikal, *The Cairo Documents* (Garden City, N.Y.: Doubleday, 1973), p. 33.
43 Alexander Herzen, *My Past and Thoughts* (New York: Knopf, 1973), p. 617
44 The classic statement on dual societies is Alexander Herzen's work, cited above. I am grateful to Robert C. Tucker for drawing my attention to the parallel between my concerns and Russian thought.
45 Clifford Geertz, *Islam Observed* (Chicago: University of Chicago Press, 1968), p. 117.
46 Immanuel Wallerstein, "Civilizations and Modes of Production," *Theory and Society* 5 (1978):7.
47 This is the position Ali Mazrui takes in several of his writings, most recently in *The African Condition* (London: Cambridge University Press, 1980).
48 Ibn Khaldun, *The Muqaddimah* (Princeton: Princeton University Press, 1967), p. 93.
49 Arnold Hottinger, "Does Saudi Arabia Face Revolution?" *The New York Review of Books*, June 28, 1979.
50 V. S. Naipaul, *A Bend in the River* (New York: Knopf, 1979), p. 234.
51 G. B. Sansom, *The Western World and Japan* (New York: Vintage, 1973), p. 338.
52 Manfred Halpern, *The Politics of Social Change in the Middle East and North Africa* (Princeton: Princeton University Press, 1963), p. 136.
53 Nadav Safran, *Egypt in Search of Political Community* (Cambridge, Mass.: Harvard University Press, 1965), p. 140.
54 Lewis Awad, *Li-Misr wa-al Hurriyah*, [For Egypt and Liberty] (Cairo, 1977), pp. 120 – 121.

NOTES

55 I am grateful to Abdul Aziz Fahad for this idea, which he shared in a discussion of Islam and its relation to the West, April, 1980.

56 Albert Hourani, *Syria and Lebanon* (London: Oxford University Press, 1946), p. 70.

57 Karl Marx, "The Eighteenth Brumaire of Louis Bonaparte," in Robert C. Tucker, ed., *The Marx – Engels Reader* (New York: W. W. Norton, 1972), p. 437.

58 *Al-Nadhir* 3 (October 7, 1979).

59 Ibid.

60 "The Disintegration of Syria?" Beirut, 1979. For obvious reasons, the author wishes to remain anonymous. But he is a most capable and careful scholar.

61 *The New York Times,* December 28, 1979. p. 6.

62 Burke, *Reflections on the Revolution in France,* p. 101.

63 Kamal Junblatt, *Hadah'i Wasiyyati* [This Is My Testimony] (Beirut, 1978), p. 106.

64 The literature on this topic is vast; one exemplary treatment (in the Japanese context) is G. B. Sansom, *The Western World and Japan* (New York: Vintage, 1973).

65 Crane Brinton, *The Anatomy of Revolution* (New York: Vintage, 1965), p. 120.

66 *Al Ahram al Iqtisadi,* February 1, 1977.

67 John Waterbury, "The Opening Part II: Luring Foreign Capital," *American Universities Field Staff,* 20, 3 (1975):15.

68 Shaykh Abdul Halim Mahmud, *Fatawa'a a'n al Shuiyya* [Opinions on Communism], 1976. The emasculation of official religion and its usage by the political order are revealed in this shallow and cynical work.

69 See *Ruz al Yussef,* August 18, 1975.

70 The research was carried out by collaboration of American and Egyptian scholars under the auspices of the Research Program on Development Studies at Princeton University. Its results are forthcoming.

71 See the magazine of the Muslim Brotherhood, *Al-Daw'a,* January, 1979, pp. 52 – 54.

72 Oriana Fallaci, *An Interview with History,* p. 268.

73 Anwar el-Sadat, *In Search of Identity* (New York: Harper & Row, 1978), p. ix.

74 Hassan Hanafi, "The Historical Roots for the Crisis of Freedom and Democracy," *Al-Mustaqbal Al-Arabi* 5 (1979):136. This is a most impressive attempt by an independent political philosopher to examine critically the style of authority in the Arab world and, as its title states, the historical roots of the problem.

75 Fadlu Shalq, in *Lubnan al Akhar* [The Other Lebanon] (Beirut, 1976), pp. 51 – 63.

76 Ibid., p. 61.

77 Ali Abdel Raziq, *Al-Islam wa Usul al Hukm,* [Islam and the Principles of Government] (Cairo, 1925).

78 *Al-Ahram,* May 10, 1979.

79 Edmund Burke, *Reflections on the Revolution in France,* p. 108.

80 See Robert C. Tucker, *Stalin as Revolutionary* (New York: W. W. Norton, 1973), pp. 368 – 394.

81 See the interview in *Al-Majjalla* with Hassan Ayyat of the Islamic Republican Party, March 15 – 21, 1980.

NOTES

82 Ghali Shukri, *Al-Turath wa al Thawra* [The Heritage and the Revolution] (Beirut, 1973), p. 23.

83 *The Wall Street Journal,* June 13, 1980, p. 31.

84 Jacques Berque, *The Arabs* (London: Faber & Faber, 1964), p. 290.

85 *An Nahar al Arabi Wa al Dawli,* February 24, 1980, pp. 54 – 55.

86 "The Receding of Civilization," editorial, *The Wall Street Journal,* November 20, 1979, p. 24.

87 V. S. Naipaul, *A Bend in the River,* p. 234. See also Bernard Lewis, *History: Remembered, Recovered, Invented* (Princeton: Princeton University Press, 1975).

88 Immanuel Wallerstein, "The Dialectics of Civilizations in the Modern World System," paper delivered at Ninth World Congress of Sociology, Uppsala, Sweden, August 14 – 19, 1978, p. 5.

89 V. S. Naipaul, *India: A Wounded Civilization* (New York: Knopf, 1977), p. 186.

90 Toru Kawajiri, "A Comment" personal communication, April 18, 1980. I wish to note my debt to Mr. Kawajiri for the sensitive parallels he drew between Japan's case and the Arab world's.

Index

ⲟⲁ

INDEX

INDEX

France, 41, 48, 58, 124, 160, 165, 170
Franjieh, Suleiman, 146
French Revolution, 182
fundamentalism, *see* Islam, fundamentalism

Geertz, Clifford, 2, 42, 58, 172, 174
Gemayyel, Amin, 157
Gemayyel, Bashir, 157
Gemayyel, Pierre, 157
Germany, 28, 42, 47-8, 50, 196
Golan Heights, 44, 45, 124, 180
Grand Mosque (Mecca), xvi, 134, 164
Gulf of Aqaba, 11

Habash, George, xii-xiii, 72, 73, 123,
    142, 143, 144, 146, 147, 150, 151, 174
Haddad, Saad, 160
al-Hajj, Kamal Yusif, 33-4
al-Hakim, Tawfiq, 96-7, 115, 116, 121
Halpern, Manfred, 176
Hamadan (Hamdan), Jamal, 81
Hanafi, Hassan, 190
Hashemite monarchy, 12, 133, 143, 163,
    181
Hassan (k. of Morocco), 63
al Hawadith (magazine), 2
Hawatmeh, Nayef, 146, 151
Heikal, Mohamed, 27, 36, 88, 93, 97, 106,
    120, 123, 131, 139, 150, 170
Herzen, Alexander, 75, 170-1
Hijazi, Abdul Aziz, 186
Hirschmann, Albert, 132, 156
Hobbes, Thomas, 137
Hottinger, Arnold, 95, 174-5
Hourani, Albert, 142, 177
Hudabiyah Treaty, 193
human rights, 199
Husayn, Taha, 40, 104, 110-11, 113, 115,
    116-17
Husein (k. of Jordan), 9, 45, 61, 75, 124,
    148
    Nasser and, 72-3
    Palestinians and, 143, 144-5
Hu Shi, 27
al-Husri, Sati, 28
Hussein, Saddam, 102, 105

Ibn Khaldun, 154, 174
Ibrahim, 80
Ikhwan, *see* Muslim Brotherhood
India, 152, 169
Iran, xiv, 7, 104, 134, 146, 167, 173, 174,
    175, 189, 195, 196
    Islam, 139
    Muslim Brotherhood in, 180
    Pahlavi regime, xvi (*see also* Pahlavi)

revolution in, 6, 10, 113, 135, 164,
    181-2, 194
    United States and, 170
Iraq, xi, xii, xiv, 28, 41, 86, 102, 105
    Egypt and, 45, 113
    elites in, 178
    Hashemite monarchy, 12
    Iranian revolution, 182
    Islam in, 138, 181
    Jordan and, 9
Islam, 177, 199
    Algeria, 58
    Ba'th party, 61, 63
    class structure, 62, 64, 180
    communism, 170, 191
    conservative fundamentalism, 63-75
    cosmology of, 6, 8
    cosmopolitanism, 104
    democracy, 187
    Egypt, 61, 82, 95, 111, 116, 117-18,
        119, 181, 186
    fundamentalism, 15-16, 18-19, 20, 24,
        38, 82, 118, 119, 164, 170, 171,
        174, 199-200 (*see also* conserva-
        tive fundamentalism, radical funda-
        mentalism)
    inter-Arab conflict, 63
    Iran, 139
    language, 58
    Libya, 193
    millennarianism, 176
    modernization, 29, 47, 69-70, 171, 189
    Nasser and, 52, 61, 63, 119-20
    nationalism and, 47, 51, 54-5, 191
    pan-Arabism, 61, 63, 126
    politics and, 144-5, 190-1, 192
    property rights, 186
    radical fundamentalism, 50-63
    radicals, 50, 56-7, 62-3
    reactionary force, 50
    resurgence of, 139-40, 176, 177, 199
    revolution and, 35, 65
    Sadat and, 117, 181, 186, 189, 193
    Saudi Arabia, 164, 166, 191-2, 193
    science and, 36
    sects in, xiv-xv, 138, 178-9, 180, 193
        (*see also* entries under names of
        sects)
    Six Day War, 30, 32, 51, 52, 55, 61-2,
        63, 64, 69, 70, 71
    socialism and, 52, 65
    Syria and, 61-2, 179-80, 191
    tradition, 194-5
Islamic Pact, 63
Ismael, 109, 110, 113, 114, 115, 116, 133,
    176
Israel, xiii, 44, 45, 59, 85, 90, 92, 94, 107,
    108

{ 215 }

INDEX

metaphysics, 29, 48, 85, 98
military
  Ba'th party, 43
  class, 55
  modernization, 56
  socialism, 62
millennarianism, 176, 181
modernity and modernization, 31, 36, 114
  dualism, 171, 174
  homogenizing influence of, 172
  Iraq, 196
  Islam, 47, 50, 69–70, 189
  military, 56
  Nasser, 29
  resistance to, 34
  Six Day War, 67
  tradition and, 59–60, 109, 172–3, 187–8
  United States, 170
Mongols, 81
Morocco, 63, 71
Muhammad Ali, 80, 81, 109, 110, 113, 176
Muheiddein, Zakaria, 122
al-Munajjid, Salah al Din, 65, 66, 67
Muslim Brotherhood, 52, 60, 62, 87, 116–17, 118, 119, 165, 176, 179–80, 188, 189, 193

Nahda (Arab Renaissance), 8
Naipaul, V. S., 175, 199
Najd, 47
nakba (disaster), 32
Napoleon, 17, 53, 82, 121
Nasser, Gamal Abdul, xiii, xv, 4, 8, 14, 49, 72, 74, 89, 95, 96, 100, 106, 117, 133, 138, 147, 148, 174, 176
  Ataturk and, 187
  Ba'th party, 11, 41, 44, 45
  death of, xv, 9, 93
  de-Nasserization, 95–6, 98
  domination of, 12
  Husein and, 72–3
  inter-Arab politics, 86, 139 (see also Egypt, inter-Arab politics)
  Islam and, 52, 61, 63, 119–20
  Jordan and, 9
  language, 27, 29, 91
  legacy of, 84–5, 155
  March 30 Declaration, 90–1
  Palestinians and, 90–1, 123
  pan-Arabism, 93–4, 109, 115, 127–8
  Qaddafi and, 125
  radicals, 79, 80
  revolution, 83
  Sadat and, 84, 94, 111, 120
  Saudi Arabia and, 104

Six Day War, 11, 25–6, 32, 36, 85, 128
  Syria and, 128
  tradition, 37
  West and, 115
Nasserism, xiii, xv, 14, 85, 93, 97, 133, 142, 154
  Islam and, 119–20
  legacy of, 155
  Qaddafi and, 125
  United States, 170
National Pact (1943), 158
nativism, 184, 200
Nehru, J., 95, 128
newspapers, see journalism; entries under names of journals
Nietzsche, F., 47
Nixon, Richard M., 106, 168
Nkrumah, K., 95, 128
nuclear proliferation, 10, 152

Oakeshott, Michael, 18
October Paper (Sadat), 99
October War (1973), xv, 2, 105, 138, 164, 171
  Egypt, 95–6, 98–9
  impact of, 5–6, 10, 15, 146, 147, 185
  inter-Arab politics, 99–100
  Islam and, 173
  oil prices, 154
  Palestinian question, 162
  radicals and, 147, 149–50
  revolution and, 147, 150
  Sadat, 95–6, 99, 100, 125
  Saudi Arabia and, 165
  Syria and, 101
  United States and, 166–7
  West and, 152–3
oil embargo, 6–7, 83
oil prices, 154, 167
oil wealth, 129–30
Organization of Petroleum Exporting Countries (OPEC), 129–30, 166
Ottoman Empire, 3, 8, 47, 54, 66, 79

Pahlavi, R. (shah of Iran), xvi, 10, 11, 63, 105, 120, 121, 135, 179, 180, 181, 187, 189, 196
Palestine Liberation Organization (PLO), xiii, 4, 27, 86, 147, 148, 151
Palestine War (1948), 11
Palestinians and Palestinian movement, xii, xiii, xv, 9, 12, 48–9, 72, 73, 78, 98, 157
  Egypt and, 82, 90–1, 121, 123
  guerilla warfare, 91–2
  institutionalization of, 150–1
  Jordan and, 74–5, 143, 144–5, 146,

{ 217 }

INDEX

INDEX

INDEX